Reviews for *The Longest Journey*

Amanda Stuart has done a superb job conveying the issues that bring people to therapy. She has highlighted themes that are central to many people who suffer for too long, and presents the stories of real clients in a way that is easy for others to relate to. Amanda is a gifted therapist who has conveyed the therapy process in a way that is inspirational. This is a 'must-read' for anyone who is debating whether or not to make that first phone call.
—*Judith Siegel, Associate Professor, School of Social Work, New York University.*

The Longest Journey: finding the true self is a profound book. It shares a powerful message that so many of us have intentionally tried to hide from. Blissful ignorance is no longer an excuse. Our children and future generations need us to learn from the lessons that are so eloquently shared by the author, Amanda Stuart.
—*Dr Angus Pyke, Pyke Family Wellbeing*

You really have to walk in someone else's shoes to understand their life, and author Amanda Stuart has done that in evolving her role as a counsellor and psychotherapist – and now author. Amanda's path to becoming a counsellor began as child growing up in a dysfunctional (yet functional) family. Her work with young children then 'turned on a light' that childhood and family nurturing moulds an adult most profoundly.

Thus began her own path of self-realisation and then the need/passion to help others deal with their childhood issues/traumas/doubts to become the adults that they could love – and in turn love others.

Stuart doesn't leave any stone unturned — physical, sexual and emotional abuse; alcoholism; absent parents; bullying; sibling rivalry. How we `survived' our childhood has a huge bearing on how we cope as adults in a complex and demanding world. Stuart's book draws heavily on clients she has helped immensely over the years.

I warn you, though, these chapters really hit raw nerves. Be brave, read this book (to help yourself, family or friends) and take a good grasp of life — and live!
—*Wendy O'Hanlon, Acres Australia*

This is a very important book that demonstrates the devastating long-term effect and the feelings of shame associated with child abuse. Confronting buried pain is pivotal to reclaiming life after abuse and for many of the survivors in this book, sharing their stories has been a powerful tool in overcoming their feelings of shame, anger and sadness.
—*Bernadette McMenamin AO, CEO and Founder of Child Wise*

The Longest Journey:

Finding the true self

AMANDA STUART

All names have been changed and permission to publish granted.

Published in Australia by Sid Harta Publishers Pty Ltd,
ABN: 46 119 415 842
23 Stirling Crescent,
Glen Waverley, Victoria 3150 Australia
Telephone: +61 3 9560 9920,
Facsimile: +61 3 9545 1742
E-mail: author@sidharta.com.au

First published in Australia 2013
This edition published January 2020
Copyright © Amanda Stuart 2013
Cover design, typesetting: Chameleon Print Design
Cover illustration by Sarah Pinniger

The right of Amanda Stuart to be identified as
the Author of the Work has been asserted in
accordance with the Copyright, Designs and
Patents Act 1988.

Stuart, Amanda
The Longest Journey: finding the true self
ISBN: 1-921829-85-0   EAN13: 978-1-921829-85-7
pp364

About the author

Since training as a counsellor and psychotherapist, Amanda Stuart has worked with individuals, couples and families. The main focus of her work with clients is to develop their sense of self, to improve their relationships (particularly with partners), and to enable both men and women to change negative patterns in their lives.

Amanda encourages her clients to use their creativity as a means to healing emotional pain, through writing, drawing, painting or music. Exploring dreams is a significant part of her work, leading clients to a richer understanding of their emotional life.

Amanda grew up in England and came to Australia in her early twenties. She worked in the library of a Melbourne boys' school for fifteen years, running the year 7 and 8 library for seven of those years. It was in this role that Amanda first became aware that young people often struggle with their feelings, and her interest in the emotional life began. Completing an Arts degree and a Diploma in Education, she taught modern languages at secondary level. Her time as a teacher confirmed her sense that many people need help to handle their emotions and improve their self-esteem. She decided to change her career path.

Amanda divides her time between Melbourne and the Mornington Peninsula. She lives with her husband and Daisy, a labradoodle.

Acknowledgements

Thirty years ago, psychologist Sid Forsey set me on the path of my own longest journey, a path which was to reshape my life. The personal development weekends mentioned in the pages of this book were structured along similar lines to those that Sid used to run several decades ago. It is hard to improve on his formula.

Many years later, I trained as a counsellor at the Cairnmillar Institute. My lecturers, Ray Hawkes, Coral Brown and Warwick Hartin, provided me with the formal training I needed and gave me the confidence to start my own practice. Jill Wright offered me support in those early days. I am grateful to all these people.

In more recent times, Mary Symes, dream counsellor, has been a gracious mentor, offering me valuable insights via the exploration of my dreams.

There are others I want to thank: the many friends who asked regularly how my book was progressing; Jim Hammerton, author and historian, who supported me from the outset; my cousin Juliet, the only person to read the original manuscript, many years ago, and Brigitte Garvey, who offered her advice when I began the process of reworking the early chapters.

In 2011, when I settled on a deadline for the first time, three people offered me invaluable assistance. My friend Ian Harrison agreed to read a few chapters and his response gave me the encouragement I needed. My brother Peter Chambers came to my rescue at the eleventh hour and assisted me in editing the final manuscript, and likewise Mary Symes, who gave generously of her time. I thank each of these people sincerely.

Sarah Pinniger's illustration for the cover captures perfectly the spirit of the book. Luke Harris, designer, translated the words into an elegant and clean design that enhances its message. I am extremely grateful to both people.

My heartfelt thanks go to my husband, Ian, who read the manuscript for the first time in Lubersac, France, in June 2011. Together we restructured the early chapters. From the time I began writing this book in 2006 Ian has offered me unwavering support. Without his belief in me, I know this book would not have been completed.

Finally I offer sincere thanks to all my clients for their courage and honesty. This book was made possible through the telling of their stories, written from the heart. Writing the book gave me the opportunity to contact clients I hadn't seen for many years. I was delighted to learn that they have succeeded in transforming many aspects of their lives. Over the years I too have benefited in countless ways from our shared journey.

For Ian

and for our children and grandchildren, with love

Contents

Introduction

They start arriving, looking apprehensive, edgy, smiling at one another weakly. It is obvious some have slept badly and look fragile. I feel pleased to see them, proud of them for taking a risk with no idea of what the weekend holds in store, knowing only that they are here because they want to make a difference to how they feel about their lives. They want to bring about change.

They are clients I have seen for a while, some for years, others only weeks, seven women and three men. I have spent a few hours thinking about them leading up to this moment, contemplating the issues I hope they will be brave enough to address in the twelve hours we will spend together over the next two days. On first meeting, you would be unlikely to suspect some of the ordeals these young people, aged between 21 and 42 have experienced in their lives: the death of a parent, emotional and physical abuse, sexual abuse. One of the men is here to address his father's suicide when he was a teenager, another to deal with the violence of his early years. One of the women suffers from an eating disorder, while one was abandoned by her father as a result of alcoholism. Two young women endured critical and judgemental mothers and while one woman has had to cope with her grandmother's suicide, another has had to face the ending of a loving relationship with her grandmother, as a result of dementia.

These men and women have jobs, friends, family, and in some cases partners. They are well-functioning, well-adjusted and 'normal' people. They may work alongside you or sit next to you in the train each day. They have also, like so many in our society, suppressed painful feelings for years.

We sit in a circle on the floor and I ask them to say, in turn, how they feel about being here. They all feel the same: scared, sick, but excited, hopeful. The ice breaks. They respond to one another, supporting in the way they hope they, in turn, will be supported. I assure them that no one story is more important than another. Each of them has struggled to deal with uncomfortable feelings, each of them has suffered.

I ask them to team up with someone they don't know and when I look around at the pairs I smile to myself. The two whose parents took their own lives are talking to one another, as are two whose fathers sexually abused their daughters. The two whose mothers were critical and judgemental turn to me and one of them asks, 'How on earth did we pick each other?'

Their task is to imagine that I have a magic wand and can enable them to change their lives in terms of their relationships, their careers and their bodies and health. How would they like their lives to be? They talk openly, recognising in the other person the same willingness to be honest, to admit to the things that are lacking in their lives. Looking at them, I know why I do this work. How often does someone reveal their deepest and most vulnerable feelings honestly, to another human being, and how often can we do this in a safe environment? I am excited by the knowledge that each person in the room will be changed by taking part in the weekend. These young people have already made a commitment in terms of time and money and more importantly, in terms of courage, to address the difficulties they face in life. What they have all understood is that they cannot change their lives alone. They need help to do so.

The weekend is underway. It is a powerful experience, one that always results in some kind of transformation. For many in this group, their time with me in counselling is nearing an end. They have already come a long way to address the suppressed feelings that have controlled them for much of their lives. They have needed courage and perseverance and have worked hard to reach this point. It is also a new beginning, as many will leave behind much of the pain they have carried with them. Each one wants to be free of the past. They want to make healthier choices. They want to know themselves better and feel happier about who they are. It is an opportunity to decide what kind of life they want to live and who they want to be. In most cases it has already been a long journey. It is time to find the true self.

I know what it is like to be in their shoes. I can pin-point the moment I changed my life, when I chose to stay alive rather than kill myself slowly. It was several decades ago and I was in hospital, recovering from an operation. It struck me, as I lay in bed the day after surgery, that my life was heading in precisely the same direction as my mother's. I was divorced, drinking too much alcohol, smoking too many cigarettes and my health was deteriorating. It was hardly surprising because both my parents were heavy drinkers and smoked, and my mother was far kinder to me when I joined her in her vices, offering me cigarettes and wine when I was a teenager. As I contemplated my life, I had to accept the fact that I was fairly miserable much of the time and I had no idea why. Like most people, I believed I just had to get on with life as I knew it. I didn't know it was possible to alter the way I felt. I knew that I needed to make changes, particularly for my children's sake. They were hitting the teenage years and observing me closely. In my mind I imagined two different paths and was reminded of Robert Frost's poem *The Road Not Taken*, which my mother often quoted:

> 'Two roads diverged in a wood, and I — I took the one less travelled by,
> And that has made all the difference'.

Alcohol and ill health was an obvious path and it was the one on which my mother ended her life when she was the age that I am now. In some ways it was a tempting path because it would absolve me of responsibility. It was a conscious decision for me, at that moment, to reject her road and to opt for another, even though I had no idea what the alternative might be. I am still struck by the significance of that turning point.

For the purpose of this book, I interviewed a number of ex-clients to find out how they believed change had occurred for them, through having counselling. Many willingly wrote their own stories while others were happier for me to write about their journey as I saw it.

There have been times when I have wanted to abandon writing this book, to press the delete button and let it all go, but the book seems to have a life of its own. Sometimes I read over a section and am surprised by what I have written; perhaps my unconscious was hard at work. What brings me back each time is the conviction that I owe it to the clients who have worked so bravely towards a better life, to tell their stories. In our time together, as a result of all their efforts, they were changed. And so was I.

It is my hope that perhaps a few who read their stories will be encouraged to risk changing their lives.

Chapter 1

Childhood revisited

All happy families resemble one another; every unhappy family is unhappy in its own way.
—Tolstoy *(Anna Karenina)*

Childhood, far from being idyllic, can be confusing, painful and even frightening. It came as a surprise to me, when I began working as a counsellor, to discover that it is invariably what we experience as a child (most of which we do not remember clearly as we grow up) which continues to control how we feel about ourselves into adulthood, at times creating feelings of anxiety and depression.

While it is common knowledge that significant events like death, divorce and illness can disrupt what might have been a happy family life, I found through working with clients that it is more often how children are treated and handled by parents, educators and carers, and what children are told (or not told) which determines their level of happiness and feeling of self-worth as they develop.

'I remember very little about my childhood' are words I hear frequently. The truth is that our unconscious mind and our body never forget. Bringing to consciousness feelings that have been suppressed can lead to significant change and to far greater happiness.

In this chapter, the way that particular clients were wounded in childhood is explored and the healing process of counselling introduced. In examining the nature of the wound, the client is able to diminish its power. This is the essence of the counselling process. It is, I believe, the journey each client needs to undertake in order to find the true self.

Being a parent is no easy task

Consider the following job description:

> *Man or woman, 15 to 45, for full-time (24 hours, 7 days a week) position. Teaching and nursing skills essential, driver's licence ditto. Able to keep house, provide nutritious, versatile meals (which may be refused), have a strong stomach and a willingness to clean up vomit and faeces. An understanding of basic budgeting is crucial. Arbitration skills required. Applicants must be able to function well even when sleep deprived. Additional (paid) work outside the home is sometimes an option and often a necessity.*
>
> *Personal qualities required include kindness, patience, fairness and selflessness. Performance reviews likely to be unfavourable. This is a lifelong contract. No leave or superannuation entitlements. Training not provided.*

Who would apply for such a role?

Parents rarely admit that they are not coping. No one knows what takes place in a family. What are the parents like behind closed doors? Do they love one another? Do they love their children equally and unconditionally? How serious are their fights? Can they tolerate their children behaving like children? Are they capable of nurturing a child? Parents generally receive attention and help only when it is obvious that something is seriously wrong in the family. New mothers (and fathers) often feel overwhelmed when faced with the demands of an infant, particularly if the child cries a lot and sleeps little. If the mother suffers postnatal depression, as is fairly common, the pressure on the family is extreme. There seems to be a code of silence among women that no one warns an expectant mother how tough it can be in the first month or two. A client told me she imagined motherhood as: 'My baby looking up at me adoringly!' The reality of caring for her newborn was a far cry from her fantasy.

It is hard to ask for help. A new mother wants to be able to handle her baby by herself, without needing to ask for advice. By contrast, most people willingly seek help in handling a new puppy. Women are choosing to have their first baby much later. The adjustment to life with a baby for a couple who have enjoyed two salaries, the opportunity to travel, to socialise and party and sleep off excesses, often comes as a rude shock.

How would you describe your parents?

Few people who seek counselling are blessed with a loving mother and father who enjoy a close relationship with one another, are in good health and live to old age. One of the first steps when an individual comes to counselling is to explore the family relationships, the early childhood and personal experience of what it meant to be part of that particular family. Clients are encouraged to consider: 'What was your parents' relationship like? Did they know how to have an intimate relationship and what kind of people were they? How did they handle stress? Were they depressed?

Were they separated? Did they have an addiction? Which parent were you closest to? What was it like to grow up in your family, with those parents and siblings?' Having explored some of these matters, a counsellor already has a fair idea of the issues a client will be dealing with.

Clients begin to understand better how they came to be the way they are in their own lives as they recognise the impact of their relationship with both parents. At times they see how they have emulated aspects of their parents' behaviour. Some have rebelled and chosen a different path, and partner too perhaps (or at least one who appears different). One of the most common reasons for people to seek counselling is relationship difficulties. Exploration of the family background and relationships with parents nearly always throws light on the choice of a partner as well as on the presenting issues. A young client was amazed to recognise in her first session that the treatment she received from her ex-fiancé was identical to her father's treatment of her when she was young.

Parents are real people too

Part of becoming an adult involves letting go of dependence on parents and seeing them as real people with their own set of goals, feelings, successes and failures. It is often a difficult task because as children we usually look up to our parents, believing that they are right in all things. In counselling, clients begin to see their parents objectively, and where appropriate, to understand how the parents were unable to meet their needs, or to offer them unconditional love and support. Young children invariably feel they are at fault when parents fight or separate and even when they die. The most common sentences

I hear when clients describe childhood hurt is: 'I thought it was my fault' and 'I thought there was something wrong with me'.

A client told me recently: 'I find it so hard to be critical of my parents and to see them as they really are. It's so much easier to blame myself, to think it's all my fault. It's what I've done my whole life'.

After some months in counselling, a client came to the realisation that having her parents' approval had dictated her entire life: 'It's so difficult to face up to what your parents are like. I just wanted to believe my parents were loving, perfect parents. I had them both on a pedestal. My whole life I tried so hard to please them. I can see now I was trying to live a life that was not my own, just to have their approval'.

While many people grow up having had their emotional needs met by good parenting, even in the best of families things can go wrong. Normal life stresses including illness, unemployment, divorce and death can affect the stability of a family and place a child under stress. On occasion, even with the best intentions, parents fail to meet a child's needs. At other times, tragically, there can be sustained emotional abuse.

In the more severe cases, children experience trauma as a result of their parents' treatment and/or neglect. The trauma can result in a psychological wound, which may remain a source of life-long distress. The incidence of childhood wounding and trauma is extremely high in our society, far higher than one would expect and in general these are the cases that I see.

The most common form of abuse is emotional and psychological abuse, described by the Australian Childhood Foundation as follows 'Emotional abuse occurs when children do not receive the love, affection or attention they need to feel good about themselves or develop properly. Constant criticism, teasing, ignoring, yelling and rejection are all examples of emotional and psychological abuse'.

A campaign by the Australian Childhood Foundation launched in 2008 aimed to destroy the perception that child abuse is something that happens in 'other families'. Many people believe that child abuse happens primarily in families that are disadvantaged, living in extreme poverty and poorly educated. Aboriginal communities, for example, receive plenty of adverse attention in the media over alcoholism, child abuse and family violence. These problems exist in equal proportion in the white population. Abuse happens in all kinds of families including the professional, educated and wealthy. Time after time, I witness this as clients recount the stories of their childhood.

Most children assume that what occurs in their family is normal and they simply have to make the best of life as they know it. Even in the most problematic families children appear to adjust because they have no choice. They cannot put up a hand and say, 'Mum and Dad, I feel scared when you fight', or 'Please could I have a kinder/ more stable father or mother'.

A client in her thirties recalled a violent fight that erupted between her parents when she was little: 'I remember my mother running out into the street, screaming that she was going to call the police. All the neighbours must have heard her, but no one came out, no one did anything. I knew then that nobody would ever help us. There was no help. We were on our own.'

For a great number of my clients, when we look at present-day concerns, what still affects them, buried deep, is the hurt received as small children.

Jenny, a young client, recalled the fear she experienced, as a result of her father's unpredictable outbursts of rage:

'He would yell at us for no reason that we could understand. I remember when I was very young, maybe two or three, being locked in a dark room with my sister because we had been naughty. I still remember how terrified I felt.'

Parents can be more frightening than violence on television

I have heard numerous sad accounts of childhood like Jenny's. Many clients recall lying in bed at night listening to their parents fighting, often with a pillow over their heads. Others waited in dread, anticipating at any moment an alcoholic father's return from the pub and the inevitable fight that would erupt. In several of these sad families, it is clear that the mother also played a part as she would lie in wait and launch an attack on her husband as soon as he walked in. The unpredictability of parents' behaviour, especially angry outbursts and attacks on a partner or child, is terrifying to the young. As a result children grow up feeling anxious, unable to trust adults and uncertain about the world around them. Many have difficulty regulating their own emotions because they are accustomed to the chaotic emotional interactions that occur in their family for no understandable reason. A female client, whose brother was always in conflict with their mother, learnt to be quiet and good and to please everyone in order to avoid her mother's wrath. She became aware in counselling that 'people pleasing' had denied her the opportunity to discover what she wanted for herself in life.

In *'Raising an emotionally intelligent child'*, John Gottman urges parents to be aware of their child's emotions and warns of the harm done to children where there is a high level of conflict: 'It hardly matters whether a couple is married, separated, or divorced; when a mother and father display hostility and contempt for each other, their children suffer … Our data show that children raised by parents whose marriages are characterised by criticism, defensiveness, and contempt are much more likely to show antisocial behaviour … they have more difficulty regulating their emotions, focusing their attention, and soothing themselves when they become upset' (Gottman, 1997, p. 138-9).

Honour thy father and thy mother

In counselling sessions, some clients are reluctant initially to see their parents as anything but loving and their child-hood as less than perfect because it feels like a betrayal and leads to feelings of guilt. Mothers in particular are often described in glowing terms in early sessions. Later I might learn that they were angry or cold or maybe obsessed with appearance. The fourth commandment, 'Honour thy father and mother' is deeply embedded in our unconscious, and when we are young it is not possible to stand up to the authority of an adult. For some people it is too confronting to continue in counselling as they are reluctant to see their parents in a true light. We would all like to believe we had a happy childhood. For their very survival, children need to love their parents and to feel loved by them.

Remembering — discovering the truth

Counselling provides the opportunity to understand why we behave in the way we do. It comes as a surprise to many clients to discover how much the conscious mind has suppressed. 'Finding the true self' perhaps sums up best for me the task faced by all clients as they confront experiences and feelings that have affected them growing up. At a conscious level they may be unaware of what occurred in their early years, but the unconscious mind and the body remember it all.

A client who was often terrified as a small child by the violent fights between her parents described the process of counselling as 'opening up a side of my brain that I didn't know was there … It opened up a new way of thinking for me … I didn't know I could look back into the past and make sense of some of the things that had happened when I was little and understand how I came to be who I am.'

Another client told me at her last appointment: 'I remember how strange it felt at first to talk about myself, about my life and what I wanted in terms of relationships with family and friends. No one had ever asked me about my feelings before. In my family, feelings were just never discussed.'

Recently a client in her early twenties came to see me. Robyn described a home life characterised by frequent outbursts of anger and violence between her parents (a doctor and a teacher) and involving the adolescent and grown-up children. Recently the police were called. My client is a sensitive, vulnerable young woman who has been upset at what happens in her family and has tried to be a go-between, keeping her family together. On the surface she has done well in coping with the situation. In getting involved, however, and trying to help her family, she has been affected deeply. Home is not a safe place. She is experiencing difficulties in her relationship with her partner. It is hardly surprising as she has no model of how to have a good relationship.

In Robyn's second session, following the exploration of a dream, she understood that she needed to find ways of keeping out of the family fights rather than engaging with them. Having counselling at this time will enable her to address the fear and the torn loyalty she has suffered for years in relation to the family violence. As a result, she will be able to choose a healthy direction in life rather than follow along the familiar path.

Case study: coming to terms with a confusing mother

Some years ago I worked with a ten year old boy whose parents were divorced. Charlie and his sister lived with their mother. She was often abusive and Charlie, the older child, was always the target. He told me of one morning when she flew into a rage because he was taking too long to get dressed. She shouted at him to get into the car and proceeded to drive him to his father's office. She told her ex-husband that he could have his son as she couldn't deal with him. She left Charlie, barefoot, with none of his belongings.

It was two years later that I saw him for a few counselling sessions. Charlie was living with his father, hurt and bewildered as to why his mother didn't want him when she had kept his younger sister with her. For this young boy, the hardest part of coping with life was trying to understand his mother and why she didn't appear to love him. When we met, I would get Charlie to draw pictures of his life, his family and friends, and talk about them. Next to a picture of his mother he wrote: 'nice, mean, rude, loveing, hopeful, angry, cruell, fulish, fustrating (sic). If I didn't do the bad things Mum wouldn't of (sic) been so mad at me'. What a confusing mother!

We worked through many of his feelings about her treatment of him, which I can only describe as extremely cruel, and he came to the realisation that spending weekends with her was pointless. In a letter he wrote to her, he explained why he couldn't stay with her: 'I don't think I should come to your house any more because we always fight over nothing. On the weekend I felt really upset that you got angry with me and I don't understand why. I would like to stay with you if you didn't get so mad at me'.

In the time that I worked with him, Charlie was able to develop a close relationship with his father, having learnt how to express his feelings. I remember one of our last sessions when Charlie asked if I would tell his father that he was worried that his father had started drinking too much alcohol in the evenings. He couldn't tell him himself. He said he would wait outside while I spoke to him. I replied 'Well, you are my client and I am happy to do that for you'. When I repeated Charlie's concerns, his father was quite shocked but recognised the truth regarding his drinking. He phoned me a few days later to say he was pleased Charlie had been able to confide in me. He added that Charlie was teaching *him* how to express feelings.

Charlie stayed with his mother on two occasions during the time he was seeing me and understood that she had major problems. He could recognise that none of what had happened was really his fault. It is, however, human nature to want love and approval from one's parents whatever they are like. I have known 60 year olds who were still hopeful of being offered unconditional love.

Physical abuse of children — parents can be cruel

I find it hard to believe that anyone harms their child intentionally. The truth, tragically, is that not all parents are able to love their children. Some parents, both mothers and fathers, are cruel and abusive, emotionally and physically, towards a child at times. Some take out their own frustrations and anger on their children because they cannot tolerate their need for attention and love. Many have not experienced unconditional love in their own childhood. They have been wounded by a parent or carer and have suppressed their pain. It is from this place of pain that they treat their own child.

It is still considered acceptable to hit children in Australia (although ironically it is a criminal offence to hit an adult). In a survey carried out by the Sun Herald newspaper in Melbourne (11 March 2010), 93% of respondents said they believed it was acceptable to hit their children.

In the same paper three months later (14 June 2010), an article headed 'Hundreds of kids bashed by parents' reported that police data reveals on average two parents are charged daily with assaulting their children in Victoria alone. The director of the Australian Institute of Criminology said the assaults went far beyond the typical smack: 'Things like caning a child, using a belt, kicking or punching a child.'

The clients I have worked with who were assaulted by a parent or witnessed someone else in the family being attacked were deeply affected, long-term, by the experience. They did not bring up the abuse in counselling sessions. It was only as we addressed other issues that the violence experienced as a child came to the fore. At times a client will have suppressed the memories because the truth about the way he or she was treated is simply too painful to bear. Defences such as denial and resistance serve to keep the memory suppressed as long as possible. In relationships with partners when they are adult, however, the past wounding is often re-enacted.

The father of a three year old told me that he regularly hit his daughter out of anger and frustration at her behaviour. He also locked her in her room. When I asked how he felt about the fact that he was treating his three year old child in such a punitive, abusive way, he replied, 'I'm not a child abuser. She needs to be disciplined.' He added: 'Everyone hits their children.'

I asked him to tell me how much he weighs and what he thinks his daughter might weigh. And then I asked how he would expect to feel if someone four times his size were to attack him? He responded: 'I suppose you have a point.'

I wondered how this man was disciplined as a young boy.

In fact in twenty-three countries it is now against the law to hit your child. The decision behind hitting a child can be unconscious. A parent resorting to this form of discipline simply wants to control a child and is using force to do so, but the violence of the hitting can escalate when a parent feels powerless to make the child obey: 'This time I'm serious. This will teach you.'

Alice Miller, a psychoanalyst and author of many books on the subject of child abuse, writes that a great many children are hit in our society: 'But the fear and anger such punishment brings with it remain unconscious for a very long time. Children have no choice but to suppress their fear and anger as otherwise they could not sustain their love for their parents, and that love is crucially necessary for their survival. But these emotions, though suppressed, remain stored away in our bodies, and in adulthood they can cause symptoms of varying severity. We may suffer from bouts of depression, attacks of panic fear, or violent reactions towards our children, without identifying the true causes of our despair, our fear, or our rage' (Articles, Child abuse and mistreatment, www.Alice-Miller.com).

Many of my clients, male and female, were hit by their parents as small children. Often they received regular beatings for the slightest misdemeanour. Several remember being sent to their bedroom or the bathroom by their mother to await their father's return from work whereupon, fired up by his wife over the child's misdemeanours, the father would carry out the punishment on his child, generally with a belt. A female client recalls her father kicking her when she was very young, another remembers her mother hitting her with a belt when she was little because she spilt the milk. Sometimes her mother used a branch from a tree growing outside the kitchen door. Her mother was proud of her strict discipline methods and would boast to relatives: 'You have to be cruel to be kind.'

Alice Miller writes of the potential damage caused to a child by physical abuse: 'Almost all children are smacked during the first three years of their life when they begin to walk and to touch objects which may not be touched. This happens at exactly the time when the human brain builds up its structure and should thus learn kindness, truthfulness, and love but never, never cruelty and lies' (ibid).

It is not my aim to attack parents who are generally doing their best. What I do hope, however, is that parents who read this book might take the time to reflect on the clients' stories.

Women cry, men deny

When female clients talk of the physical punishment they were subjected to twenty or thirty years earlier, they invariably become upset and cry. Male clients, on the other hand, usually try to laugh it off. They do their best to convince me: 'It didn't affect me.' Some even try to tell me it did them good. When pressed, they usually reveal their hurt and anger at the treatment. Several men were shocked when they broke down and cried in front of me. They had no awareness of the buried pain. Not one of these clients was aware that childhood treatment was affecting his or her emotional state. Releasing old hurt is powerful.

I believe parents who assault their children often do so in an unconscious state. The child's behaviour triggers suppressed rage and the parent reacts in an attempt to diffuse his or her own anger (possibly at treatment received several decades earlier). Of great concern is that some parents will no doubt hit their children when they are intoxicated and/or so angry that they are unaware of the force they are using.

In the last book she wrote before her death in 2010, *Free from lies*, Miller invites parents who have hit their children to 'summon up the courage to admit their errors to their children'. She suggests they speak honestly to their child, along the following lines: 'When you were small we hit you because we were brought up that way and believed it was the right thing to do. Only now have we realised that we should never have done it, and we want to apologise'(Miller, 2007, p. 13).

I suspect it is only an unusual parent who could follow this advice. An apology from a parent to a child is rare, but I believe it would make a great difference to the child.

A question I am asked frequently by clients (and by others) is: 'How can you bear to listen to so much misery, day in and day out?'

The answer is simple: I know that by addressing buried pain and hurt, clients can heal and can improve their lives greatly. They can become who they want to be. To witness the transformation — the letting go of old pain and sorrow, the growing confidence and increased energy — is not only rewarding but exciting. To be able to do this work, a therapist needs to be able to tolerate the clients' pain in order for healing to occur. And it does require patience on both sides.

Case study: parents who abuse alcohol and drugs

Jo was in her late twenties when we first met. She was referred to me by one of her friends. She was happily married and expecting her first child, something she had anticipated with joy for years. What brought her to counselling was the fact that she was becoming increasingly anxious and depressed and she had no idea why.

No one presents for counselling because they want to explore the treatment they received as a child. It is unusual to attach great importance to what took place when we were young. Many of my clients state that they remember little of their early years. When I ask about childhood experience, however, it becomes apparent immediately if the client has suppressed painful feelings. The memories are all there, buried inside. With little prompting they recall significant events and the way they were treated.

Jo's parents had always had a stormy relationship, often fuelled by alcohol. Looking back Jo suspected that her mother had been an alcoholic for many years, but this was never discussed. Both parents were physically and verbally abusive towards her when she was growing up, she told me in her first session: 'I remember them hitting me when I was very little. I was an anxious and hyperactive child and they tried to discipline me. The more they hit me, the worse I behaved. I think eventually I invited it, but I never understood why. Perhaps the physical pain was better than the hurt I felt inside. I was really skinny, so it hurt a lot when they hit me. What made it worse was that they never touched my sisters, even when they were naughty. They were never sent to their room whereas I was always being banished. I have never understood why my mother made me the target of her rage.'

Some parents work hard to preserve an outward appearance of good, loving parenting but behave differently behind closed doors, as Jo described: 'My mother was always nice in front of other people and I started to dislike her. When I was a teenager she tried to get close to me and encouraged me to confide in her but I couldn't. I have never been able to trust her because I can't forget how mean she was to me when I was little. She has never apologised or acknowledged her part. I was always identified as the problem — a difficult child.'

Jo was aware that she had become defiant in an attempt to defend herself (and in fact to defend her personality). She realised that her defiance simply made her mother angrier. As a young girl she knew of no other way of dealing with the anger she felt towards her mother.

In counselling, Jo was able to recognise that her sadness and hurt had surfaced as she approached the birth of her own child. It was clear she needed to revisit the way she was handled by her parents when she was little.

What came to light over the following months was Jo's belief, deep down, that growing up she was in fact 'a bad child' and deserved her mother's treatment. She was able to recognise the hostility she felt towards her mother. Fear that she would treat her child in the same way that she had been treated was terrifying. She wondered if she would know how to be a loving, supportive mother.

When I asked about other significant relations, Jo told me she was very close to her grandparents and would stay with them in school holidays when she was a child. I commented that Jo appeared to soften and relax when she spoke of her grandparents and it was clear they had shared a close relationship. She felt quite hopeful following this discussion.

Jo contacted me when her son was a year old, to say she was thoroughly enjoying motherhood. She felt that having counselling when she was pregnant had helped her greatly. Jo said she had begun to discuss with her mother the sadness of her early years. At times she found herself becoming irritable and annoyed with her son, but she was able to recognise it as an old pathway and not the one she wanted for her own parenting. She had another role model firmly in mind.

Children of parents with an addiction

Parents with an alcohol or drug addiction are at best unreliable. Usually they are quite inaccessible to their children because their main focus is on feeding their addiction. The addiction serves to conceal their pain. Those with an addiction, a mental illness and/or personality disorder face an enormous challenge in bringing up children. If I learn that a client's mother or father is an alcoholic, I know there will probably be a number of emotional difficulties for the client.

Case study: yearning for a normal mother

Maya was just twenty when she sought counselling. Most of her difficulties concerned her mother whose behaviour was so extreme as to raise the question of a mental illness. Maya's mother was addicted to alcohol and marijuana and was often abusive to family members. Her mother refused any form of treatment or help. Maya told me she had fantasised throughout her childhood about the mother she longed for: 'I yearn for a mother who is warm and nurturing, a confident woman who smiles, who laughs, who is strong. In my mind she should have employment, a nice house with a mortgage, a nice car. A normal mother.

'There was no normality in my family growing up. Everything that I craved was missing. Constant turmoil describes my family life.

'The mornings: "Mum, wake up Mum! Wake up … we have to get to school." Carrying my backpack, I walk in to school, knowing how embarrassed I will feel when I walk into the classroom. I wish I didn't have to go in. I walk through the door. Everyone is suddenly quiet. I feel my face go red. I am late for school once again.

'Kindergarten, grade 1, 2, 3 and so on. Waiting on the brick wall after all the kids have gone home with mothers who picked them up on time. I wait and wait, looking in one direction and then another. There's no sign of her. A teacher comes over to me: "Are you sure she is coming to pick you up? Would you like us to phone her?"

'Again the embarrassment as I walk with the teacher to the office to call my mother. I don't want the teachers to think badly of me. I look up to them.

'I feel ashamed to be the last one to arrive at school and the last one to be picked up.

'In counselling I realised I needed to address the shame of my early years. Shame comes from my mother, the shame of living with someone who is mentally ill, someone incapable of functioning in everyday society, a non-conformist with delusional views, irrational thought processes, someone filled with anger and bitterness, towards my father, towards us, her children, towards total strangers, anyone who upsets her. I have grown up with this person, my life dictated by hers, my emotions dependent on hers. Even my weight gain was hers. I was a little sponge, soaking up all my mother's poisonous ways of thinking. She taught me to hate the world, to hate my father and she turned us children against one another. For years my brother and sister hated me. Now we know the truth. We know she poisoned our thinking. My mother says to me: "Shame on you!"

'It is time for me to hand back all the shame to my mother and learn to love the world.'

Fortunately for Maya she is young and fiercely determined to make her life a positive one. She worked hard in counselling to face the effects of her early years by confronting her feelings of shame and her need to please others. Between sessions she used writing as a tool to help her and in doing so she was able to promote her own healing. She is now clear that her mother's condition is not her fault or her responsibility, but she is also a daughter who cares, so her task is not easy. Her mother is likely to get worse as time goes on. While her mother refuses treatment, there is no help available for Maya and her siblings. Maya was able to recognise that she needed help for herself.

Maya now has a close relationship with her brother and sister. She has a career she loves and she has bought an investment property. She is just 22 years old.

Sadly, siblings are rarely able to help one another when the family is in turmoil although the companionship of a brother or sister makes the experience less lonely. The situation is different for every child. Each one has to focus his or her energy on surviving on a daily basis. In the pages of this book are the stories of two pairs of sisters, clients I saw at different times. Their stories differ greatly. No two children experience exactly the same parenting.

There is plenty of research into the effect on children of a parent's alcoholism. Judith Siegel describes the way adult children are affected:

'High on the list of dysfunctional lessons is the silencing of feelings and the denial of individual needs....[most] adult children of alcoholics do not know how to recognise their own feelings and pay attention to their internal states. In alcoholic families, the drunken outbursts and conflict are looped together, either because the drinking directly leads to arguments or because an alcoholic who has been provoked will turn to liquor for comfort' (Siegel, 2000, p. 121).

Losing a mother to alcohol

A sensitive, caring daughter is likely to blame herself for not supporting a parent. Sam's mother was unable to get her life in order and after she died, in her late thirties, Sam felt enormous guilt: 'My mother had a very sad life. I hate myself for what I put her through when I was younger. I wanted her to try and feel good about herself. It was so frustrating. I loved it when Mum would try. She had a heart of gold and she was generous, caring, beautiful. But she didn't want to help herself. She had a drinking problem. She was killing herself. In the last six months she was drinking so much she would fall over at home and really hurt herself. I didn't feel she was a mum; she was always in bed. I moved out when I was fifteen and lived with my older sister. I still feel guilty that I left her.'

In counselling Sam was able to understand that as a child there was nothing she could do to help her mother. Her mother needed to choose to get help herself.

It is true that Sam's mother had a sad life. She was very young when she gave birth to her first child and her relationship with Sam's father didn't last. For the previous two generations, contraception was not readily available, nor was it reliable. How many young people get pregnant because they take risks in the heat of passion, when the last thing on their minds is conceiving a child? I have worked with several women who were struggling with the dilemma of an unplanned pregnancy. Not one of them felt comfortable having an abortion.

A number of my clients' mothers were young, some only fifteen or sixteen. At such a young age it is hardly surprising they were unable to parent in an effective manner. In most cases they were also single parents or had a dysfunctional relationship with the child's father. A client whose mother was sixteen when he was born found out as a teenager that the man he thought was his uncle was in fact his father. In counselling he came to the realisation: 'I was never parented by anyone. I had to take care of myself throughout my childhood, as well as my two sisters'.

Parenting is hereditary

In exploring the way my clients' parents were raised by the previous generation, often what is apparent is that they too were deprived of love and security growing up. Tragically, many repeat the same destructive patterns with their own children, acting out of suppressed feelings. Some parenting is primitive and harsh. Children may be treated in the same brutal way as the parents were. The punitive treatment may be unconscious; it is all that is known. I have spoken to a number of parents who cannot recall beating their children while the children, now adult, remember only too well. The parents have most probably suppressed the memory. Parents do not always question why a child is behaving in a particular way. They react to behaviour that feels intolerable. Some of the values and ways of treating children have been passed down through the generations, often unconsciously. It is for this reason I like to work with young people before they have children so they can avoid repeating old patterns.

As a parent it is horrifying to hear yourself sounding exactly like your mother or father did when you were little. It is the last thing you expect: 'Did those words come out of my mouth?' I still recall stopping myself from uttering some words my mother said to us a number of times when we were young: 'You'll be the death of me'. Was I the perfect mother? Absolutely not! My one regret is that I did not get the help I needed before having my own children.

Recently a young mother of a two year old girl came to see me. She was concerned that she had screamed at her on a few occasions (for behaving like a two year old). When she shouted at her daughter, she found she was shaking uncontrollably but had no understanding of why. It wasn't difficult to help her access some of the buried feelings from her own childhood which led to her screaming at her toddler, and to reassure her that it was worth doing this work for the sake of her child and her relationship. While we can suppress hurtful memories, our unconscious mind and our body store everything.

Children should be seen and not heard

A client told me that many of her friends had wanted to have children, but once a child needed attention on a daily basis, they found it hard to tolerate. They wanted their children to occupy themselves, in the way they were expected to take care of themselves when they were little. It isn't so long ago that children were expected 'to be seen and not heard'. It was a phrase I heard throughout my childhood. I am sure my mother believed that was how children should be. No doubt she heard it when she was a child too.

Generally speaking, most parents do the best they can. In the one truly honest conversation I had with my mother the last time I saw her before she died, she told me that of her four children, I was the one she believed was 'fine and happy', but that later, when I was living in Australia, she became aware that maybe that wasn't the case: 'I realised that somehow I had gone wrong with you, but I didn't know how or why, or what to do to put it right.'

I have never forgotten those words. In that moment I went a long way towards forgiving her for being such a negligent mother because she was willing to acknowledge some responsibility in her treatment of me. If only she had chosen to tell me decades earlier. An apology of any sort from a parent is rare, and it can make all the difference.

Phillip Larkin, the English poet, puts it well:

'This be the verse':
They fuck you up, your mum and dad,
They may not mean to, but they do.
They fill you with the faults they had
And add some extra, just for you.

Larkin concludes his poem with the recommendation that readers don't have children of their own.

I do believe another solution can be found for the problems facing parents and children. There is plenty of help available today, but parents have to admit they are not coping and seek help. Parents are the only ones who can do something to improve the quality of their children's lives.

Thankfully many men and women find parenting an immensely enjoyable and rewarding experience. They are fortunate, as are their children and their children's children.

If parents fail to offer unconditional love and support, does it mean they are guilty? No, not guilty, but parents must be responsible for their children's wellbeing. Unfortunately there is no training available before embarking on becoming a parent and no test to determine suitability for bringing children into the world. It is hard to know, before experiencing it, whether you are really suited to having children. Perhaps child welfare payments should be awarded only after both parents have completed sound parenting training.

The long-term effect of childhood trauma, whatever form it takes, is significant and can affect every area of a person's life as they go out into the world, attempt to form relationships and have their own families. Until recently, little notice was taken of the rate of child abuse. I have often thought that people are more concerned about the state of the economy or who will win the grand final than they are about the welfare of children and families. It is a topic that is rarely discussed.

Counselling offers hope

Uncomfortable feelings of anxiety or depression are the most common triggers for people to seek counselling. I generally find out in early sessions how dependent the client is on alcohol and/or drugs, and whether they are taking medication, including the contraceptive pill. Many people are not aware that alcohol is a depressant or that alcohol and antidepressants do not mix well. A few clients I have worked with were taking antidepressants, drinking a fair amount of alcohol, smoking marijuana and were on the pill — quite a cocktail. While I always address ways of reducing physical symptoms (healthy diet, exercise, sound sleep, meditation, yoga), a counsellor's task is to uncover the source of the discomfort.

No matter what the presenting issue might be, for most clients what lies beneath the surface is a sense of sadness and emptiness at how they feel about themselves and their lives. Often they know deep down that life could be more enjoyable. As they go about their daily lives — work, home, friends, family — week in and week out, they begin to wonder: 'Is this all there is?' and 'Is this who I want to be?'.

Clients want to have better relationships with the people who matter to them, and at the heart of it I see all counselling as being about relating, whether it be to others or to ourselves. For all the advances that modern society has achieved, particularly in the area of technology, relationships continue to be far from satisfying with more than forty per cent of marriages ending in Australia, and that does not include de facto or gay relationships. Nor does it mean that marriages that do survive are necessarily happy. Many of my clients grew up with both parents. Children tune in to what is occurring between their parents. I can recall several clients who described growing up with parents who were critical, hostile, or indifferent to one another. Physical contact and intimate gestures were rarely observed. How can the children know how to have a close, intimate relationship? Siegel comments: 'The ways in which children react to tensions between their parents is one of the most important discoveries of family therapy … In these families children take on predictable roles so that one may become super responsible while another becomes the clown or the problem child. The problem child may act out in a serious enough way to bring the entire family to therapy. However, all of the children have the same underlying issues and are vulnerable because of what they learned from their parents' marriage' (ibid., p. 12). The clients whose journey in counselling is explored in later chapters often observed conflict and tension in their parents' marriage.

It is hard to go it alone. We all need help at times.

An adolescent who grows up without a supportive adult in her life may find it hard to have a sense of her own worth. In my experience, the supportive adult doesn't have to be a parent (although that of course is preferable). One relative or adult who is able to offer unconditional love and support can be enough. Some people's lives are changed by the attention and care offered by a sensitive teacher.

I was blessed in having two wonderfully caring aunts when I was young, who I am sure were aware that I needed more love and nurture than was on offer at home. Throughout my childhood and adolescence, I stayed with one of these extraordinary aunts in school holidays. I would simply write to her before every holiday to ask if I could come on a certain date. I was never refused and I was even made to feel she enjoyed having me.

When I left home, I had a room in my other uncle and aunt's house in London while I adjusted to living away from my home (although in fact leaving home at seventeen was a thrilling experience). I still remember being made to eat a boiled egg for breakfast with the family because my aunt was worried I wasn't looking after myself. I have never really liked eating eggs for breakfast, but my aunt's boiled eggs were different. They were prepared with plenty of love.

Those who are unfortunate in having no one who can offer this degree of care can often turn their lives around if they seek counselling, preferably before marrying unwisely and perpetuating the cycle. Sometimes a counsellor's role is to be a 'parent' to a client. I know that on occasion my role has been to 'mother' a number of clients, male as well as female, who were denied that relationship in their family.

Through committing to counselling, clients can understand the past, integrate their experience and make positive choices. They can learn to relate as a result of the trusting relationship that develops between the therapist and client. For some, this can be a very new experience because all they know is the way their parents and family members relate to one another.

Most people only decide to act for themselves when the pain they are suffering becomes unbearable or when they find themselves repeating the same mistakes in one relationship after another. It is too difficult to explore these painful feelings without help. The task in counselling is to strengthen the client to the point that he can bring about the changes he wants for himself. One client told me when he finished counselling: 'I now have a tiny counsellor in my head. In any difficult situation, I can imagine what you would say to me.'

Counselling — only for the brave

Not everyone is suited to the process, however. Some people are not ready to take responsibility for their lives; others are deeply defended and in denial to the point that they cannot see their own behaviour plays a part. It is tempting to blame others for our misery, or fate for dealing us a poor hand. Blaming others is a sure way of remaining stuck. Committing to counselling requires courage; some choose not to continue when it becomes too confronting. It can be exhausting emotionally. A client, a psychologist, told me at his last session that for six months all he had done was focus on healing his emotional life. He compared the energy it required to climbing a mountain.

The relationship between the client and therapist is crucial. It is imperative that the client feels comfortable and believes the therapist can help him or her to change. There must be many people who give up because their first experience with a therapist is not positive. The second or third may not be right either. A friend told me that she felt so intimidated by her psychologist she needed a gin and tonic before her sessions! I know that I am not the right person for everyone.

Counselling brings about change

For those clients who are willing to make a commitment to this strange way of spending time and money, the rewards are considerable. In a very short time they begin to know themselves better and to understand what it is they want out of life. They learn how to improve relationships and make positive choices in relation to partners and friends. Many clients have chosen an entirely different and more fulfilling career. Invariably clients report a significant improvement in their health, even in the case of long-standing illness. Many lose weight they have struggled to shed for years. As they feel themselves changing and enjoying life, they feel excited at what the future might hold. As a client wrote in a Christmas card: 'Thank you for a year free of anxiety and depression. Let's hope next year brings an orgasm!'

There are numerous pitfalls, however, even from the first counselling session. A desire for honesty in their own relationships is one of the first changes experienced by nearly every client, and it is a change that is not always welcomed by family and friends, who may prefer not to hear the truth and feel threatened by changes they observe. This is why it is often a lonely path, because many friends, perhaps better described as acquaintances, get lost along the way.

The following poem was given to me many years ago. I have since learnt that the original poem, which was considerably longer, was written in 1954 by Dorothy Law Nolte. It spells out quite simply what children need to feel good about themselves:

If a child:
... *lives with criticism, he learns to condemn*
... *lives with hostility, he learns to fight*
... *lives with ridicule, he learns to be shy*
... *lives with shame, he learns to feel guilty*

But if a child:
... *lives with tolerance, he becomes patient*
... *lives with encouragement, he displays confidence*
... *lives with praise, he gives appreciation*
... *lives with security, he develops trust*

And a child living with approval learns to like himself;
And through living with acceptance and friendship
discovers love in the world.

Chapter 2

Learn to trust yourself: confront your abuser

Child abuse casts a shadow the length of a lifetime
—**Herbert Ward**

As discussed in the first chapter, many clients, both men and women, experienced some form of neglect or abuse in childhood. This chapter explores the way clients are helped in counselling to understand the source of their difficulties, to face disowned feelings and learn to trust themselves. These feelings can be caused by parental mishandling or neglect but also by events that may be outside a parent's control. In addition, the tragic reality of the sexual abuse of children is discussed. Clients subjected to sexual abuse when they were young are faced with a difficult and painful journey if they decide to face their past. The rewards for doing so, however, are considerable.

Only a small percentage of people suffering anxiety, depression or emotional distress on a regular basis will seek counselling. Of that small number, an even smaller percentage see it through to a point where they free themselves of the discomfort and feel happy, able to pursue positive goals and choose loving relationships for themselves.

The process of counselling

Children who are blessed with good parenting and a trauma free childhood are likely to become confident adults, with a strong sense of self and the ability to deal with difficult situations in an effective manner. They are unlikely to seek (or to need) long term counselling. I can recall a number of clients over the years who came to see me because they needed help in addressing a particular issue. They were people who had good self-esteem and just a few counselling sessions were usually sufficient to clarify their concerns and resolve the problem.

There are, however, many people in our society who have suffered severe emotional trauma in childhood. Such trauma is damaging to the sense of self and creates the basis for unstable relationships, personal unhappiness and a general lack of fulfilment in life. At times, the psychological trauma runs deep into the personality and people affected in this way often suffer from anxiety and depression. In my experience, depression may be a signpost, pointing to an earlier wound.

In this book, I use the word 'wound' to describe the type of emotional damage that has been inflicted on a client, generally in childhood. For the child, the traumatic events that have occurred create significant distress and anxiety and a range of conflicting emotions. With no means of expressing her painful feelings, the child has no option but to suppress them and to attempt to live her life as if the trauma had not occurred. These are the disowned or unacknowledged feelings that continue to exert a powerful influence on the child's emotional state and behaviour in later life. While these memories are buried from *conscious* awareness so deep that they may be lost forever, they remain active, at times influencing decisions, choices and actions as well as emotional states. This continues throughout life unless the child, when she becomes an adult, chooses to look inside herself. The way the buried feelings continue to control the client when she attempts to form relationships is also explored. This is the wound referred to in this book.

In this chapter, I will be exploring ways to re-own and restore to the personality the feelings that were suppressed. Each step along this path creates more strength, more energy and a greater enjoyment of life. All clients who continue to work at this process reach a point where they develop greater self-esteem and a more resilient personality. They also enjoy more effective and satisfying relationships. And they have a real enjoyment of life.

To reach this point, a client needs to remove the bandage, uncover the wound and acknowledge its source. In my experience, the wound is always old. Clients will willingly discuss the treatment received at the hands of an ex-partner, for example, convinced that he inflicted the wound. In time they come to see that the ex-partner is a symptom, selected (often unconsciously) to maintain the wound. What is familiar is comfortable. What is unfamiliar creates anxiety. In order to change, we have to be prepared to take a risk. We have no way of knowing what the outcome will be.

Most clients have to reach a point of desperation: 'I'm sick of feeling like this' or 'Why do I keep repeating the same mistakes?' before being forced to confront the source of childhood wounding. Sometimes it takes the form of a collapse — prolonged sickness or one infection after another.

This week two of my female clients have managed to contact the wound and a third is very close. All three have defended themselves from looking at the real source of their wound for weeks. As defences, they have used denial, avoidance, distraction, (and at times alcohol and/

or drugs). Why? And why do I allow them to continue to defend themselves? Because sometimes the truth is hard to bear and they need to be strong enough to handle whatever it is they are so afraid to face. Only the client can determine when the time is right. I know I must wait.

Long after a relationship ended, with betrayal and lies, one of these women would attempt to distract herself from looking at the real wound (and do her best to distract me) by repeatedly focussing on the hurt inflicted by her ex-partner, yearning to be with him again. A person who had been spared early wounding would have valued herself more highly and let him go without a second thought.

As adults, many clients find themselves attracted to partners who reproduce the same patterns laid down in childhood, thereby creating a major source of instability in their relationships. Through their work in counselling, they are able to heal the past and relationships become easier.

As Judith Siegel writes in *What children learn from their parents' marriage*:

'All too often these emotional issues stay submerged until the child is almost grown and begins to date... it is not surprising that these young adults are attracted to partners who struggle with similar issues, and that they repeat the dynamics they were exposed to in their childhood home' (Siegel, 2000, p. 13).

The wounds suffered by these women were inflicted in childhood. They experienced their wounding in different ways according to the treatment received as children. For one client it was a feeling of being 'lost and lonely', for another it was the belief that she was 'worthless, never good enough' and the third, Dina, had taken into herself her mother's accusation that she had always been 'an angry child'.

In a counselling session I put to Dina that the early wounding of her childhood was still affecting her, causing anxiety, preventing her from feeling comfortable in a loving, affectionate relationship.

She responded: 'You might as well be speaking a foreign language. I can't get past the belief that it's my fault because my mother told me, from as far back as I can remember, that I was an angry child.'

'So do you believe you came out of the womb angry?'

'Well … no … but …'

'If you were to have a baby now, what would that baby need to thrive?'

'Love, affection, food, shelter, education …'

'Which of those things did you receive as a child from your parents?'

'Well, I was given food and a home and an education, but I can't remember any affection or love being given to me by my mother.'

Looking back, Dina can recognise that all she wanted was attention and love (what every child wants). A child has no way of expressing the hurt and anger she feels towards a parent for depriving her of her basic human needs. Any feeble attempts are met with further punishment. The language used by parents is all too familiar: 'Don't speak to me like that', 'Don't use that tone of voice with me' and, as unconscious memories rise up: 'How dare you …' The child absorbs these words, passed down through the generations. Dina's story is told in greater detail in Chapter 3: *The girl becomes a woman*.

The sexual abuse of children

Sexual abuse is an uncomfortable topic to write about; in our society it is still a taboo subject, rarely discussed. It is rarely addressed, even in books on parenting. And even in books on shame. To fail to mention the sexual abuse of children — which includes a number of my clients — would be cowardly however, and would distort the picture of what it means to be a child in our society.

It is rare for a client to tell me she was sexually abused until I am seen as an adult who can be trusted, and this can take a long time. When one considers the physical and emotional violation, the loss of trust and the over-whelming shame and guilt experienced by most victims, it comes as no surprise. Sexual abuse isolates young children who are victims in a lonely place. Usually they have been forced into silence and are afraid they would 'get into trouble' if they were to tell anyone. Children are skilled at wearing a mask to hide their pain. One client learnt very early in life how to present a 'happy face' to the world, however desperate she felt inside. Her mother would be irritated with her if she looked miserable and would exhort her to 'put on your happy face'. She is aware she still puts on her happy face at times.

From speaking to clients, I sense the damage caused by sexual abuse is a wound to their deepest sense of self. Over time they try to push the abuse out of mind but the memories remain. Many victims have told me that the more they tried to forget what took place, the more anxious and depressed they became and the greater their need to suppress the feelings with alcohol or drugs.

The extent of sexual abuse in our society is horrifying. According to Child Wise, a child protection organisation which focuses on the prevention of sexual abuse, one in five children is sexually abused in Australia. Only 3% of children ever tell anyone of the abuse. It came as a shock to me to learn that in 94% of cases, the perpetrator is known to the family or the child. Once I began working with clients, these figures were shown to be accurate.

Most of my clients who experienced sexual abuse, both the men and the women, were abused by a teenage or adult male, generally someone known and trusted within the family circle. In almost every case the abuser was a relative, a father, brother, stepfather, grandfather, cousin or uncle, someone they could expect to trust and someone whom others in the family trusted implicitly. In a number of these cases the abuser was an older brother (older by at least six years) possibly exploring his own sexuality. Who would suspect a brother? In one case, the abuser was the child's mother, and the victim her young son.

Several of these clients were young children, four, five, six years old when the abuse occurred, and sometimes it continued for years. In many cases it involved sexual penetration. Only one of the victims told her mother, many years after the abuse, when she was in her teens. It was fifteen years later that she decided to seek counselling. Often the abuser swore their victim to secrecy, threatening fearful consequences if they told anyone, such as: 'your mother might die/you will get into trouble with the police/we'll both go to jail/your parents will send you away', and assuring them: 'This is our secret' and 'You know you are special to me' and the all-confusing 'I love you'.

It is important for me to state at the outset that I believe all the clients I have worked with, who told me they had been abused, were being truthful. They stood to gain nothing by volunteering the information. A number of these clients confronted their abuser after working on doing so in counselling sessions; not once did a perpetrator deny the abuse.

For most people, it is impossible to comprehend how children can be sexually abused. How can anyone do this to an innocent child?

When a child is sexually abused by a close relative it is extremely puzzling for the victim. A client recalled her confusion: 'Doesn't this man love me? Is this why he is doing this to me?'

Deep down what is happening feels wrong and a child believes either: 'There is something wrong with me' or 'I must be bad'. Or both.

Counselling — a huge step

In Chapter 7: *Start loving, stop punishing your body* I have included a client's 'journey of healing'. It is a detailed account of confronting abuse, written by Alex, a young woman who was sexually abused by her uncle when she was fourteen. It is also a valuable account of the different stages my client went through as she worked to heal her past. I believe it would benefit anyone trying to come to terms with sexual abuse and unsure about whether or not to seek help. The reason that I have included her story in Chapter 7 and not in this chapter is because it was her body that forced her to confront the abuse. Each time she was tempted to give up the struggle to face her past, because it was simply too painful, it was her body that forced her to keep going. Alex is a successful athlete, a gymnast, who has to rely on her body to excel in her chosen field. She is accustomed to training on her own and relying on herself, so having counselling, asking someone for help, was not something that came easily to her. I have included here her description of reaching the decision to seek counselling as it demonstrates how hard it is for a victim to reveal the shameful truth about sexual abuse to anyone. As she wrestled with the decision of whether or not to come to the first session, her mind played tricks on her, as though encouraging her to avoid taking that crucial step.

The first task for Alex was telling her husband, who was deeply concerned for her and encouraged her to get help. In her words: 'Opening up to him gave me renewed strength and I believed I could handle it on my own, so with great determination I scoured the Internet and purchased self-help books. The problem was they all recommended a counsellor. I was still not convinced. But then the final straw — my body let me down — I tore my hamstring and was unable to train. Complete focus is required to complete difficult gymnastic skills and gym was the one place I could clear my mind and not be consumed by my suffering. Lying on a chiropractic table with my children right there I had my first breakdown in front of people I knew. I could not stop crying and blurted out that my uncle had hurt me when I was younger. My chiropractor was a close friend and a wonderful man. He comforted me and recommended I see a counsellor and he knew the perfect person. He gave me her card and urged me to call her. The thought of seeing a counsellor terrified me, but with support from my husband and close friends I made the decision to do just that.

'From deciding to see a counsellor and actually making the phone call took about two weeks. The first time I called it went to message bank and I could not believe it, but she sounded like some kind of spaced out, foolish hippy! I hung up without leaving a message. It took me over a week to admit it to myself, but I knew none of this was true. I was just scared. So I called again and it went to message bank again. It was the same message, but this time I heard the compassionate voice of someone who was offering help. I left a message and we made an appointment when she called me back.

' "To go or not to go?" That was the question I asked myself a thousand times every day leading up to the appointment. Then the day arrived. I was a mess. I decided to go to the chiropractor on the way to my appointment and get some background information on the counsellor. I was distraught. I was obviously in a state of panic and I cried as I searched his answers to my questions for an excuse not to go to the appointment. He simply answered my questions about how he knew her, what he knew about her and how she could help me, with calm and reassuring answers. I had come this far, so I went to the appointment and took another step towards choosing to heal. The counsellor looked much how I expected but quite unexpectedly I felt immediately comfortable with her. I felt that maybe, just maybe, she would be able to help me put all of this behind me.' Alex's story is continued in Chapter 7.

Over the years I have worked with a number of women who had the confidence and strength to say no when their fathers attempted to have sex with them around the stage of puberty. One woman was in her early sixties when she came to see me, concerned about other aspects of her life. She still recalled the terror she felt, fifty years earlier, when her father came into her room one night and woke her. She shouted at him to leave her alone. After trying unsuccessfully to persuade her to let him into her bed, he left the room. She lay awake for the rest of the night, petrified. The following day when she saw him on his own, she told him: 'If you ever try to do that again, I'll go to the police.' Needless to say she was deeply affected by his behaviour. Her father was no longer someone she could trust. Her courage saved her from far greater trauma.

The loss of a trustworthy father for a young woman, the one man she should be able to go to, to be hugged and held, the one man who should protect his daughter's vulnerability and innocence, is immeasurable. It only takes one episode to damage an individual. If your father is not to be trusted, what man is?

A client who was sexually abused by her stepfather from the age of seven told me she heard her mother in the passage outside the door, on her way to the bathroom. She was terrified and bewildered by what was happening to her. She believes her mother knew. Her mother would never listen to criticism of her partner.

The feelings that have been suppressed are difficult to access. Clearly a child subjected to abuse who remains silent does not feel sufficiently confident in herself or trusting of her parents and most likely believes she was to blame for what had occurred. The feelings are too hard to understand and therefore to process. The child becomes overwhelmed and bewildered.

Jenna was sexually abused by her grandfather when she was very little and struggled with addiction for many years. Facing the truth of what he did to her was a nearly impossible task: 'It was so hard for me to look at the truth. This was the person who abused me. This was a man I loved, who loved me. I had to acknowledge the truth of who my grandfather really was and how someone who I thought loved me ignored my innocence and my spirit. He manipulated my vulnerability to get what he wanted for his own selfish desires. What did that make me? Who did that make me? I am left with the core of the wound and while it's incredibly painful, it's a relief not to be destroying myself any longer through denial. He has no power over me now.'

What I understand from the clients who found the strength to talk about their experience is that it has affected every one of their relationships — with school friends, with relatives, with colleagues and especially with partners. How can you place trust in another human being when someone you believed to be trustworthy has shown they are not and has violated you?

A client who was sexually abused as a child by her uncle worked hard in counselling to change the way she was in the world, in all her relationships. She told me she learnt very early to be 'dishonest and untruthful'.

I asked her who *had* she been honest with in her life. She replied, 'No one.'

I asked: 'Are you honest with yourself?'

She replied, 'No.'

Reaching a point where she was ready to look at herself was the beginning of significant change. A few months later she told me she had started being truthful with everyone, and while it felt very strange, she had begun to like herself more as a result of her new honesty.

Children believe adults to be in the right (and an adult to them is anyone older than 17 or 18). This means it must be their fault. At a fundamental level, they need to believe that adults (parents, grandparents, teachers) are good. It follows, therefore, that they must be bad, because what is happening feels wrong. A lonely child craves affection, physical as well as emotional, and many clients believed that in part they were complicit in the abuse. At the start they may have welcomed the attention and the affection but had no idea what was to take place. Deep down many believe they were responsible for the abuse.

One client was just eleven when a man whom her parents had invited to stay for several months sexually abused her, threatening to kill her if she told anyone. She told me, tearfully, that she believed it was her fault as she had invited the abuse.

'How did you do that?'

'I thought he was a kind man at first and I would talk to him after school, before my parents came home from work. I was nice to him.'

Most victims of abuse feel such shame and guilt that they cannot reveal the awful truth to a soul. Secrecy becomes a way of life and it distorts their view of themselves. Over the years a number of clients revealed that they had been abused and while they could handle facing the abuse in the safety of the counselling sessions, the idea of revealing to family and friends what had happened to them was simply too horrifying; the feeling of shame, the belief that in some way the abuse was their fault, make it impossible. The client wonders: how would people react? What would they think of me?

A need to be liked by others often controls victims of sexual abuse, affecting their relationship with everyone they know and preventing them from forming healthy friendships. Even more tragic is the fact that some will seek out abusive relationships because these feel familiar, normal. It is what they believe they deserve in life.

Confronting the abuser

For most clients who have suffered sexual abuse, healing is a slow and gradual process, at times extremely painful. The first step involves facing the truth of what happened. I refer to this stage as 'removing the bandage', because invariably clients have chosen to bury all memory of the abuse in an attempt to protect themselves. The memories are horrible — most clients feel physically sick when they talk to me about what actually occurred.

A client usually begins by contacting the feelings associated with the experience, invariably hurt, betrayal, shame and guilt. Many clients had found ways of defending themselves from the feelings because they were so uncomfortable. Some had turned to alcohol or drugs; others had had a series of abusive relationships and focussed their energy on their partners. My clients were young when the abuse occurred, between the ages of four and fourteen. For a very long time, therefore, they needed to maintain a false image and to behave as though they were unchanged. The truth is that they were no longer the same person; they were changed forever.

Through contacting the painful feelings in counselling sessions, the client begins to see that instead of being someone who is party to a guilty secret, she is a victim. The person who took advantage of her innocence is her abuser. Confiding in a counsellor is a crucial step as he or she is often the first person the client has risked telling about the experience. Will she be believed? Can the counsellor be trusted? How will the counsellor react — with understanding or with horror?

An abusive relationship is particularly confusing to a child because her genuine feelings have usually been engaged by her abuser. This is the grooming process and it is important that a client understands this is what happened to her. She did not invite the abuse. Slowly the client begins to heal, to trust and value herself and to believe she is not responsible for what occurred. There is a long process of recognising that this was a breach of trust and she does not need to feel shame or guilt. Her abuser was the one with power and the one who ought to feel the shame. Once the client feels more comfortable with discussing the abuse, she may decide to tell parents, family members or friends. At times the client is fearful of doing so because of possible repercussions within the family, if (as is quite likely) her abuser is a relative.

Every client that I have worked with who was sexually abused has reached the point where she feels anger at the way she was treated. I believe this is a healthy and appropriate emotion, which often results in the client being able to free herself to some degree of the damaging feelings caused by the abuse. It is at this stage that many clients decide they want to confront the person who abused them. An expression I use when encouraging clients to stop blaming themselves is 'put the shit where it belongs' and for a client this message is a powerful one. It involves the recognition that she was not to blame for the events of her childhood. She can express her anger at being violated and regain her power.

Several clients decided they would write to their abuser while a few were determined to confront the person face to face. Others wanted desperately to confront the person who abused them but were afraid of the consequences. These are decisions I believe only the client can make. A counsellor's role is to support the client and to ensure that she feels sufficiently confident and has the necessary support in place if she chooses to face her abuser.

The sad truth is that the trauma of being sexually abused (even attempted abuse) does not go away easily. It always leaves a scar. A client, abused as a young child, told me she found it hard to be intimate with men as an adult: 'I am aware that I hold back and keep my true feelings locked away. I am always reminded of what happened when I was little and I can't let myself go, however much I want to. I can't stand feeling exposed, vulnerable and trapped.'

Zara, who was abused at the age of five by a much older cousin, asked her parents to come to a counselling session. When she was a teenager she had told them what had taken place but felt they didn't really believe her and certainly didn't take the abuse seriously. Both parents were defensive in the session and said they didn't even know exactly what had occurred. What did he do? My client was so distressed she was unable to speak and asked me to tell them. When I did so, they were shocked. I suspect they had been in denial to this point, wanting to believe the abuse was minor.

Clients have responded to the idea of 'putting the shit where it belongs' in a number of different ways, even to the point of travelling overseas to confront their abuser. It is important to state that the confrontation does not need to be aggressive. By the time these women had done the necessary work with me in our sessions, they were able to express anger without exploding. Sometimes it is not desirable or possible to address the person who caused the pain and healing occurs within the trusting relationship that is developed with the therapist.

Many therapies today reject the notion of confronting one's abuser and instead recommend we practise forgiveness and 'turn the other cheek'. In my work I have seen, time and time again, that it is necessary to get in touch with one's anger first, before there is any point in attempting to forgive. Contacting their anger has been a crucial step with several clients, who were previously attacking themselves and becoming ill.

As a counsellor it is thrilling to see a client who has struggled for a long time with debilitating and shameful feelings reach a point where she has learnt to like and to value herself.

One of the most rewarding birthday treats I can recall was in 2010 when I received a text message: 'I f****** did it'. I knew what it meant. After working hard for over a year, Alex had reached a point where she valued herself sufficiently to face her abuser. She had driven to her uncle's house an hour away early one morning and confronted him over the sexual abuse he subjected her to as a young girl. When she told me a week earlier that she was ready to confront him, I made sure she was prepared for his possible response which might disarm her and prevent her from carrying out her mission. I said he might apologise profusely, he might assure her he had thought about her continually over the past twenty years or he might try to put the blame on her by suggesting she invited his behaviour. Incredibly, he did all three things. She was prepared for him. Alex told me in a phone conversation later that day: 'I knew I would feel different if I confronted him. I didn't know just how good I would feel.' Her story is told in Chapter 7: *Start loving, stop punishing your body.*

Case study: the odd one out

Annie, a client in her mid twenties when she came to see me, had learned that her father sexually abused her sister when she was little. Initially he denied that he had done anything, later conceding that he abused her 'only once.' He said that at the time he believed the seven year old child he was abusing to be his wife, my client's mother. He maintained it had happened 'a long time ago' and couldn't understand why the family was making such a fuss.

For Annie, her father's actions were shattering: 'I feel betrayed my own father could sexually abuse his daughter. I was devastated. Hearing about it turned my life upside down. It's something I will never forget — it will probably be with me for the rest of my life — even though I'm not the one he abused.

'When I was about twelve years old I remember hearing a school friend had been abused by her stepfather and I also remember how disgusted my dad was about it. Yet he had done the same to Rhiannon.

'I was very angry when Dad denied what he had done. Not wanting to confront him about it has been extremely hard. At times I felt, and still feel, that I'm gutless. Most people I know would confront an issue like this, but I cannot bring myself to do so. I'm not even sure why. But every time I think about what he's done to Rhiannon, to my family and myself, I go back to feeling angry and disappointed in him. I'm not sure I will ever feel differently.

'I don't understand why I am the only one in my family who feels this way. My family seem to have moved on very quickly, especially my older sister. And Rhiannon, whom he abused, even asks Dad for money and has let her seven year old daughter spend the day with him on her own. But I also know that Rhiannon is very messed up. She drinks heavily, has terrible relationships and doesn't always treat her daughter well.

'I seem to have bad relationships with men too. I choose the wrong type. In the past year, however, since working on this in counselling sessions, I feel I have improved and am choosing much better partners.'

It is not the first time I have heard a story like Annie's. In some families, secrets and lies are common. No one wants to create a rift or to spoil family relationships, preferring to ignore what has happened. Sometimes the consequences of standing up for what you believe in are far-reaching and may draw criticism from unexpected quarters.

In Annie's case she was left on the outer, no longer able to speak honestly with anyone in her family because they colluded in support of a father who abused his daughter. Annie had no support. It was a significant loss for her, as she was very much in the centre of the family before the abuse was known about; for years she had strived to keep her family together and to have a good relationship with each person. She was deeply concerned that her seven year old niece was suffering neglect and was a child at risk. For her own development, however, letting go of her old attachment to family members was a painful but necessary process.

Annie's situation illustrates clearly the way the client's relationship with the therapist is crucial in the healing process. In understanding Annie's distress at both her father's behaviour and her concern for her niece, it was possible to validate her feelings, to acknowledge her indignation and to support her in her response to the situation. Her family, on the other hand, behaved as though she was overreacting. They preferred to ignore the facts and discount the effect on each family member of a father's abuse of his daughter.

How long will it take me to get through this?

This is another question I am asked and it is not one I can answer easily. What I can say is that clients will know when they feel comfortable, free of the controlling feelings from old wounds and ready to leave counselling, as illustrated in the following case study.

Case study: a brother's love

Reuban was in his late twenties when he first came to counselling on the recommendation of a close friend. He had decided it was time to get help in dealing with the effects of being sexually abused by his older brother.

In the early stages of counselling, Reuban would often cancel appointments and disappear for long periods between sessions. What I came to understand was that the counselling was extremely confronting. Reuban had to access painful, dark and shameful feelings in order to heal. He felt ashamed of the abuse, and ashamed of some of his subsequent behaviour. He needed time out to gain in strength before being able to confront the next layer of wounding. There were times when he would block out all thoughts of the trauma, because it became too overwhelming. When he felt stronger and able to face the abuse once more, he would contact me again and we would continue where we left off. The risk in this situation is that the client will feel ashamed of his erratic behaviour, too ashamed to ring for an appointment after a long absence. For this reason, I usually contact clients who have disappeared without explanation — a brief text message or email — to make it easier for them to return.

It was more than a year before Reuban believed in himself enough to confront his brother in a letter. This is part of what he wrote:

I was an impressionable 7 year old when you changed my life forever, robbing me of my childhood and my innocence. For 10 years you abused me and I am left feeling empty, hollow and unable to trust myself in a relationship. I have suffered enormous pain, guilt and shame. I have difficulty connecting with men intimately and have had problems with drugs, alcohol and sexual promiscuity. I have had one relationship breakdown after another. I should have been able to look to my older brother to protect me from the world and shield me from harm, to look up to him and trust him. I am supposed to love my brother but instead I am filled with hatred and disgust for what you subjected me to for ten years. For a very long time I was too afraid to face what was happening. It has taken me years to accept that it was not my fault.

You were the one in a position of power and abused it by taking away what can never be brought back. But despite the constant nightmares, pain and loss, I know I will survive and with help I will be able to heal my life.

Reuban didn't receive a reply to the letter, so a month later he phoned his brother whose only concern was that their parents should never know about what took place.

As a result of his infidelity, Reuban's relationship with his partner Simon was put under great pressure. Reuban was fortunate in that Simon came to understand the effects of the abuse he had experienced as a child and cared enough about him to support him as he faced the damage of his past. He agreed to come to a few sessions with Reuban and was able to assist the counselling process by revealing the way Reuban's difficulties affected their relationship.

Not surprisingly, Reuban had avoided contact with his parents and the relationship had become strained. While he wanted to reveal the truth to them regarding his anger towards his brother, he was afraid of what effect this might have on the family. Keeping the secret, however, was creating paralysing feelings of anxiety. Reuban had stopped seeing me for a time because he sensed that I believed he should tell his parents about the abuse. While I aim not to give advice, I was concerned that Reuban was suffering deeply, turning his anger on himself and becoming depressed. He was isolating himself from everyone, including family. I received a phone call one day: 'I want to tell my parents the truth.'

For the next six months, Reuban prepared himself for what felt like a terrifying ordeal — telling his parents that he had been sexually abused by their oldest son.

Four years after confronting his brother, Reuban asked his parents to come to a counselling session with him. It was certainly one of the most painful sessions I can recall; I felt deeply for each person in the room, most of all for Reuban. Distressed and tearful, he read a letter to his parents, revealing what had taken place when he was a child. He reminded them of the time they found and read his diary when he was about fifteen. In the diary he had written in detail what was happening to him. His parents questioned him at the time but accepted his explanation that he had made it up. He had often wondered how they could have let this go. 'Why didn't you drag me, kicking and screaming, to a counsellor?' he asked in the letter.

It was shattering for his parents. Both were in a state of shock when Reuban finished reading. Not only had one of their sons been abused, the perpetrator was another son. To their credit, they believed everything in the letter and his mother stated that it was now her responsibility to confront her oldest son and force him to seek help. Reuban's relationship with his parents improved immediately.

Within a month of this meeting, Reuban was a transformed man. He was feeling good about himself and as he put it: 'I'm getting to know the real me, and to know that I'm a good person, not evil as I was made to believe by my brother.'

Three months later, Reuban told me he was feeling happy. What he had discovered was that he was capable of giving and receiving love, for the first time in his life.

It is clear from Reuban's story that the long period he spent in counselling (four years) was necessary. It allowed him the time to gain sufficient strength first to face the trauma of the abuse and then to reveal the truth to his parents. In some ways confronting his brother was a less demanding task.

Often clients found it hard to understand how their parents could be unaware that something was wrong.

They puzzled about this: 'Surely they noticed something different about me?' Alex (who was abused by her uncle at the age of fourteen) recalled how strange it felt at the time, that no one knew: 'I have always found it so difficult to believe and even more difficult to accept that I could be so completely traumatised and no one could see it. It made me feel invisible, worthless'.

What I have come to understand is that at times the child's parents were not attending closely to their son or daughter for a variety of reasons. Some were embroiled in their own relationship conflict or emotional traumas, while others were preoccupied with work and spent long hours away from home. In two families (one of these being Reuban's) the parents' attention was taken up by a child with a severe disability. Sometimes, warning signs are ignored. Several parents have told me, on learning the truth: 'I did think it was a little strange at the time, but then I just thought …' If parents are not watching closely, a child is easy prey and is at risk. We all need to be mindful of the statistics of child abuse. I should like to hope that my writing about sexual abuse would alert even a small number of people to what is happening to children in our society, even today.

In some cases, the parents had placed their trust in someone they later learned was anything but trustworthy, such as a teacher or priest.

In April 2011, I attended the presentation of Chrissie Foster's book, *Hell on the way to Heaven*, to the parliamentary library in Melbourne. Her book is an incredibly moving but shocking account of her two daughters' sexual assault by a Catholic priest at their primary school in Melbourne. Chrissie Foster describes the way the priest drugged one of her daughters before assaulting her, ensuring she could not tell anyone what had occurred. She was later told by a court official that the priest had done this to other children. Chrissie was clearly an involved, loving, protective and devoted mother. All her care of her children wasn't enough, however, to protect her little girls from a paedophile priest. In the following weeks I corresponded with Chrissie as I was greatly affected by her book. In Chrissie's words: 'After the utter shock of finding out that sexual assault had happened to my daughters and then discovering how easily it had happened, I felt it made all my efforts at protecting my daughters a sham. In the eighties it was 'stranger danger', but nothing could be further from the truth given the fact that 95% of sex offences against children are by someone known to you or your child. Why wasn't this up on billboards for us all to read? What chance did any parent have without this knowledge?'

Counselling offers the client the opportunity to heal old wounds and to validate the uncomfortable feelings that have plagued them. Whatever form the abuse takes, I believe victims are helped by facing what happened to them, if the right support is in place. They need to be able to trust that person and it is crucial it is someone with experience and competence who understands what the client needs. In this sensitive situation, a therapist needs to be aware of the risk of re-traumatising a client unintentionally. By avoiding the truth, victims can find themselves suffering from anxiety, depression and other illness, or reliant on alcohol or drugs to numb the pain. Chapter 7 explores the way buried pain has a way of affecting us for years.

Invariably, through examining old wounds, clients are able to reconnect to who they believe they were before life events changed the path they were on. That is why it is a long journey. We need to feel strong enough to face the feelings we have buried in the past and reclaim the parts of our self we abandoned.

Chapter 3

The girl becomes a woman

'What is my life for and what am I going to do with it?
I don't know and I'm afraid.'
—Sylvia Plath *(The unabridged journals 2000)*

This chapter explores the lives of eight women who came to see me for counselling, bearing the wounds suffered in childhood as discussed in the first two chapters. Each one was willing to tell her story and to write of her experience. Invariably, past parental wounding had resulted in anxious feelings and a lack of confidence in handling relationships. I believe many of the parents of these women would be shocked to learn that the way they parented and disciplined their children had led to emotional difficulties and a loss of self-esteem in their daughters. As discussed earlier, this is the way they believe children should be brought up. This is the way they were disciplined. It is all they know.

Struggling with problematic relationships, both in the workplace and in their private life, persuaded seven of the eight women to seek counselling. Just one was in a good relationship. What each woman lacked was a robust sense of self and the confidence and resilience to handle adult life.

As young children these women behaved in ways that were unacceptable to their parents and were criticised or punished for it. They then shut down their feelings, at times concluding that they were flawed in some way. As seen in the previous chapter, one client believed she was 'never good enough' while another was convinced she had always been 'an angry child'.

For three of the women, the damage to their self-esteem occurred in early adolescence. Family trauma such as death or divorce had a big impact and the young girl believed she had to deal with her distress alone. In most cases, her feelings and response to the trauma were ignored. In their families parenting styles differed, but in nearly every case my client had been denied the opportunity to get the help she needed and to express her feelings, particularly if these were perceived as negative. Clearly most of the parents were not comfortable with their own emotions and chose to ignore them, thus having no capacity to understand the suffering of their 'difficult' daughter.

In controlling a child's behaviour and silencing her, parents are unknowingly preventing their daughter from handling emotions in any real way, and down the track, preventing her from knowing how to be in a healthy relationship. Initially, all eight women spoke of their lack of confidence in relating to others, to partners and work colleagues. All but one (married to her childhood sweetheart) despaired of ever having a loving relationship with a partner.

I believe that parents can help their children to understand their feelings from a very young age, in particular the negative emotions such as anger, jealousy and resentment. If parents ignore or punish children for showing these emotions, the child learns that certain feelings can't be shared and so shuts them down. Mark Greenberg says that this makes the child overstressed, both physiologically and psychologically, 'because the emotion is still there, and it puts an obstacle in the way of developing a basic trust between the child and adults' (Greenberg, 2003, p. 259).

Each of the eight women presented as vulnerable and lacking in confidence when they came to counselling. Not only did they experience difficulty in trusting others, they were unsure how to trust themselves and looked to the outside world for approval. They spoke of feeling 'insecure', 'insignificant' and 'worthless'. Buried beneath the lack of confidence were feelings they had suppressed, or as Mark Greenberg puts it, 'shut down'.

In reflecting on the eight women, it is apparent that what they shared was not only the lack of confidence and self-esteem as a result of their early experience of inadequate parenting. They also shared a strong belief that there was a different path open to them if only they could discover what it was. They were hopeful that counselling could offer a new way of being in the world. They wanted to know and to like themselves and to be able to act with confidence. They were also willing to form a relationship with me that involved committing to the counselling process. To this end, they needed to be honest and trusting. For a number of these women, whose mothers were clearly not to be trusted, this was a leap of faith. The alliance that forms between the client and therapist is crucial for healing to occur. In my practice, many young women come through the door. The length of time they remain in counselling varies greatly. The women whose stories are told here all stayed in counselling for a considerable length of time because they believed it was necessary to treat their wounds, the roots of which went very deep. As a result, they transformed almost every aspect of their lives.

In spite of major changes in society, the stereotype of the 'nice girl' lives on. While little girls are expected to be well-behaved and compliant, we are still quite accepting of the idea that 'boys will be boys'. Boisterous behaviour is deemed acceptable for a 'real boy'. (In Chapter 4, the experience of male clients is explored.) The instruction to be a 'good girl' rolls off the tongue so effortlessly. Even as a grandparent I found it hard to avoid saying these words.

Many of my clients learnt in their families to be obedient, quiet and submissive. Looking back at their early years, they describe themselves as 'a good girl', both at school and at home. Often they chose to behave in this way to please others, mainly parents but also grandparents and teachers. A client told me she was criticised by friends at school for being 'too nice'.

What are little girls made of?
Sugar and spice and all things nice.
That's what little girls are made of.

At times, 'being nice' was the only way these young women could imagine surviving, having observed the repercussions that followed for not being nice or good. Several clients remembered seeing the punishment meted out to their brothers while others had experienced personally the pain brought about by misbehaviour. A client said she was always good because it was 'too frightening to be naughty'. She recalls being terrified of her father when she was very young, possibly three or four, because he would lose his temper with her brother who was two years older. Another client remembers the distress she felt when she saw her father hitting her little sister who was lying on the floor. Often a young girl has no idea what has prompted her father's violence. Docile behaviour is an obvious way of avoiding trouble.

If not addressed, the paralysing fear of growing up with a violent father who is given to explosions of rage continues to exert influence into adulthood. Mothers, of course, can also be terrifying but generally a father's size, aggression and explosive behaviour is the more frightening. Fathers, moreover, are usually stronger and can hit harder.

Respect your elders

Tanya, a young client, raised in a fairly harsh, authoritarian family, told me with pride that she had spoken up for the first time recently when she felt angry at something a family member said to her. She felt better straight away. Over the following days, however, she was aware of powerful feelings of guilt that caused her to feel anxious. In the counselling session she was able to see how acting for herself, doing something completely out of character in her family, had led to her discomfort: 'I was brought up to believe that my parents knew what was right and I didn't. You had to respect your elders whatever they said, listen to others, sit down and be quiet. If I expressed an opinion I was told it was wrong anyway. This is what I lived with my whole childhood and adolescence and it was too hard to fight against it. If I tried to stand up for what I believed in, I was punished.'

It is hardly surprising that Tanya felt anxious when she stood up for herself for the first time. Both parents had punished her for minor crimes in the past. Leaving an unwashed plate in the sink could be enough to inflame her mother's wrath. At the age of twenty, an angry exchange with her father led to Tanya trying to run out of the house, but her father blocked the doorway and fought her, knocking her to the floor. Tanya left the house. That night her father ended up in hospital with what turned out to be kidney stones. Tanya was blamed: 'What kind of daughter are you?' asked her mother.

Moving away from the conditioning of her upbringing was quite unfamiliar and therefore frightening. The expectation that she would submit had been a powerful force in her early years, particularly since her parents resorted to physical punishment if they were disobeyed.

Tanya addressed many of the experiences of her childhood when she took part in a weekend group with six others. Initially she was reluctant to criticise her mother as it aroused feelings of guilt. The indignation and anger felt on her behalf by others, however, enabled her to address the abuse and to see that she had not deserved her parents' violent treatment.

She was able to express the hurt of her early years, and the damage it had caused: 'I lost myself as a person. For many years I despised myself. I have never felt safe. I have always been scared of my mother. She belittled me and criticised me constantly. I honestly believe she beat me because she felt like it and as a result I don't even like being touched.'

What Tanya realised was that she could no longer remain silent. For the first time she could feel for the young child she was once, frightened of her mother and critical of herself. What was apparent also was that she had begun to value her new knowledge and to know her true self. There was no going back.

It is in fact terrifying to a young woman, forced into submission as a child, to contemplate the possible repercussions of speaking out in support of herself. Quite apart from beatings, she may be risking her parents' withdrawal of affection, their abandonment. For her survival, a child needs to believe she loves her parents and is loved by them.

When they first came to counselling, many female clients were afraid to stand up for themselves. Some had lost touch with their real feelings in the trauma of life in their family. Helping them to find their true self was clearly not going to be a simple task. This is the only life they know. The idea of changing, for a young woman, is unimaginable at this point. Her distress, however, demands her attention. Before she can change, she needs to find her inner strength and increase her self-esteem. She needs to believe she can achieve this.

For some it is simply too hard and perhaps it feels too late to act. Recently a woman in her sixties cried tears of anger and hurt as she spoke of the emotional abuse inflicted on her by her mother, now in her nineties. She has not been able to find the strength to stand up to her mother and to tell her how hurt she feels. It is too difficult for her to change. I suspect her mother will go to her grave unchallenged.

A number of my clients are the children of European migrants who came to Australia after the war, seeking a better future for the family. Many arrived in this country with no more than a suitcase and had to start a new life far from home. In some cases the parents were unable to adjust to a different culture and chose to preserve the values of the one they had left. No doubt in their country of origin society has changed and relaxed over time and parenting styles have softened. For the children growing up in Australia, it was difficult to reconcile the two cultures, often feeling they fitted in to neither. How do you find a place for yourself with no role model? To get on in this country, the younger generation needed to embrace the Australian way of life but were held back by parents who relied on them for support while disapproving of the freedom they were seeking.

Many of the parents had no other family in Australia and I suspect that in some cases they were choosing to leave problematic family relationships in their country of origin. I suspect, also, that they parented in much the same way as they were parented. Often, boys and girls are raised very differently in these cultures. It is important to stress, of course, that many European families who came to this country are extremely nurturing and do not fit this picture.

Case study: finding her own voice

Jemma's family had migrated from Italy. When she first came to counselling she was in great distress. A concerned friend had contacted me on her behalf. Jemma was unhappy in her marriage (her second), and it was clear she was being exploited by her husband. She felt extreme shame at the prospect of another divorce as in her culture divorce was considered a disgrace.

Jemma described a harsh and punitive childhood. Her brother was ten years older, but the two siblings were brought up very differently. While he was allowed considerable freedom — a motorbike, an active social life with friends and no responsibility within the family — Jemma was expected to stay at home and help her mother and to act as interpreter for her parents because their English was poor. She was not allowed to go to friends' houses or to invite anyone home.

On one occasion a school friend's mother insisted on

accompanying Jemma home after school to suggest to her mother that the two girls play from time to time at one another's houses. Jemma's mother declined the offer, closing the front door on the other parent. Jemma was punished for allowing this encounter to take place.

Around the age of nine, Jemma asked her mother if she could learn to play the piano. She was told she had no talent. What she wanted for herself was never a consideration for her parents. For much of her early life, her brother bullied and taunted her because she was forced to stay at home while he was free to live a more normal life by Australian standards. Jemma described her childhood and adolescence as 'living an invisible life.'

When I first met Jemma I was shocked at the degree of her submission. She was clearly an intelligent, sensitive young woman with strong values who had put everyone else's needs before her own. She had no sense of her own self; her life was governed by her mother's expectations. Jemma suffered deep guilt if she failed to behave like a dutiful daughter. She believed her very survival depended on having her mother's approval.

In Jemma's own words: ' "Shush, don't talk, just be a good girl". This is all l heard growing up. My early conditioning robbed me of my voice and my rights as a person.

'Being a good girl was the only way to get a smile in my family, maybe some love and attention. I learned early on that this was all l could do. Ours was a fairly brutal migrant background and law and order was enforced in the home. Things were done a certain way and if you did anything wrong you were in massive trouble. There was not much room for error, so I just didn't make mistakes. I strived to be perfect in a world that is so far from it. My mother only showed me attention if I did my chores. At an early age I cleaned, ironed and generally helped out to obtain a little bit of love, or maybe just some attention. I strived to do well, not just at school but in everything I did. It was exhausting living like this but I knew no other way. My parents behaved as though they were only just surviving. They clothed, fed and educated us, but there was not much time for fun. I sometimes don't blame them because they knew no better.

'I transferred this 'good behaviour' into my adult life, believing that the only way to have love and friendship from friends or partners was to run around after everybody. I put everyone else in my life before me. It meant becoming a slave. I knew no other way to behave.

'I felt as though I were living my life in a prison, and all I thought about was how to escape. There was an obvious way, which at the time seemed like the only solution — get married.

'When I was nineteen, my father suffered an aneurysm. It was devastating watching him turn into a vegetable in hospital. He died shortly after. I felt as though my whole world had been turned upside down. My father was the one person in the family who offered me a little understanding, even though he was very strict. Then I met my first boyfriend — a policeman, someone with authority. Looking back, I can see I thought that maybe he was someone who could guide me. How wrong I was. When I think about the person I am today, it's hard to understand why I was attracted to him, other than a desperate need for support. By the age of twenty-two I was married. It was the beginning and the end of my life. I was shocked at the way he treated me, but I put up with it. I foolishly thought the more I did for him, the more accepted I would be and the better he would treat me.

'In fact he did exactly what he felt like. He drank heavily, pleased himself, socialised with his colleagues and treated me with contempt. He called the shots and I followed like a lamb. He was very motivated by money and would have sold his grandmother for a dollar or two. I am honest to the last cent. We were totally unsuited. I knew I had to leave him.

'Shortly after separating I met someone else. Basically I had learned nothing about myself and relationships. I now know that I was trying to fill the void inside me, ignoring all warning signs. I remember a friend advising me to take time out, see a counsellor and get some advice. I couldn't believe she was suggesting that I speak to a stranger about my problems. The rule in my family was clear: "speak to nobody about our business and never discuss your problems". I thought this is what you did — you just handled things alone. Needless to say, my second marriage turned out to be no better than the first. I ended the relationship, feeling deeply ashamed at a second divorce. I knew that it was time to look at the way I was allowing others to treat me.

'I realised that as well as my two partners, many friends had just used me. The only person to blame was myself because I virtually laid out a mat on top of me and encouraged people to wipe their feet on me. I never spoke up for fear that using my voice would lose me these people who treated me so badly. It's hard to believe that is how I lived for so many years. I was afraid I would upset people, but I was happy to allow others to make me feel very upset.

'I came to the realisation that my upbringing was a contributing factor and that the cycle needed to be changed. I couldn't continue the way I was.

'I decided to try counselling. By this time I was nearly thirty and in a bad way. I saw a few people, but it was hard if you had no relationship with the person. Some counsellors simply looked and stared at me, others just nodded and showed not one ounce of compassion. It was disheartening and I was losing faith that counselling could help me. Fortunately I then heard of another counsellor through a friend at work. At my first appointment, I knew this was the right person for me.'

Jemma spent several years in counselling before she believed in herself sufficiently to change her behaviour, to stop running around after her friends, to challenge abusive treatment from several men in her work place, to limit her visits to her mother (every evening after work when I first knew her) and to consider what she wanted for herself out of life.

I knew at times the counselling sessions were confronting. I regularly questioned the way she was allowing others to treat her and I used the word 'slave' to describe the treatment she was prepared to accept. Initially the thought of losing her 'friends' was frightening. In time she understood she could not move forward while she allowed people to exploit her, and that included her mother.

Around this time, Jemma had two frightening dreams which she brought in to discuss. In the first, a dog was caught under the wheels of a car and was being dragged along. It was obviously going to be killed. An old man, bald, European, was watching. He was laughing and seemed not to care.

In the second dream, Jemma looked out into her front garden to see lots of dead dogs lying all over the garden, their feet in the air.

The dreams were terrifying. Jemma's own dog was her main source of comfort at the time, so the dreams upset her greatly. When we discussed what the dreams might be alerting her to, Jemma came to see that the dogs represented the parts of her that had been killed off, first as a result of the harsh driven values of the old European culture and in the second dream, by the way she had been treated by many in her circle of 'friends'. The dreams marked a turning point. Recognising that she couldn't look to others to nurture her forced Jemma to start looking after herself, to stand up for herself and to confront abusive relationships.

I remember a desperate phone call from Jemma the first time she had found the courage to challenge her mother. She sounded terrified, sensing that her world was about to come to an end. I was delighted for her. In her words: 'With a lot of help in counselling, I learned to respect and value myself and to find my voice. I began to stand up for myself and say what I needed to say, maybe at times hurting people along the way but letting them know that I wasn't prepared to be treated badly anymore. I learnt to stand on my own two feet. I learnt to look inside myself to know what is best for me. I am still learning. Thirty odd years of abusive treatment becomes a normal way of life. I have to work at it constantly because standing up for myself is not a natural thing for me to do. To be a good girl and shut up is what comes naturally. I know I cannot do that to myself ever again. I know I want to be treated well by the people in my life.'

As Jemma described, over time she learned to value herself. In her late thirties she met 'the love of my life', a man who saw her for her true self. She experienced the joy of giving and receiving unconditional love for the first time.

In Jemma's case, the family operated on a set of rigid, fixed rules that were applied regardless of the situation. This is described by Virginia Satir as 'a closed system'. She says that such a system is invariably 'dominated by power, neurotic dependency, obedience, deprivation, conformity and guilt. It cannot allow for any changes, for changes will upset the balance'. She adds that people find it hard to break away and the members of the system 'are kept ignorant, limited and ruled through fear, punishment, guilt and dominance. A closed system has to break down over time because one or more persons comes to the end of their coping ability'. (Satir, 2008, p.119)

Both Tanya and Jemma's families fit with Satir's description of a closed system. It is clear that when they came to counselling, both women were at the end of their coping ability. And both were experiencing fairly severe health problems.

In discussing how family systems come to be created, Satir states: 'I believe that a system is based on what the adults, who are in charge of the family, bring from past experiences, their hopes, knowledge, information and values. This is woven together through their self-esteem, communication, emotional rules and survival vulnerabilities' (ibid., p. 118).

Abandoning the role of the 'good girl' invariably leads to extreme guilt. Any thoughts of teenage rebellion are far too terrifying. The silencing of feelings, the sadness and loneliness, count for nothing when compared with the fear of disobeying parental expectations and being seen as 'bad'. Satir comments that: 'Human beings seem willing to pay whatever price is necessary to feel loved, to belong, to make sense, and to feel as if they matter, even if the price exacted doesn't really accomplish that. The self is willing to adapt to almost anything to try to get those things. This makes it possible for closed systems to continue as long as they do' (ibid., p. 119).

In counselling it takes a long time for a client to believe that caring for herself, expressing her wants and feelings, even revealing her anger, does not make her selfish or 'bad'. It takes even longer for her to accept that her parents did not nurture her or meet her needs and that she has a right to feel indignation. I see this as a crucial step, which leads to the client being able to see her parents objectively and to begin the process of forgiveness. In telling her story, Jemma says: 'I sometimes don't blame them (her parents) because they knew no better.'

It is clear from Jemma's story that over time she found the strength to rebel against the oppression of the system and to break free of its dominance. Before seeking counselling, she would revert to being the good girl, following the rigid rules of her family. With support and encouragement, she found the will to challenge the control exercised by her mother and others. She came to know her true self.

It is not only the daughters of European migrants who take on the role of 'the good girl' or 'mother's helper' in the family. Several women I have worked with over the years often found they could only gain approval from parents for being good. Choosing the role of the good girl, however, often comes at a high cost. It may prevent her from caring for herself and protecting herself in her relationships with others. Expressing feelings, in particular admitting to her anger, can be challenging because good girls don't get angry. A client told me recently: 'When I feel angry with someone and I want to tell them how I feel, my voice disappears so that I can't speak and my whole body feels weak.'

In suppressing anger, girls deny themselves the opportunity to explore their wants and feelings and to pursue their goals with confidence. Instead they focus their energy on meeting the needs of others.

Case study: was I born angry?

Dina was in her mid twenties when she came to see me. She was doing well in her career and was in a good relationship, but anxious feelings were damaging her enjoyment of the relationship. She was aware of the anxiety that controlled many aspects of her life and wanted to understand the reasons for her discomfort.

Dina had always had a difficult relationship with her mother and found it hard to accept that she was not solely to blame for their problems. Dina's mother told her often that she had always been 'an angry child' (discussed in the first chapter). Her attempts to fight back when she was a child were understandably ineffectual and only resulted in making her feel guilty. I remember asking Dina whether she believed she had come out of the womb angry. She had difficulty believing this was not the case: 'I got a lump in my throat the minute I began to write about the feelings associated with being called an angry child. According to my mother, I have always been angry. In some ways I feel I was an angry child. My counsellor tells me I wasn't born angry, but I find that hard to believe sometimes because I know I have a fire in my belly.

'When I wasn't at crèche I would be with my parents at their bakery. I liked being behind the scenes, playing and eating dough, scraping the tops off the sticky buns and pretending to be a customer. But I think I did all those things just to get attention. And of course, how could my parents give me attention when they were running a business, talking to suppliers and customers and trying to make a living? I got my father's affection but never my mother's. I quickly learnt that to get her attention I had to act out — yell, scream and even swear at times. This often happened in front of customers. I think I really wanted to say: "Hey, what about me?" But as a three or four year old, how do you find the words to say that you feel desperate for attention?

'One day, I remember pulling on the back of Mum's dress, screaming, crying and swearing. I felt pure rage flow through my veins for the first time. With all that energy boiling inside, I ended up ripping my mother's uniform. When I think back to that time I get mixed emotions. I feel guilty and I remember when I was growing up, remembering how awful that day was, I would apologise to my mother. I would be in tears. Now, I realise I didn't know any better, that it was my way of trying to get her attention. It's sad, and sad that I don't think my mother realises this because in her eyes I was just an angry child.

'In grade three or four, I remember drawing a picture of my mother as a witch. I tried to make her look as horrible and ugly as possible. I really didn't like my mother and am only learning to now. I pressed the pen deeply onto the page to make obvious marks. I was releasing the tension I had exploding inside me. My mother ended up finding that picture. I felt embarrassed and like a terrible daughter. I drew it for release because I couldn't explain in words the hurt my mother's neglect was causing me.

'It's strange, but when I think about the times I expressed great anger or frustration, 90% of the time it was associated with my mother. So I suppose that's why she thinks I'm an angry person. There wasn't anyone else I felt anger towards.

'I'm twenty-six years old now, and my mother still calls me angry. I still wonder sometimes if it's true that I was an angry child. It's hard to get rid of the voice inside my head telling me I was and occasionally I believe it.

'Sometimes I can pinpoint what it is about my frustration towards my mother. I think I felt cheated as a child. I felt deprived that money was always the excuse for my not being able to do extracurricular activities, that I didn't have parents who loved each other or cuddled me profusely, and that my mother never mixed with other mothers. And I suppose I feel I missed out on a traditional family upbringing as my parents divorced when I was only five. I don't know if I can forgive her for not giving me memories of a happy or normal family. Now the lump in my throat has turned into tears.

'In counselling sessions I was able to release my thoughts and understand the feelings that had controlled me for so long. I wanted to feel normal and to know that I wasn't the only person who feels this way. I wanted to know if I was crazy. Anxiety can play funny tricks. Now I know I'm not crazy and I know that others feel the way I do.

'Counselling is the one place where I feel understood and where I can cry about the pain deep down that other people don't understand, things that are serious to me but may seem petty to others. I like the challenge of counselling. Even if it's painful, it makes me feel like I'm getting somewhere. It gives me hope.'

It is hardly surprising that Dina suffered anxiety and found it impossible to enjoy a loving relationship while she believed her mother's label, 'angry child'.

Satir is clear on this question: 'A bad boy or girl was never born. Only beings with potentials are born. Something in that human being has to be denied, projected, ignored or distorted for him or her to become some kind of bad, sick, stupid or crazy boy or girl, man or woman … All infants are necessarily a captive audience for the beliefs of their parents and the society of which they are a part' (Satir, 2008, p.119).

Somewhere buried underneath Dina's hurt was the

knowledge that there was another way of living her life, and it was this knowledge that brought her to counselling. Her first task was to refute her mother's label, to believe she was not born angry. This took a considerable time. If we are told something on a regular basis as small children, we believe it. Once she stopped believing her mother's words, Dina could begin to explore what was behind the label and to begin to know her true nature, her real self.

What prompts women to seek counselling?

It is generally the distress of anxious or depressive feelings that bring a woman to counselling, searching for some relief from her pain. I cannot recall a single client who came to me, sometimes decades later, who was aware that old wounds were at the root of her distress. The long-term effect of childhood trauma is rarely identifiable. It occurred 'a long time ago' and there is an assumption that the child is resilient and will get over the painful experience in time. One often hears the words 'Children are resilient'. I believe the truth is that children are good at concealing their feelings and appearing as though they are fine. Adults often choose to cover over the wound of poor parenting and pretend to the world that all is well and their child is being parented adequately. But the emotional upset of neglect or abuse does not go away; it is stored in the body and in the child's unconscious. In adulthood it is this suppressed pain, experienced as anxiety and/or depression that eventually spills out (often in close personal relationships) prompting the search for counselling.

Case study: peeling the layers of an onion

Melissa was in her mid twenties when she came to counselling. Her mother suffered from a mental illness and died when Melissa was eleven. Melissa believed she needed to be exceptionally conscientious and good, to step into her mother's role and care for her father and brother. When I first knew her, Melissa was very distressed and suffering severe anxiety. She was not ready to talk about her mother to anyone. At our first counselling session, Melissa told me she was worried that her mother's mental illness could be genetic. When she was young she had overheard relatives discussing her mother's illness, expressing concern for Melissa, and resolving 'to keep an eye out'. As a result, Melissa had expected to develop a mental illness as her mother had done. I was able to assure her that she was not mentally ill; she was merely suffering from extreme anxiety. In her words:

'When I started going to counselling, I was highly anxious, very self-conscious and suffering from low self-confidence. I initially wanted to work on my anxiety, which I soon discovered was just a mask to all the bigger issues that I hadn't dealt with since childhood, the most important being the death of my mother when I was eleven. I remember being told by my counsellor that counselling is like peeling away layers of an onion, and that describes it exactly. As soon as you deal with one layer, the one underneath starts to show through. As I addressed some of the causes of my anxiety, new issues were revealed. The anxiety became a subsidiary concern to other, newly discovered areas of exploration. While I'm still a slightly anxious person, it's nothing like the debilitating affliction I suffered for all those years. I can now see where the anxiety comes from and the reasons behind it: loss, abandonment and a lack of nurturing and proper parenting. Counselling has made me feel so much more comfortable with these things. I can now think about my mother's death without feeling a deep sense of shame and hurt.'

Following the death of her mother, Melissa's father was not able to nurture her. He very quickly formed a new relationship with a woman who was not willing to parent Melissa although she was a devoted mother to her own daughter, close in age to Melissa. Within six months her father had moved in with his new partner. Melissa's mother was never mentioned in the family and she was too afraid to ask about her. Childhood ended abruptly. She was forced to care for herself (and her brother) from that time. Adolescence was a sad and lonely time without her mother for guidance. While she was going through puberty, no one nurtured or guided her. Melissa had to turn to her older brother for advice about the physical changes she was going through. It could be said that when her mother died, Melissa lost both parents. She then lived out the classic Cinderella story.

Melissa's father, I suspect, was too afraid to stand up to his new wife and as a result he chose not to acknowledge his daughter's suffering.

Once Melissa had gained sufficient strength from our work together, she decided she was ready to find out more about her mother. She asked her father to come to a counselling session with her. This is something I suggest from time to time because it is often easier for a client to raise sensitive issues with the support of a third party. Talking about her mother was still a frightening prospect.

After thanking her father for agreeing to come (I could see he felt uncomfortable), I remember saying that Melissa wanted him to be there because she would like to know about her mother. His response revealed just how unaware he was of his daughter's needs: 'But that was such a long time ago …'

It was clear he had no understanding what the loss of her mother had meant to Melissa, or that she was still traumatised by her death, fifteen years later. Melissa would have suffered far less had her father been prepared to parent her and to realise she needed to know about her mother. I asked him to talk to Melissa about her mother. He told her she was a beautiful and highly intelligent woman. He spoke about the work she did. He also talked about her mental illness, which Melissa had been too afraid to ask about. I asked him what Melissa's mother looked like. Was she fair-haired or dark, was she tall or short? His face softened as he looked at his daughter: 'She looked just like her.'

Being able to speak about her mother with her father marked a significant change for Melissa. Sadly, following our joint session, her father didn't raise the subject of her mother again.

Post script. Just this week I heard the wonderful news that Melissa and her husband have a baby daughter.

Where are the fathers?

Many of the young women I have worked with grew up without the influence of a nurturing and trustworthy father, either because he was not around, he was always working or because he was not emotionally available. As discussed earlier, several fathers abused their daughters, emotionally, physically and/or sexually. Young women like Jemma and Dina would have had far easier child-hoods had their fathers stepped forward to compensate for the harshness of their mothers' treatment.

When emotional issues arise in the family, many well-meaning fathers are ill-prepared and lack confidence to address the feelings. They abandon discussion of personal matters to their wives, assuming they are more proficient in this area. As a result, their daughters may lack any sense of a strong, present masculine figure who can handle what is happening emotionally.

A client overheard a conversation between her parents. Her mother asked her father why he didn't talk to his daughter (my client, who is thirty-three) about the difficulties she was going through. He replied, 'You know the girls and how to talk to them. I don't.'

A young woman who is able to enjoy a close and trusting relationship with her father is blessed. What I observe is that she will display greater self-confidence and have a far clearer idea of what she wants in life. She will value herself in relationships rather than complying with the wishes of others. She will also seek out a positive relationship for herself, rather than choose a partner who will reproduce the wounds and unmet needs of the relationship she had with her own inadequate father when she was growing up. Sadly the majority of the women I have seen in counselling were deprived of this positive father relationship.

Ian Grant emphasises the importance of the father-daughter relationship: 'A father has a tremendous impact on how his daughter sees herself. If a father sees his daughter as intelligent, capable and attractive, she will tend to see herself that way. A father's approval of his teenage daughter defines her identity and worth, as well as her sense of the possibilities in her own life and of her ability to achieve her goals' (Grant, 1999, p.105).

Negotiating adolescence

As they enter adolescence young girls are extremely vulnerable, particularly if the adults in their lives are emotionally absent or preoccupied with their own concerns. It is normal for an adolescent girl to want to be noticed, to be seen as grown up and to be liked by others. This is all part of working out who she is.

It can be a time of great confusion. A number of my clients grew up in families where feelings were simply not discussed. Some mothers appeared incapable of guiding their daughters through this time of enormous change. One can assume that they were not helped by the previous generation and so the wound of unmet needs is passed on. Many girls were not told about menstruation. It was never mentioned. One client remembers being at boarding school in her first term, thinking she was bleeding to death when she had her first period. Many recall walking around with their shoulders hunched because their mothers hadn't noticed they needed a bra. Several clients remember embarrassing episodes from this impressionable time in their lives and the feeling of utter loneliness when there is no one to go to for help.

An article in *The Age* (15 March 2010) discussed the way sexuality is taught (or not) in schools. As a teacher in the 1990's I remember filling in for an absent staff member and being instructed to spend the fifty minutes getting the students to put Lebanese cucumbers into a condom! When I asked what I should teach them about sexuality, the advice was: 'Whatever you like.' I wondered if I should begin: 'In case you haven't seen one, a penis does not look or feel like a Lebanese cucumber and it's not green.'

In some schools I am sure sexuality is taught effectively

but it is in the family that, as well as the practicalities of sexual intercourse, the emotional issues of an intimate sexual relationship need to be addressed. I have worked with many women who were told little or nothing about sex and sexuality growing up. They picked up whatever they could from friends, often discovering later (too late in some cases) that the information was inaccurate.

Many parents clearly feel inadequate and wounded in this area. No doubt no one discussed intimate relationships with them when they were growing up. One client remembers a biology textbook mysteriously appeared next to her bed when she was twelve. I recall overhearing an argument between my parents over who should discuss sex with my brother. It was obvious neither felt very enthusiastic. Recently I learnt from my daughter that this was a task I accomplished pretty well, but I made the mistake of cooking sausages for dinner that night!

Young women develop and mature at different ages. It can be a time of great embarrassment if you are either an early or a late developer. Women talk of painful bullying experiences at this time. Some were sexually aware long before their peers while others recall feeling under pressure to engage in sexual activity, simply because 'everyone is doing it', or so they claim.

If the adolescent child/woman has been brought up to be compliant and good, she might have difficulty knowing how to manage relationships with boys because she is not used to saying no. One client who got involved in an unhealthy sexual relationship when she was far too immature recognised the damaging effect it had on her later: 'I remember being very angry when I realised how that first relationship had affected me because it changed all my relationships and I would let boys get away with things. I would just go along with what they wanted. I got a reputation as a result and I lost a lot of friends.'

A girl needs to feel sufficiently confident to resist the pressure of an insistent, sex-obsessed adolescent boy and to understand that her behaviour may be misinterpreted. She also needs to learn to value herself and to appreciate and respect her own body.

Naivety around alcohol and drugs also puts an un-parented girl at great risk. A report *For Kids' Sake*, released in Australia in September 2011, includes some alarming statistics: an increase from 28 to 38 per cent in female school students experiencing unwanted sex between 2002 and 2008, and a doubling in the rate of hospitalisation for alcohol intoxication for women aged 15-24 between 1998-99 and 2005-06 (*The Age*, 6 September, 2011).

When I was a teacher, a student in year 10, a naïve, sensitive girl, confided to me that she had drunk alcohol for the first time at her older brother's party and was then persuaded to have sex by one of his friends who was twenty-eight. She was terrified she might be pregnant. She described the experience as 'horrible, disgusting.' What a sad introduction for this young woman to the joy of sex.

On another occasion I spoke to two fifteen year old girls who were distracted in class and clearly unable to concentrate. When pressed, they admitted they were in a dilemma. They had been given a tablet to take before going to a dance party that night and were unsure as to whether they should take it. When I inquired what the tablet was they said they didn't know. They thought it was 'like ecstasy.' They trusted me sufficiently to listen as I told them of the dangers of taking an unidentified drug that, apart from anything else, could lead them to engage in risky behaviour. I was aware I had simply delayed their doing something of this nature but I also sensed that my concern for them had touched them at some level.

Adolescents generally want to blend in rather than attract too much attention. It requires high self-esteem to stand aside from the crowd and act independently of your peers. The desire to conform is especially strong for young women who lack clear guidance and a strong sense of self. Growing up with parents who are incapable of offering love and support invariably leads to sad and lonely feelings; from this place, pleasing others and at times allowing males to take advantage of them sexually, is a common and desperate reaction to assuage these feelings.

By the time they sought counselling, several clients had had numerous sexual partners but no relationships they felt proud of. Some had contracted STDs, unaware they could choose to protect themselves, and the males said nothing to warn them. Most of the young women whose stories are told in this chapter grew up being good and compliant because they were rewarded for that role. They came to understand later how detrimental this was.

Case study: the vulnerability of the good girl

Susanna was one of the young women who lost their way in adolescence. She was in her late teens when she first came to see me for counselling. When talking about her childhood she recalled being told by her parents when she was eleven that they were separating. She described feeling intense emotion 'as though my throat would burst', and remembers the embarrassment she felt at crying in front of her parents because no one had seen her upset before. She still remembers trying to force down the feelings and the shocked expression on her parents' faces at her tears.

Looking back Susanna can see she was avoiding facing the truth as her parents were clearly going through a lot of turmoil in their marriage. In spite of this she had not anticipated that they would separate.

'At the age of eleven I was trying to be the one that had it together even though my family was falling apart. If I pretended I could hold it together, everything would be all right, so when I heard them say they were separating I felt completely overwhelmed.

'My parents were totally focussed on their own lives after the divorce. My dad got remarried and I didn't see him much on his own. I spent every second week with him and my stepmother, but that relationship got into difficulties too. I felt very lonely around that time. My mother also had a new partner. I know I resented the step-parents. I suppose I always blamed them for coming into our lives. It was easier than blaming my parents.

'Before my parents separated I had a strong sense of who I was. I felt I could stand up for myself and I knew what was right for me. I could trust my gut instinct. I remember when I was very young — the first time a boy tried to kiss me — I felt very strongly that I didn't want to have anything to do with it. I didn't care what anyone thought of me, I just pushed him away instinctively. I suppose I probably made him feel awful, but now I look back at that little girl and wonder where she disappeared to during my teens. I no longer felt I had a strong sense of who I was.

'Somehow over the years I lost the confidence in myself and I didn't voice my opinions strongly enough. At times I wasn't sure what to do and I felt really lost. I didn't feel my opinion was important enough and I would make every effort to make others feel comfortable. I wonder if it's something to do with when Mum and Dad used to fight. I remember wanting to appear as though everything was fine and to appear happy because I so wanted everyone else to feel that way. Sometimes I still find myself trying hard to make others feel happy.

'Around the age of fifteen or sixteen I started rebelling, smoking and going out a lot. At school it was a different space and I didn't feel comfortable. I was used to being such a good kid, so good in school. I was very conscientious both at school and at home. I saw all these kids around me having fun and joking around at school. I felt I wasn't part of it. I couldn't focus on my schoolwork any more. When I saw the kids enjoying themselves but also working hard at their studies, I felt an outsider. School just didn't seem important any longer.

'My parents' divorce had such an effect on me. I just saw the world in a different way. I had wasted a lot of years in terms of pursuing a direction for myself. When I was about nineteen, I was ready to have counselling because I knew I needed to talk to someone. I also went back to study, having worked out what I wanted to do in terms of my future. I started to feel better about myself. I met someone then (actually he is now my husband) and for the first time I felt he was someone who could understand me. I knew he was good for me.'

When she first came to see me, Susanna was feeling lost. Self-doubt, confusion and vulnerability controlled her relationships with friends and with partners. In counselling, our task was to reconnect Susanna to the young girl she was before her parents separated, a girl who had a strong sense of self.

Susanna came to see me earlier this year and the fruits of our work together are clear. She is happily married and has two children — a daughter and a baby son. She is working in a creative field, which she enjoys.

The people I see are, for the most part, well-functioning, educated and employed. They are all ages, but perhaps because my earliest clients were young women in their late twenties, early thirties, they are still the age group I see most frequently because they refer their colleagues and friends who have often observed them making positive changes and looking happier. They feel motivated to get help for themselves. Many of these young people are on fairly low incomes and they apply themselves wholeheartedly to counselling because they know that it is a large financial commitment, particularly if they need counselling over a considerable period of time. They also know they want to change. In their late twenties, early thirties, many young women face difficult challenges in terms of where their life is heading. Frequently it is an awareness of the discrepancy between where they are and where they want to be that brings them into counselling. At times they speak of feeling lost and lonely, a feeling they have known for a very long time. Recently a client revealed she fantasises on occasion that she will be involved in a car accident and be killed, 'because it would be easier not to be here.'

Case study: peeling back the layers

Lucy initially came into counselling following breast cancer in her late twenties, feeling overwhelmed by the shock of the experience and terrified that the cancer might return. Looking back, Lucy described the process of counselling as follows: 'It was like peeling back the layers of my life and getting to the vulnerable core of who I was, which I didn't know before. I could describe it like opening up doors inside myself, having an honest look at who I was. In counselling you can open those doors slowly, in a safe environment. You open one door and go inside and it's okay, and then you open another door and go into another room. And because you are not alone you feel safe. All these rooms contain emotions, and you learn it's okay to feel these emotions and to own them. It's okay to be vulnerable. The trigger for me was having had cancer at the age of twenty-nine. I had recently come out of it and couldn't get over the fear of it happening again. I didn't want to keep living in fear, so I decided I had to talk to someone. From there a whole lot of other things came up, in particular how I was seen in my family and how I was brought up. The effects of family are such a major influence. I was given everything I needed materially by my parents, but emotions were not discussed or addressed. As a result I was not open with my emotions. I would just keep quiet and shut my feelings away. "Just get on with it," was the family motto and occasionally I still find myself slipping into that way of thinking.'

Lucy's parents' motto is one I have heard frequently, and as she states, she simply learnt to shut her feelings away because they were not important to her parents, who presumably were uncomfortable with their own feelings. Judith Siegel stresses the importance for parents to be emotionally available to their children:

'…there are many families who are uncomfortable with emotions … and because they do not know how to soothe their own feelings, they tend to deny or dismiss emotional upset in their kids. …They might convey a belief that bad feelings are not something to dwell on. Because feelings create discomfort for them, they easily get impatient and tell their child through words or gestures to "get over it".

The child misses an opportunity to learn how to soothe unpleasant feelings and how to use the emotional realm as an important source of information' (Siegel, 2000, p. 52).

Lucy moved from the country to Melbourne at the start of grade 6. She had been very happy at her first school and achieved well. The adjustment to living in a big city and a new school was difficult and Lucy was shocked to find herself the target of a number of cruel bullies. Lucy felt she couldn't ask her parents to support her. She believed she had to deal with the bullying on her own. She was aware the bullying affected her deeply and destroyed her confidence in relating to others.

'In adolescence, my relationships were all about my wanting to be loved; I pretty much did anything to feel I was loved. I would go out with anyone who I thought loved me, rather than consider what I wanted or needed from the other person in a relationship. If someone paid me any attention, that's all I needed; I didn't think about myself. I would usually meet people in bars and clubs where everyone was drinking, hardly the best way to get to know someone.

'I went out with several people for a couple of years, but they all had significant problems — "like attracts like" I suppose. For a very long time I equated sex with love. Most of my relationships were based on sex until I sought counselling, in fact. It was all about sex rather than an emotional relationship. I didn't talk to anyone about what I was doing. My parents certainly had no idea about my life because personal things were never discussed at home. I didn't even know how to talk about my feelings.

'At that time I had no sense of my own value. I didn't ask myself how I felt or what I wanted. The people I went out with were educated, lovely people, but basically they took a different path in life. One in particular was a lost soul who could never settle down. Looking back I can see he would never have reached his full potential. He's probably still drinking in bars and playing pool today.

'Several months into the counselling I met someone. It was completely different from every other relationship I had experienced. We didn't even kiss for five weeks and didn't have sex for quite some time. We really got to know each other first. We were older, and both of us were looking for a serious relationship.

'In all my other relationships sex clouded my judgement. I was so used to the sexual side happening first. Getting to know someone first as a friend was very new to me. I was not sure how I felt about him at the start, but the more we got to know each other, the deeper the feelings grew.

'Having gone through counselling I was more open to doing things differently. I had learnt a lot about myself and I knew that it was okay to ask for things in a relationship with another person, and to express my wants and needs.

'Before I sought counselling, I really didn't know the core of who I was. It was only through peeling back the layers in a secure environment, exposing the vulnerable part of me, that I reached a point where I liked — no, where I loved myself for who I was. I suppose I always knew those doors were there, but I was too afraid to open them. It takes time too. Sometimes it really felt very hard. I knew, however, that while I felt guided in the counselling, I was the one who had to do the work. I've now got the tools to keep moving. I learned that it's okay to ask for help. I've done so a number of times with different aspects of my life.

'Counselling made a big difference because I was able to trust another person with the most vulnerable parts of my being, in a secure environment. I ended up understanding my feelings and valuing my strengths while still accepting the vulnerable part of myself. I could not have achieved this on my own.'

Where are the knights in shining armour?

Frequently when working with single women, it is apparent that their main preoccupation in a new relationship is: 'Will this man want me?' and 'Can I hold onto him?' Perhaps a more empowering question a young woman needs to ask herself is whether he would be a good partner for her, one who would respect and value her and make her feel good about herself. What kind of man in fact is he? Does she even know?

I remember working on this issue with a young client who was repeatedly disappointed in relationships. Soon after realising that she was obsessed by the question: 'Will this man want me?' she understood how she needed to change. Just a few months after making this discovery, she met a man she warmed to as a person. She knew that he would be a good partner for her. Within a year they were engaged.

For many single women, turning thirty is a time of crisis. They feel society's pressure to have in place the right partner, a home of their own, a satisfying career and most of all, a clear decision about whether or not to have children while they are still able to. The fear that she will never meet anyone can have a controlling influence on a young woman who is still single, when most of her friends have paired off and maybe had a baby. Desperate feelings destroy her enjoyment of life and make it harder to relax in a new relationship.

I have seen tremendous ambivalence in women who are unsure as to whether they want to have a child. Others are in a relationship that feels stable and they want a child but are afraid to raise the topic with their partner because they sense his reluctance to become a parent. Often their fears are realised.

A thirty-five year old client broached the subject of having a baby with her de facto partner of two years, saying that she would like a child within the next three years. Ten days later he ended the relationship. I have worked with several women who were abandoned by their partner (the father of the child) while they were pregnant because a baby was not something he could envisage. I asked one of these reluctant fathers-to-be to come and see me. He told me that he just didn't want to be a father. When I told him that he was the *only* father his child would ever have, he was genuinely puzzled. (He is now the adoring father of a little girl).

I have also worked with a number of gay and bisexual women who want children but realise that it is not an easy decision as the issues are very complex in a same sex relationship. So many girls grow up believing they will be a wife and mother because that's what women do, and to see this natural choice disappearing is disturbing as it shatters their own and society's expectations. Several clients believed the fantasy of romantic love, and as one expressed it: 'I always believed a man would appear in my life and he would rescue me.' Many young women have told me they first began imagining themselves walking down the aisle on the arm of the perfect man when they were very young. One client was nine or ten when the fantasy first took hold. The attachment to romantic fantasy can impede a young woman from having a mature and fulfilling relationship, with all its imperfections and humanness.

Case study: a father's betrayal

Asher's reason for coming to counselling was something I hear frequently: 'I was turning thirty and my life wasn't where it was supposed to be, according to society. By thirty you should be married, or at least in a stable relationship, and know what you want in terms of having children. You are made to feel there must be something wrong with you if you are still in a full-time job after thirty and single.

' "Why can't someone nice like you meet someone and settle down?" People actually asked me that question. They might just as well have asked, "What's wrong with you?" And on days when I felt low it made me feel there *was* something wrong with me and I would wonder, "What's so bad about me? Why am I still single?"

'I knew there were things I hadn't dealt with in my life and I had to admit to myself that I was upset a lot of the time. I felt lonely and in despair about ever having someone in my life who cared, genuinely, about me. I didn't have a relationship with my father and I wanted to understand how this was affecting me. I knew I needed to talk about it to someone. I also knew I was not a bad person, but I always felt I was someone who had done something wrong, that it was my fault. It was time to deal with it.

'I was the eldest of three girls and as a child my father and I were very close. We were good friends and I helped him out, but then I became a teenager and I wanted to do other things, to see friends and go out. My father would say no, and when I was in year 8 we began to have huge arguments and we wouldn't speak for a week at a time. Then he stopped talking to me altogether. He ignored me completely at meal times and would talk to my mother and sisters and behave as though I wasn't there. I remember he didn't even wish me happy birthday when I turned thirteen. Mum and Dad had each other, and no one talked to me, so I was very lonely. I didn't understand what I had done wrong.

'My middle sister was favoured by my parents and even though she was naughty at times, she never got into trouble. I was seen as the troublemaker and my sisters were told to stay away from me. I thought I must be a pretty awful kid.

'Then Mum started to realise how Dad was treating me and she began to stand up for me. From then on Dad turned on the whole family. He started looking after himself, making his own meals. This continued until I was sixteen.

'Mum was very controlled by him in those years, bullied really. My father didn't let her work, so she was stuck at home with very little money. No one knew what was going on or what we kids were going through because my father was nice in public and a lot of fun, but he was a ratbag at home. There were lots of fights in front of us children. He terrorised us.

'I remember one day putting music on very softly, but he burst into the room, took off the record and threw it across the room. As soon as his car appeared in the drive, one of us would call out, "Oh my god, he's here!" and we would turn off the TV and run to our rooms.'

Asher began staying away from the house, riding her bike around the streets, watching videos at friends' houses and staying overnight whenever she could.

Asher believes now that it is possible her father had a mental illness, but this was not recognised or addressed and she was left wondering why her father targeted her after enjoying a close relationship with her when she was little. What she does know is that her father's parents separated when he was fourteen and he didn't see his father for many years. It was around the same age (when Asher was fourteen) that her father changed towards her so dramatically. Had the map of 'father' simply run out for this man when his daughter reached the age he was when his father abandoned him? Was he overwhelmed by repressed feelings?

After several years, Asher's mother decided to leave with the children and at seventeen Asher moved out of home. In counselling sessions, Asher came to understand the effect her father's treatment had on her subsequent relationships with boyfriends: 'I had lots of boyfriends and slept with a few of them. I usually got drunk at parties and would set out to meet someone, but most of my relationships went the same way. I wanted to be number one in their lives, but I was never their main priority. They would take me for granted and I often felt pushed aside. I can see now that I was used to being treated badly, to being pushed aside and feeling hurt. I would have an anxious, sick feeling inside me at being treated as though I were of little value, and the feeling became normal to me. I began to anticipate being treated poorly and I can see I contributed, inviting this kind of treatment. There were times I would hold on tight, scraping up every little crumb, trying to convince myself it was a good relationship and that it would last. But I learnt to recognise the warning signs in myself as I became suspicious or clingy and I would start to push and push as though I were testing them to find out how far I could go, to see if they would still accept me, still want me, before they dumped me. Deep down I knew what I was doing. I had come into counselling to address my feelings about my father's betrayal, and I was reliving that hurt in my relationships with boyfriends. As a child I had a close loving relationship with my dad, but he abandoned and betrayed me and I expected all other males to do the same.

'Through counselling I was able to see that I was drawn to men who would hurt me and in time I was able to change. I am now in a good relationship with someone who treats me well and who stops me if I become destructive. He just says: "We're not getting into this, you're being silly." And for the first time I know I am valued for who I am.'

Asher's relationship with her partner has continued to thrive. Their daughter has celebrated her second birthday. When I contacted Asher recently and discussed her story, she told me: 'My story seems surreal now and feels like it was a long time ago. Sometimes I feel a little sad about my past, but I have so much in my life now. I feel incredibly lucky to have a wonderful family and to be close to my sisters now that we all have children. I am blessed to be a mum and have an amazing, loving partner to share it all with, despite my upbringing!'

Divorce reform in Australia

In Australia, divorce laws were reformed in the early 1970s, making it possible to have 'no-fault' divorce. Literally thousands of couples filed for divorce as a result. When I consider the clients I have worked with, it is (in general) the women who have been most affected by divorce. The absence of a solid father/daughter relationship clearly weakens their self-confidence.

Until the 1990s there was little understanding, however, for how divorce impacted on children. There was also little in the way of counselling support. In many cases the parents were doing their best to deal with their own emotional distress and were oblivious to the suffering of the children. It was some years before it was recognised that divorce did have a profound effect on children of all ages. Research indicates that the incidence of mental health problems is far greater amongst the children of divorced couples where the divorce was conflicted and arrangements concerning children involved tension and hostility. Many of my clients, now in their thirties, are the children of those couples who filed for divorce as soon as the laws were relaxed. It is important to state that being the child of divorced parents is not necessarily worse than living with two parents who do not respect and love one another and who fight in front of their children. Many clients faced considerable emotional difficulties, in spite of growing up with both parents.

Thirty years ago children generally stayed with their mother. The father, even if he lived close by, would only have limited contact with his children. Some men, possibly persuaded by their ex-wives, believed it was 'better for the children' if they were no longer involved in their children's lives and they stayed away, sometimes having no contact with the children. Judith Siegel comments on the need for children to be able to stay close to both parents after separation, but this is often not the case:

'... fathers tend to withdraw from their children when they are not the custodial parent. Some researchers speculate that fathers give up when they feel they have no real say or control over what is happening in their children's lives. Others speculate that the loss of the separation is just too emotionally difficult for fathers to live with on a daily basis'(ibid., p. 111).

In my experience of working with a number of separated fathers, I observe that the feelings of loss and sadness are often overwhelming. Some cannot admit to their children that they miss spending time with them. At times a father doesn't value himself highly, or appreciate how important he is in his child's life. I want to stress that I believe most parents do their best but are often overwhelmed by their emotional state. In many cases their own experience of being parented was also inadequate.

Separating couples I have worked with in the last few years are making their children high priority, treating one another civilly, sharing custody or at least ensuring the children spend plenty of time with both parents. They also endeavour to provide two homes that are welcoming and comfortable wherever possible. If handled with good will by both parents, children do not need to suffer greatly when parents divorce, provided their feelings are taken into account.

Case study: a father leaves home

Natasha was in her late twenties when she overheard a friend talking about the difference counselling had made in her life, and she decided to make an appointment for herself. Six months earlier her boyfriend had ended their relationship and she was still feeling rejected. In our first session, when Natasha described the relationship, I remember commenting that it was just as well it had ended as it was clear she was offered little by her ex-partner. I suspected that her feelings of rejection stemmed from a much earlier wound. At that time, Natasha did not value herself highly and it was not surprising she was prepared to tolerate poor treatment from a partner.

Natasha remembered being told by her parents that they were separating when she was twelve. She recalls feeling upset and crying as she walked to school. Her parents did not in fact separate until Natasha was around eighteen. She remembers feeling miserable for much of those six years. Natasha was not warned when her parents did eventually separate.

After Natasha's father left, contact with him gradually declined. By the time she came to counselling, Natasha had convinced herself she didn't want to know her father and didn't care that she had no relationship with him. She was in touch with her anger rather than the hurt that lay underneath. It was clear she was choosing partners who would hurt her and not value her, echoing the experience of her father's abandonment.

One of the ways clients are able to address these wounds and start a healing process is by writing a letter to the person who has hurt them. The writing of the letter, even if it never reaches the addressee, is always therapeutic. Expressing hurt, putting it into writing rather than dwelling on it, is an effective way of releasing painful feelings that have been stored in the unconscious. It always amazes me how clearly and honestly clients are able to express their true feelings when they set about writing that letter.

For many months Natasha considered writing to her father. While she wanted to do so, she found it an impossible task. Eventually she decided to book into a hotel for the night with the express intention of writing to her father.

Natasha was surprised how easy it was to write her letter. She was able to access her feelings immediately:

I'm writing this letter because I'm sick of feeling I don't matter to you. You walked away all those years ago and it seemed as though you didn't care about me at all. The day you left, you didn't even speak to me. It proved to me that I wasn't important to you. I couldn't help feeling totally rejected by you. At first you used to buy us Christmas presents, but that only lasted a couple of years and since then you haven't even bothered to wish me a happy birthday. Little things like that would have made all the difference over the years.

I was just a kid when you left. How was I meant to understand what really happened? At the start I blamed you entirely for the marriage break-up, but now I'm old enough to understand that it wasn't all your fault. But what I know is that if you had kept trying with me, we would still have a relationship today.

I'm not even sure if I want a relationship with you now. You have hurt me so much inside and I don't know if I'm ready to forgive you and have you in my life. Your walking out and deserting me has affected me in ways that even I cannot comprehend. You never showed me what it feels like for a daughter to be loved by her father and I know it has affected every single relationship I have had with a man.

So now I'm thirty years old and I'm still single because I'm attracted to men like you who are arseholes, who will end up hurting me and rejecting me like you did. I try not to get too close to them for that reason, but it doesn't make any difference because every time they move on it still hurts like hell and it's because you wounded me all those years ago. I don't want to keep repeating this pattern in my life and I will until this shit with you is sorted out.

I often think about you and I know that you must really be hurting. If you think I don't give a shit about you, you are wrong. I don't even know if writing this letter is going to help me. I don't even want to send it to you because I'm scared of the repercussions it may bring. If I send it and don't hear anything I will be pissed off. If I send it and you contact me, I don't know if l really want that.

There was more to the letter, but this extract addresses the main things she wanted to say. Natasha felt better after writing and was surprised how clear her feelings were when she put pen to paper. I found it interesting that through writing the letter, she was able to contact her feelings of hurt (more than her anger) and also to recognise her father must also be suffering. In spite of the hurt he had caused her, she cared about him deeply. Natasha was the one who decided to make contact, not her father. Children are very forgiving of their parents.

Natasha did not in fact send the letter, but a short while later she heard through family members that her father was going to live overseas: 'I knew that the day would come when I would have to face my dad. I was really scared about doing it. I didn't know what kind of reception I was going to get. He may not have wanted to know me and I think that would have really hurt. The chance of that happening stopped me from doing it. So I kept putting it off.

'One day I heard on the grapevine that he was moving to Hong Kong for two years. When I heard that I freaked out. I knew I would contact my dad one day and I was pretty sure it was going to be in the next two years, but if he was moving away, what was I going to do?

'I decided that I would go and see him that week and I contacted a friend who agreed to go with me. I didn't even know where he lived. I looked him up in the phone book and arrived at his house later that night. I was looking at five units and had no idea which one was his, so I just started knocking on doors. Once someone told me which one was his, I felt terribly nervous, overwhelmed by so many emotions. I stood on his doorstep and waited a couple of minutes before knocking. He answered the door and he was really surprised to see me. I went inside. I can't remember what was said, but he was happy to see me. He gave me his phone number and I gave him mine. I stayed for about half an hour. I remember telling him that I had wanted to come for a while. Later that night after I left, he sent me a message telling me that he loved me. It was the first time I had seen my father in twelve years.

'It took a while for us to get a relationship going. He would contact me and we would go out for dinner, but for a long time I felt uncomfortable. Slowly over time it became easier. He'd been in a relationship for a few years and I think that helped a lot. I can honestly say that through contacting my dad, my life changed. Knowing that he loves and cares for me has made me feel so much better about myself. I don't choose arseholes anymore. I don't have the anger and resentment that had built up inside me anymore either. We have quite a good relationship now. Getting to know him again opened the door to spending time with his side of the family and it's one of my favourite things to do. We all get together and have a great time. I used to love doing that as a child and that enjoyment disappeared from my life for the twelve years that I didn't have contact with my dad. Now, as well as my dad, his family is back in my life and I feel I am part of something special.'

I sent Natasha her story and asked her to describe the way she has changed as a result of counselling. She is aware that she is no longer the same person: 'I first began counselling six years ago, (although I have had several breaks in that time) and I can *almost* say I no longer need counselling. I honestly believe that I wouldn't be the person I am today if I hadn't decided I needed help. Although I couldn't see it at the time, I was angry and resentful towards men in general, because I felt my father had abandoned me. I was attracted to men who treated me badly.

I didn't stand up for myself, even when I knew I should. I just let people walk all over me.

'Over the years I learnt to value myself and to believe that I deserved to be treated with respect by everyone in my life. I now stand up for myself and say how I feel in any given situation. I realise that what I feel and think is what matters most. I'm prepared to take risks with my emotions, in order to care for myself and to feel happy. I have also gained a sense of independence and I no longer feel I need others' approval in making decisions. I know what is good for me.

'Having counselling wasn't always easy. There were times when it seemed too hard to face my hurt and I just wanted to run. I am glad that I persevered. As a result I know myself and I am true to myself.'

When we consider these sad father/daughter relationships — the young girl bewildered at the loss of her father's love, feeling rejected, abandoned — it is hardly surprising that several young women whose stories are told in this chapter found themselves in relationships with men who would re-wound them. In counselling much of the focus is in helping to strengthen them to the point where they value and like themselves and subsequently choose relationships with partners who will treat them well, partners capable of offering love and commitment.

Case study: a mother leaves home

Milla was also the eldest of three girls and in fact as I started to think of the clients who worked through the difficulties of their lives with me, I realised that by far the largest number were the oldest girl in the family. The expectation falls on her to be reliable, to help her mother run the house and to take responsibility for younger children. I was the oldest girl in my family; as my mother struggled to nurture her children, I worried terribly about my younger brother and sister and tried to be a little mother to them.

Following constant fighting when she was growing up, Milla's parents separated. Milla had few memories of her childhood, but she could recall the fear she felt when she was shouted at and shut in her room. Milla and her sisters were told the day their parents' relationship ended. Their mother moved out of the house to pursue a relationship with someone else, promising the girls that she would come back for them, and they would live with her in a nice house. At the time Milla was just thirteen.

In Milla's words: 'Initially we thought things would improve because the fighting would stop and to some extent this was the case, but Dad just withdrew and became depressed. He had no idea that his anger problems had been part of the reason Mum decided to leave. In the meantime my sisters and I kept the house running as best we could. I felt more like a mother, keeping the house clean, cooking dinner, doing the dishes and looking after my sisters.

'Dad was also quite dominating and controlling. He was against us watching television because he disapproved of it, but at the same time he would watch it himself. There were many times when he was quite hypocritical.'

While she was having counselling, Milla's father was diagnosed with cancer and he subsequently passed away. It was a confusing time as she was working on feelings of anger at how her father treated her in her childhood and was then catapulted into all the feelings associated with his death: grief, loss, sadness. Milla was aware she put her father on a pedestal at this time because he had died and she felt too guilty to explore her anger. At the same time, the memory of her father yelling at her was hard to let go of and she would find herself becoming angry with her boyfriend.

'I would find myself in one bad relationship after another and I couldn't understand why I was attracted to men with problems. It wasn't until I was dating a boy with an alcohol related illness and was abused mentally that I decided to seek help. In counselling sessions I quickly realised I was searching for my father whom I had felt so sorry for growing up. All the men I dated had problems that were similar to my father. I also felt worthless. I didn't think I deserved to be treated any better. Perhaps in some ways I was also replicating my mother's behaviour towards my father.

'My mother left the marriage to pursue another relationship and in spite of her promise to us, we didn't end up living with her. She was always making excuses as to why it couldn't happen, often blaming her new husband. My relationship with her became very difficult. Most of her energy was focussed on her relationships with other men, which she would discuss in detail with me. As a result of the work I did in counselling, I came to see that I was being asked to parent my mother and I worked hard at altering the relationship, to make it clear to her that I didn't want to know about her affairs. It was very difficult to do this initially. I was afraid she would abandon me again as she had done when I was little. I remember in a counselling session writing down some of the ways I could tell her I didn't want to know about her love life, and keeping the note near the phone. Without the note, I was lost for words because it was so unfamiliar to confront the way she had always been with me. I came to realise that in my relationships with men, I was behaving just like her — having consecutive affairs — which made me feel very ashamed.'

Addressing the ways in which she was emulating her mother's behaviour was quite confronting. In behaving like a parent we inevitably feel closer to them, and to abandon living like her mother, having affairs which offered her little, involved Milla in considerable distress. It is clear her mother had not addressed her own emotional difficulties.

Milla described the change she went through as: 'being in mourning for the old Milla. It seems very strange not to be going out chasing boys.'

Early in 2011 Milla contacted me and we arranged to meet. She brought her two young daughters with her. Milla is in a loving relationship and working in her own business. She feels very fulfilled in her life today: 'When I first met my partner I thought I saw my father and his issues. I often labelled his behaviour as controlling and dominating. In coming to understand more about relationships in counselling, however, I had learned that I couldn't change him. After much arguing and talking about our past issues we learnt that communication is what matters. There is no blaming or mistrust between us now. Coming from a similar background, we both understand what could potentially trigger a painful reaction. I love him very much. I never thought I deserved to feel this happy.'

Leaving the familiar path

It is something I observe frequently: in order to live a healthier life than our parents, we often have to reject their path and choose a different one. It generally involves feelings of loss and uncertainty. The new path is unknown and can feel extremely frightening. The known path is familiar, even if it is not how we want to live. It is hard to leave one's family emotionally. From birth our family is there for us, we share a long history and we are bonded to its members on countless levels. It takes enormous courage and maturity to recognise that attempting to remain close with family values might not be beneficial and could in fact have a destructive effect. One only has to think of women who remain in violent relationships, who have often experienced violence within their families growing up. If they do succeed in leaving an abusive partner, but don't understand their wounded pattern of relating, they often seek out another. What is familiar is invariably easier. For clients this is often the point where they get stuck. Do they really want to risk moving away from the way their family lives life?

A client who underwent change on many levels over her time in counselling told me she was concerned about two aspects of her transformation: 'How do I introduce the 'new me' to people who have known me all my life? And will people like the new me?'

The eight women whose stories are told in this chapter all knew when it was time to leave counselling. They reached a point where they had a real enjoyment of life, they could trust themselves to judge what was good for them in most situations and they had the confidence to handle relationships. When they reach this point, I am happy to see my clients leave. A young woman who returned to her native France to live, illustrated how she had changed over the time we worked together, at her last session. She gave me two photos of herself and asked me to comment on them. In the first, she was looking straight at the camera, her mouth open wide, and she was laughing, a forced laugh, much like celebrities have to put on for the media in an attempt to appear happy. She didn't look happy. In the second she was looking into the distance and smiling; she looked calm, relaxed and genuinely happy — at peace and in touch with her true self. She told me they were her 'before and after counselling' photographs.

In every case, the clients discussed in this chapter were responsible for the transformation they achieved in their lives. They were prepared to face their early wounding and to overcome old hurts and old patterns of relating. They have chosen good, loving relationships with partners. Several of these women are now mothers — good mothers.

Chapter 4

The boy becomes a man

Everyone thinks of changing the world, but no one thinks of changing himself
—Tolstoy

n this chapter, I focus on the men who come to see me for counselling. Why separate the men from the women? The patterns that I observed among male clients appeared to be different, in terms of what men were looking for in counselling as well as their preoccupations, their disconnection from feelings and at a deeper level, their sense of alienation. All these things came as a surprise to me when I began working as a counsellor. In this chapter I explore the journey of six men who came to see me for counselling, at times reluctantly. As their stories reveal, they transformed how they felt about themselves as a result of committing to the process.

My first experience of men was my relationship with my older brother as my father was often away and, when he was at home, only rarely involved himself with young children. He responded very differently to his grandchildren, however, when they were little. He enjoyed our visits, delighted in my children's exuberance and would even buy chocolate biscuits and lemonade for them — a treat unheard of in my childhood.

From around the age of eight, my brother regularly subjected me to various forms of torture, from painful although harmless Chinese burns to more serious assaults on my body, all in the name of fair play between siblings. One memory stands out. After weeks of begging to join his 'boys only' club, I remember having a cross scratched onto the inside of my wrist with a penknife, by way of initiation. When I pointed out that neither he nor his friends had bleeding scratches on their wrists, he replied, 'We're boys.' My only means of retaliation at that young age was to resort to reminding him periodically of the rhyme:

What are little boys made of?

Slugs and snails and puppy dogs' tails.

That's what little boys are made of.

At the time I think I actually believed he was made of 'slugs and snails'.

Many decades have passed since I was that child, prepared to be tortured because he was a boy and I a mere girl, desperate to join his gang. I should add that, while he took delight in tormenting me, my brother was not in fact a bully. As a young girl I idolised him. I should also admit that a few years later, realising with delight that of the two of us I was suddenly the taller, I launched a savage attack on him using every underhand tactic I could think of. Utterly shocked, I saw tears in his eyes. It was our last fight.

Men — the stronger sex

I grew up believing that because he was male, my brother was stronger than I was, not just physically but in all things. I adhered to the idea that I belonged to the weaker sex, along with my mother and the women in the family. My father, an army officer, and all my uncles, epitomised the strong male. They were taller than average and this only added to my belief that they were powerful. It was men who acted in the world, who commanded in all things, in terms of careers, earning money, decision making and of course disciplining children. I was born at the end of the war and many of the men in my family had fought in the war. This was proof to me of how strong men must be. Clearly they were superior. When I joined the work force in my twenties, I continued to believe in male superiority and assumed that men in positions of power (including senior management) possessed a range of qualities which included confidence, strength, integrity, honesty, fairness and a strong moral sense.

I came to understand, much later in life, that in our family it was my mother who really dominated, not my father. What I'm describing is a patriarchal family seen through the eyes of a small child. It is the way society functioned. While the changes in the last fifty years have been enormous, men still have the edge over women in our society in terms of earning power and promotion to senior levels in medicine, government, the law and business, with notable exceptions of course. I obviously cannot ignore the fact that, for the first time, Australia has a female prime minister and governor-general.

Real men don't need counselling

When I first began as a counsellor, ninety per cent of my clients were women. The men I did see were usually dragged into counselling, reluctantly, by wives or partners. Just a few chose to continue in individual counselling because they recognised the benefit for themselves. Hearing about the men in women's lives, from the abusers in childhood, the bullies in school and the workplace, to the unfaithful partners and absent fathers, I decided I both wanted and needed to work with men. As though my thoughts were heard, the men started to appear and nowadays half my practice is made up of men.

It took me a while to understand that the men who came to see me for counselling were looking for something different from my female clients. For a start, most men do not want to admit to needing counselling at all and only do so when forced to concede they are not coping. I suspect there are many men, of all ages, who would not consider asking for help unless it is of a practical nature. Over time I have learnt how to work more deeply with men who are suffering. Perhaps as I became stronger and more assertive in how I counselled them, they sensed I could handle their agony. In the first counselling session, women usually cry as this may well be the first time they have revealed the extent of their distress to anyone. Men, on the other hand, do everything in their power to avoid showing their vulnerability.

When a woman turns thirty, she is acutely aware that she needs to make important life decisions with regard to career, a partner and children. This applies equally to gay women, many of whom are choosing to become mothers. Without a biological clock to sound the alarm, men often continue to cruise in relation to these major life decisions. It is common for men to come to see me for the first time in their mid to late thirties when the prospect of turning forty fills them with horror. Surely our parents were old at forty! Sometimes painful feelings resulting from the breakdown of a marriage or relationship prompt a man to seek help. Often it is the despair when they look back over their life as they head towards forty and feel regret that they haven't achieved more, been more successful in their careers, bought a house, met the right partner or raised a family. At times they recognise they need to get help because their old coping mechanisms and defences fail them. Some are forced to admit to themselves they are too dependent on alcohol or other substances. The men who see me for counselling come from all walks of life. What unites them is the uncommon acceptance that they need to seek help.

Who says I need therapy?

Graham, a man in his thirties, described his initial reaction to the idea of counselling: 'It was my wife Georgina who suggested we have counselling. I wasn't comfortable with the idea because of the preconceived stigma attached to it, that I couldn't cope on my own and needed guidance in life, that it meant there was something wrong with me, that there was something seriously wrong with our relationship. In addition I didn't see myself as needing to pay for help. That too was part of the stigma I attached to it.'

Graham's attitude towards counselling was typical of many men: 'I should be able to do this on my own. Asking for help is a sign of my weakness.'

When another client, Chris, came to his first appointment, he was terrified, he told me later: 'I had no idea what to expect, or what it would be like. Counselling is something that you just don't discuss because it means there's something psychologically wrong with you and no one wants to think that. But I also knew that I was lost and needed help.'

While it is unusual for men to feel comfortable 'seeing a shrink', I believe many men in our society are in desperate need of help. If they were able to recognise this, all society would benefit. Certainly relationships with their partners would improve. It is mostly men who fill our prisons, who commit violent crime, abuse, incest, murder, rape. As a result of the Internet there has been a huge increase in the activity of paedophile rings, nearly all male offenders. We expect to admire our leaders in business, but time and again they are in court facing charges of fraud and embezzlement. Most of our leaders are men. Where are the positive role models for our youth?

In not wanting to have counselling, both Graham and Chris were expressing their reluctance to reveal vulnerability and what they saw as weakness. The expectation placed on a man, even today, is that he will be strong and in control — of himself, his work, his relationships. This is how many men wish to be perceived. I believe many women also still hope for these qualities in a male partner, believing that if the man is in charge, they will feel protected and safer.

Needless to say, only a few referrals come my way via male clients because most men don't want to tell anyone they are having therapy, whereas women are happy to recommend counselling to friends and colleagues. It is a rare man who will admit to a (male) friend that he is not coping emotionally. Most women have at least one or two friends they can confide in.

What does it mean to be a man? Am I a real man?

A client who was struggling to work out how to proceed in life described his difficulty in this way: 'I want to be a manly man, talk like a real man, do manly things. Sometimes I don't even know what it means to be a man. It's uncomfortable to speak about feelings. That certainly doesn't seem manly.'

His comments were made when he was involved in a group of eight men and women who met with me on a monthly basis. I asked whether he thought the other three men in the group could be described as 'manly'. He replied: 'I don't actually see *any* of us as real men.'

In his mind, real men were assertive, aggressive and in control. They certainly didn't cry or reveal deep feelings.

It takes great courage for a man to face up to his emotional difficulties and reveal what he would perceive as weakness and vulnerability to a counsellor, and particularly a woman.

Ten foot tall and bulletproof or ...?

Through working closely with men in counselling sessions, I have come to see that many have an inner and an outer persona. 'Ten foot tall and bulletproof' was an expression used by several men I counselled over the years. This of course describes them when they are feeling invincible and on top. 'Little boy lost' was how one of these men described himself on the inside. He was convinced no one knew that at times he felt extremely vulnerable. When out of curiosity I googled 'ten foot tall and bulletproof', I discovered it is a 1994 pop song by singer/songwriter Travis Tritt. The first verse is as follows:

I'm a full-grown man
That's plain to see
But nowhere near as full-grown
As I'd like to be
But I'll find a bar
And I'll have a few
Until I'm ten feet tall and bulletproof.

Several male clients have told me that before going to any social gathering they need a few drinks to increase their confidence.

Bernard, a client who saw me for a few sessions before moving overseas for his work would probably fool most people into believing he felt 'ten foot tall and bulletproof' from the way he dressed, the manner in which he presented himself and the way he spoke. He could even come across as a little intimidating in his demeanour. He was obviously a highly intelligent and talented man who had achieved success in his career. What he revealed to me, however, was someone who had suffered deeply. He had always found it hard to fit in, both as a young boy and as an adult. Perhaps appearing invincible was a way of keeping others at arm's length. When he came to see me, he had just experienced yet another relationship break-up.

I only saw him a few times. I was aware it was very hard for him to reveal his real feelings to me. At our last session he handed me a letter saying he had taken my advice and written to his father although he had no intention of giving him the letter. Writing the letter had made him feel a little better about himself, he told me.

This is part of what he wrote: 'Dad, you are a lot like me. You don't like kids much. I felt that you didn't like me. You made me afraid of you. You made me feel that I was always useless and wrong, especially at manly things.

You didn't teach me the things that might have helped me to fit in. I felt I had no one to help me. I felt weak and worthless. You and Mum provided all the essential stuff like shelter, food and a good education, but I needed more. I needed to feel loved, I needed to feel I belonged. Now I'm middle-aged and somehow I've worked things out so I can get by, but I'm alone and I don't feel whole'.

Bernard's letter expressed the tragedy of feeling unloved and unsupported by one's parents. I have often wondered how he has fared in his life.

One of my clients who had been obsessed with football from an early age and was still playing competition in his late twenties talked to me of the fear he experienced as he psyched himself up to play his best on the field. While he wanted others to see him as 'the big fella', he often felt like 'a scared little boy'. He admitted to me that on occasion he relished the opportunity to hurt other players as it released his own feelings of suppressed anger. At other times he felt afraid of the ball and hoped it wouldn't come his way. While he would be able to admit to his occasional violence towards other players, his fear of the ball coming in his direction was something he would hide from other men because it was far too shameful.

The six men, discussed in this chapter, had all experienced at least one failed marriage. They had no real insight as to why the relationship ended. In every case, they also had no real sense of their true self and it is hardly surprising they were unable to make a relationship work.

Psychologist Peter O'Connor considers that men have an immense fear of their unconscious feelings. He believes that they find it difficult to access these feelings and prefer a fixed and socially acceptable view of themselves. He says: 'To welcome the feelings into consciousness is to challenge the supremacy of the acceptable male view that logic and reason are the only legitimate ways to be in the world'. He considers that the end result is: '...a severance within men between their inner and outer lives, which often compounds and brings much distress into their personal relationships, particularly with women' (O'Connor, 1993, p.3).

Case study: A mother's love

Patrick, a man in his mid thirties, expressed concern about his marriage and his part in the conflicts when he came to his first counselling session. He was aware that every couple of months he would change in his attitude towards his wife. Patrick had been a high achiever, school captain, a straight A student and star on the sporting field. He presented as an articulate, intelligent man with a considerable amount of personal charm. One could expect success to follow him in life, in relationships as well as career. When I first knew him, he was working in the corporate world as a derivatives trader, earning a high salary.

Patrick had been married before and was aware that his second marriage was in trouble. He told me that he was an ex-alcoholic. He no longer drank but from time to time became angry and abusive towards his partner, deliberately hurting her in the things he said. He could, in fact, recognise the warning signs when he was about to change from being a kind, considerate and loving man to one who was hurtful and destructive. He was powerless to control the overwhelming rage he felt, and his subsequent behaviour.

Exploration of the family background revealed that Patrick's father, a doctor, was 'never around' and his mother 'ruled with an iron fist'. Like other men I have worked with, if he angered his mother in any way, he would be hit or sent to his bedroom to await his father's return, and a beating would ensue.

Feelings were never spoken of in the family. His mother drank heavily. Growing up it was his mother who taught him everything he needed to know and who drove him on to achieve highly. She often used physical punishment to attain her end and Patrick believed it was 'for my own good'. She criticised many of his achievements, even on the school sporting field. If he failed to do what was expected of him, his mother would stop speaking to him. This led to Patrick feeling abandoned. He referred to his mother as his 'guiding light' and worried about letting her down. As a child he felt great discomfort when he angered his mother and would apologise — 'I'll be good, Mummy' — out of fear of her retaliation. It was clearly a confusing and complex relationship.

I asked Patrick to write for me what it was like growing up in his family. This is part of his story:

'It's hard to know, when you are young, if your upbringing is significantly different from the norm but I started to get the sense that mine was. It formed in my mind as a feeling of injustice. Friends the same age could go outside and kick the footy after dinner, during summer months. I was forbidden to do so. There was so much that was forbidden. I learnt what to do by memorising the ever-increasing list of things not to do. There was always a pressure to be a certain way, to meet other people's expectations and if what I wanted to do or to say contradicted those expectations, I would just submit.

'It was like constant grooming. Never letting up. "I'm doing this for your own good" my mother used to say. It was relentless. And everything seemed to be driven by an alluring and elusive fuel called approval, satisfaction or recognition — that never came.

'It was very difficult to be my mother's eldest son. I felt a great weight. I felt responsible for taking on the new generation of our family name and I needed to give it the respect it deserved. How dare I be responsible for bringing ill-repute to the family name?

'Growing up was a real slog. Conflict and confrontation were the norm. Table manners, the clothes my brothers and I wore, what we said, how we acted, what we spent our time doing was all controlled. I remember weekends and holidays as being excruciatingly boring. Living a greater distance from school than many of my friends meant that they didn't play at my house often. Later, I found out my friends wouldn't ring our house for fear that my mother would answer. They thought they were in trouble from the way my mother used to answer the phone in a gruff voice.

'I still remember one morning, around the age of 7, playing in my parent's bedroom. I obviously did something to upset my mother and she took off her slipper and struck me on the back of the right thigh. I collapsed in excruciating pain. I had no idea why this hurt more than the usual smacks, but for some reason my eyes saw sparks and I was in real pain. The only thought I had was "Please … Mummy… please don't do that again … it hurts too much" and I extended my arms to hug her, saying "Sorry, Mummy, I'm sorry … I won't do that again … please don't hit me again …" and I honestly thought she had heard me. Then smack — the back of the other leg. I remember just lying there in absolute bewilderment and asking myself what I had done to deserve this amount of pain.

'My mother's best friend, a high flying corporate executive proclaimed to my mother that I would be a "Captain of Industry" while my mother was in hospital having just given birth to me. I think my mother felt she would have failed if I didn't become one. So my future was set in stone. Work like none other to beat all others and fulfil my potential. I have felt the weight of this my entire life. It has delivered me many achievements and a lot that I am proud of. But it has not afforded me peace, happiness or the ability to interact in a meaningful or intimate relationship ... yet!

'Growing up, there was a complete absence of touching, hugging, kissing, support and positive reinforcement. I was very lost in my life. I had little idea how to express myself, but I could deliver to others (particularly adults) expectations very effectively. I needed to be good — and not just good, but the best — at everything. Other parents used to tell my mother that I was the student that every mother wanted. I think that just fuelled her. I guess I felt proud of this and it fuelled me too. I knew how to achieve at school. I was being built for things like that. But anything else — having an opinion, a point of view, knowing my feelings or being myself — I had absolutely no idea. I could never focus on what I liked, what I was naturally good at. The only thing I know that I hung onto was that my favourite colour was green. It seemed to get recognition and notice by the power brokers of the family (notably my mother and grandmother) and so this was my thing. It is the only decision I can remember making for myself, from my own choice. The colour green.

'Another vivid memory. Mummy was driving us to school one morning when I was about 16. I was in the front, my youngest brother (about 11) in the back. In response to something my mother had said to him, he replied, "Shut up, Mummy." Before I even realised what was being said, I felt the back of her hand across my face. "See what you taught him?" she yelled at me. I spent the remainder of the ten minute journey trying to make the other cheek as red as the slap mark on the first, so that no one at school would realise what had happened. I didn't want to be accused of doing something wrong by the school when I hadn't. I hadn't taught my brother to say anything.

'I just felt ridden. Used for what I could do. I was pretty capable, but it seemed like it was never enough. It was exhausting, painful and unrelenting. I was never good enough. I was in a lot of pain. I thought this was a little odd, but convinced myself it was only a little bit worse than what others were going through. If I tried harder, it would make it better. But it never did.

'I am really hurt by my father in all this. He is a kind, soft man. I think he genuinely cares, but I really wish he had stood up and looked at the situation. I was a good kid. Surely he could have seen that something was going on between my mother and me to the point that every night he would have to come home and sort me out. "Wait till your father gets home ..." And I knew that my side of the story had just evaporated and I was going to cop a belting as he would believe my mother's version of events. My father didn't help me or see me or look at the situation. Ever. He just followed what my mother said. I was just a child. I needed help. I had no voice. Where could I go? My father is a doctor. He provides family counselling advice to people and families under stress. He approaches things from a logical viewpoint. I think he really is a caring and sensitive person. He has spent his life dedicated to helping people. I feel I missed out with my father. I was so overshadowed by my mother, I never really got to know him. Maybe that was why he didn't stick up for me and instead let the misery continue. I don't know. She's pretty strong, my mother. She broke me.

'Later I drank a lot of alcohol. It seemed to make things go quiet in my head. Settle things down and anaesthetise my feelings, but of course I didn't find any answers, and I finally succeeded in giving up alcohol entirely.

'I had a child adopted out when I was 19. I had just left school and my girlfriend fell pregnant. The last thing I could do was tell my parents. My life would have been over. The investment they had put into my education and upbringing would have been for nothing. I was in real trouble so I didn't tell them. Years, probably fifteen years later, they did find out. They came to me and said: "We didn't know what went wrong. You went completely off the rails. We thought you'd killed someone." They had never mentioned this before. I was absolutely floored. They had seen I was in real trouble and did nothing. They showed no concern, no support. They just let me handle it myself, at the age of nineteen. This is how I felt my entire life with them. There was no safety net, no support mechanism, no safe place to go.

'It is only since having extensive counselling that I have begun to put some names to the feelings I experienced as a child. The big one for me was despair. Struggling to identify my feelings in a session one day, I remember my counsellor suggesting that the feeling was 'despair'. That describes it exactly. It was how I felt throughout my childhood. Despair is like acid running through you, rendering your whole being useless — for now and perceptively for ever. I boxed it up. And when I think about it now, I can see that throughout my thirties I found a vehicle to escape the feelings of despair — anger.'

It was a revelation to Patrick as he began to understand the effect of growing up in his family. While he was not close to his father, a younger brother enjoyed an easy relationship with him and as a result Patrick chose to invest a great deal in his relationship with his mother. It was no coincidence that he had an alcohol dependence. In behaving like a parent, we inevitably feel closer to them. Discussing with Patrick his mother's treatment of him was a sensitive issue in our early sessions because he was still looking to her for approval. It took some time before he was able to see that he had given over his life to her authority. Around this time Patrick participated in a personal development group with six others. The response from the other men and women — their shocked reaction to the way he had been treated by his mother and to the fact that he continued to call her 'Mummy' (even though he was in his mid thirties), made a strong impression on him.

Exploring the family relationships helped Patrick to understand why he behaved in the way he did and why he needed to feel in control in any situation (just as he had felt controlled since childhood). He was unaware, initially, that he had been affected by shame at the way he had been treated and by his mother's alcoholism. He understood why he treated his partner badly at times. He had internalised his mother's pattern of abuse and emulated her behaviour in his relationship. In so doing he was also perpetuating his feelings of shame.

Patrick had had several experiences of counselling previously but was left feeling hopeless about being able to change. He had a powerful incentive when he came to see me. He wanted to make a success of his second marriage and to be a trustworthy father to his children. Several violent outbursts had taken place in front of his young daughters.

I had the impression, quite early in counselling sessions, that Patrick was looking to establish a relationship of trust with me. He wanted to believe that I could help him to change. Putting trust in a female counsellor was a positive sign.

We had to begin at the beginning. Patrick needed to find out what he wanted from life. What he did know was the ways in which he had succeeded. Being so completely controlled, however, had prevented him from knowing anything about himself, how he felt, what he wanted for himself, what he liked: 'I was not allowed to move a millimetre to the left or the right ...' At one level, Patrick's success in his career counted for very little.

As Patrick stated, the one thing he knew that he liked, growing up, was the colour green, and he had clung to that knowledge as the one thing he did know about himself. At our next meeting he told me that he had learned something else about himself during that week, that he loved his wife and children. An important beginning.

As with many clients, the first dream that Patrick brought in (having assured me he didn't have dreams) indicated where we needed to begin. Patrick dreamt that he was whittling a piece of wood. He was feeling happy and free of anxiety. That was all there was to the dream, but it marked a significant turning point. He was feeling good about himself for the first time in a long while. The journey was underway. Through committing to counselling, Patrick was able to separate emotionally from his mother and take charge of his own life.

In Chapter 6: *Trust your dreams*, Patrick's dreams are explored in detail. It was via dreams that Patrick was able to negotiate the adjustment to adulthood. Six months after coming to counselling, he decided to train as a teacher. While the financial rewards are considerably less, his heart is in his new career.

Douglas Gillette writes of the mother-son conflict 'One of the most important developmental tasks, which a boy must successfully accomplish in order to achieve satisfying intimate relationships with women later in life, is that of separating emotionally from the mother. The boy must come to experience himself as profoundly independent of his mother — of her emotional states, of her needs, and of her sexual identity' (in Biddulph, 2004, p. 90).

Gillette goes on to say that the boy can do this most successfully when he has a strong and present father in his life. Without the positive male presence 'even good-enough mothers are frighteningly overwhelming' to the emerging boy.

Steve Biddulph maintains that boys in our society are 'horrendously under-fathered and are not given the processes or the mentor figures to help their growth into mature men. With no deep training in masculinity ... they grow into phony men who act out a role — a complete façade which does not really work in any of life's arenas'.

He goes on to say: 'Boys and young men never know the inner world of older men, so each boy makes up an image based on the externals, TV and peers, which he then acts out to 'prove' he is a man.... men often have little sense of their true selves.' Biddulph believes that 'the enemies, the prisons from which men must escape are loneliness, compulsive competition and lifelong emotional timidity' (Biddulph, 2004, p. 3).

Finding the true self

How does one go about 'finding the true self?' The first step is to enable clients to respond to the question: 'What do you feel?' It is a harder question than one might imagine. Often men respond with 'I think ...' rather than 'I feel ...' They are unaccustomed to getting in touch with feelings. It came as a great surprise to me to discover that many people are not even aware of their feelings.

A client knows his true feelings, deep down, but often is disconnected from them until ready to face them. I have worked with a number of clients, mostly male, who had no idea they possessed feelings until they were guided to access them. Many of the feelings we suppress are intensely painful, so why would we choose to look at them? There may also be a fear that unleashing deeply buried feelings might lead a client to wonder: 'Am I a psycho?'

There are numerous ways of avoiding unpleasant feelings, such as gambling, eating or drinking excessively and taking drugs. The only problem is that the feelings do not go away. They usually return with a vengeance! Siegel says that men who are uncomfortable with expressing difficult feelings '[may] turn to alcohol and other substances that can numb or distract. One response is to get angry. An alternative solution is to emotionally withdraw or shut down' (Siegel, 2000, p. 46).

To be aware of feelings and to be able to express fear, sadness, anger, etc. enables one to initiate change. It may come as a surprise to a man to know that there are aspects of himself which have been suppressed and it can be overwhelming to contact those buried feelings. I recall one man who was shocked initially at his newly discovered feelings (having told me emphatically that he didn't have feelings), but as the session continued he decided, 'This is quite exciting really!' As the client gets in touch with the previously hidden parts of himself, he begins to grow and to change.

In order to contact the true self, it is necessary for the client to engage with the process and to reveal truths about himself which he might consider shameful or 'bad' and which he would normally keep hidden.

As one client expressed it: 'The hard part for me in counselling sessions was that I had to get in touch with feelings that I didn't like at all and which I felt very uncomfortable about. Then I had to try them out with someone I could trust ... I had to find out what reaction I would get if I revealed the truth about myself.

'If you are really ashamed of what you've done or what you've thought or who you are, you are not going to talk to anyone about it because you are trying to impress others, to present yourself as a likeable person, a competent person and this image you are trying to portray doesn't fit with shameful experiences. Instead of being competent and strong you actually feel weak and a victim and that's the last thing I would want to think of myself as being. But I was. I was a victim throughout my childhood. That is the truth. It took a very long time to reach a point where I was able to talk about uncomfortable feelings that I felt deeply ashamed of.'

By engaging in the counselling process, revealing dark, hidden truths about himself to another person, the client begins to free himself of shameful feelings and to change his view of himself.

Ian McKellen: finding the courage to be myself

An interview by Virginia Trioli, with the actor Ian McKellen when he was in Melbourne in October 2010, struck me as a very clear illustration of the way we are controlled by feelings we keep concealed:

Ian McKellen: 'I had to learn how to be real ... I was always dressing up, not being myself.'

Virginia Trioli: 'So that's what it's about — the naked actor on the stage, and being truly you?'

Ian McKellen: 'Well, why was I so keen to put on false noses and put on wigs and make-up?'

Virginia Trioli: 'Was it insecurity?'

Ian McKellen: 'It was insecurity, and the insecurity I had was because I knew what other people didn't, that I was gay. If you have this big secret in life, and you are not free to show the truth of your emotions to other people in a public way …

'It was only when I came out, aged forty-nine, when at last I was brave enough to say 'I am who I am', that my acting fired up and the emotions could get past what had been a block. Now my emotions are bubbling up near the surface where they belong, not banked down.' (ABC, Artscape, 2010).

In the following case study, it is clear that Graham didn't feel he couldn't look to his parents to help him to deal with his emotional life or to negotiate the difficulties he faced in adolescence.

Case study: The misery of depression

Graham and his wife Georgina came to counselling for a time when their marriage was in trouble. Sadly they parted ways. Some months later, Graham phoned me to make an appointment as he wanted to look at aspects of his own life, including feelings of depression about the marriage ending. He continued counselling for over a year and as well as the breakdown of his marriage, he addressed several other issues, including his parents' divorce. It was a significant step for Graham as initially he had serious reservations about counselling because of the stigma attached to it. In particular he didn't want to believe there was something psychologically wrong with him. His experience in marriage counselling served as a stepping stone and convinced Graham that he could benefit by seeking help.

Like many people I have worked with, Graham had been bullied throughout his school years, particularly in secondary school. He was shocked when the bullying continued at university. His account of the cruelty he suffered is possibly one of the most horrifying I have heard. The main bullies were also supposedly his 'friends'. Later the bullying escalated into attacks on his sexuality. Graham told no one of his suffering, keeping the pain inside for many years. He did not feel that his parents could help him so he didn't confide in them. If a child who is bullied feels he can go to a parent, the suffering he endures will be considerably less. He will not feel so desperately alone.

Boys who are fortunate in having a solid group of friends in adolescence, female as well as male, generally develop a strong sense of self which supports them as they go out into the world to form relationships. The wounding from the bullying that Graham suffered in his formative years was still painful and had left him with a low opinion of himself and a sense of despair about forming another relationship after his marriage failed. Not wanting to burden his friends with his problems (nor to be reminded of his marriage) he withdrew into himself. He couldn't trust anyone, and that included himself. When he came to see me he was experiencing a very bleak depression, which he later described: 'It was affecting my work. I was becoming indecisive about everything. Not having trust in myself led to my believing that I wasn't good enough to cope with life. A depressing thought in itself. The indecisiveness added to the downward spiral in that I couldn't choose a direction for myself that I felt would bring happiness or that would rekindle any passion for life. I was just simply living, taking one breath after another but not having any hope for things becoming brighter.'

Graham struggled over many months with severe depression, to the point that he couldn't work for more than a few hours a day. Some days he didn't work at all. It was clear that he felt suicidal at times and I discussed my concerns with him, suggesting he take antidepressants for a time. He was reluctant to go down that path, having tried medication for just one week when he was married (not long enough, in fact, for most medication to take effect). When a client is depressed over a long period, I always ask about suicidal thoughts because it is obviously something they have contemplated. Graham replied that he wouldn't act on his suicidal feelings, 'but I sometimes consider joining the bush fire fighters so that I can be killed honourably.'

Graham was fortunate in having a very sympathetic boss who was prepared to keep him on, even though his work was erratic. I felt reassured that Graham believed there was hope and wanted to persevere with counselling, without medication, even though he was having a hard time. In general it is easier to work with people who are not taking medication because it can numb an individual's feelings, making it harder to address underlying pain. Obviously medication has a place when treating clinical and prolonged depression.

Graham later described for me why he felt resistant to the option of medication: 'I felt deeply that I would be somehow losing the 'real' Graham by taking something mind altering. Even though I was doing it hard, I wanted to be the one doing it, however miserable I felt. Not an artificially happier version of myself. If I was going to become happier, I wanted to experience the thrill of knowing I was turning some corner for myself and that it was part of my own growth. Not for something I'd swallowed. I was beyond any stigma regarding counselling because I'd come to realise that no matter what insight or guidance you gave me, it was ultimately up to me how much I put into it and got out of it. I didn't want my life to be a sham. I wanted to be happy because I *was* happy.'

We continued with the process. Graham addressed the painful experiences of being bullied and his deep sense of betrayal in view of the fact that the ringleaders were supposedly his friends. He was able to face the way his parents were unable to help him in terms of feelings and relating to others. He had, in fact, always felt alone in his suffering.

One weekend Graham participated in a personal development group. When the subject of bullying came up, five of the eight people, male and female, revealed they too had been bullied at school.

One of Graham's problems, around the time of his darkest depression, was the fact that he had withdrawn from his friends. As I pointed out to him one day, the only two women that he knew well were his mother and his ex-wife. It was time to establish a database on women. We were able to share a joke about this at the time, but later he told me that he had set about doing just that after our discussion, realising that he was in fact isolated socially and knew little about the female species. In order to begin living life, he needed to form some strong friendships, something that he had been unable to do following the experiences of bullying when he was young. He pursued new interests and started meeting people and was surprised to discover that they warmed to him and wanted to know him. From that new start his life began to change. He was able to risk trusting again and to appreciate his own worth.

Graham contacted me a year or so after finishing counselling to tell me how he was faring: 'I'm actually happy being single and really enjoying the fact that I've developed a warm circle of friends. Feeling good about myself has allowed me to acquire just as many female friends as male. Needless to say, because I've been happy to be single, I've ended up falling into a good relationship. Ironically if it weren't for our failures in life, we wouldn't have come together to enjoy this experience. We'd be living the lives that we thought we wanted, and now seem somehow mundane. The realisation has made me aware that relationships can be so much more than I expected. There doesn't even need to be drama. It is all part of having to experience the bad to appreciate the good. I haven't yet come close to experiencing the love that I had with Georgina, but I do know the answer to my most frustrating question: was that marriage harder than it should have been? The answer is a very calm and at peace 'yes'.

'I've come a long way since the days when I was depressed. I missed my marriage for a long period, but now I enjoy a life without the drama and stress that that relationship brought with it. Likewise if I were never to have children I know I could easily enjoy a life without them. I won't have failed for not experiencing my own children. There are always close friends' and family's children to enjoy. In other words, whatever direction life moves me in will be okay by me. Sure I may well miss out on some things, but missing those would allow me to experience and enjoy other things that may otherwise have been less available to me. Through overcoming my resistance to getting help, I have been able to take charge of my life and learn how to enjoy relationships.'

For the first time in decades, Graham felt good about his life, accepting of a different path from the one he had expected to follow, and optimistic about his future. To reach this point, it was necessary for him to examine his life and his relationship with his parents. Confronting his depression, painful as it was, forced him to get to the heart of his difficulties.

As a counsellor it is immensely rewarding to witness a client emerge from a long period of depression and start living a productive and fulfilling life. In the time that he worked with me in counselling, Graham learned to trust that I cared about him. He was aware that I saw him as a worthwhile person and this gave him greater confidence in relating to women.

Graham mentioned that 'there are always other people's children ...' Graham has been in a relationship for four years now. His partner has five children and he has been a very involved person in their lives.

Case study: the family supporter

Many clients, both men and women, have described the way they often had to be supportive to a parent, even from a very young age. I hear of mothers who fall apart in front of their children, cry inconsolably or take to their beds. It is overwhelming for young children to witness an adult parent in this state. They feel inadequate to help, and their own distress at the parent's collapse prevents them from caring for themselves or even acknowledging their pain. Who can they go to? Who can they tell? And is it their fault?

Chris, who was terrified at his first counselling session, was thirty when his partner ended the relationship. Concerned for him, she suggested he sought counselling. Chris threw himself into counselling. In his first session he admitted to feeling lost and having no direction for himself. A memory from his early childhood was imprinted on his brain. Around the age of six, coming home from school, he was surprised that the babysitter was nowhere to be found. He wondered if his father had come home and went to look for him. His father and the babysitter were in bed together, in his parents' bed. Chris left the room, unnoticed. He sat on the couch watching television until his mother returned from work. When she asked where the babysitter was, and where his father was, he told her. The trauma of the violent eruption that followed — his father thrown out of the house and the babysitter leaving for good, all played out in full view of the neighbours — had remained with him for twenty-five years.

Following the separation his mother became depressed and for several years would sit with Chris in the evening, telling him of her distress and crying on his shoulder. In counselling sessions he was able to get in touch with his feelings of resentment at his mother's behaviour. He was expected to parent his mother and comfort her, and he was only seven years old. Later Chris had offered the same support to the women with whom he formed relationships, who eventually betrayed him or ended the relationship once they had got their life in order. He had turned himself into a 'leaning post' for women. It was a role that he could easily fill; he was a kind, sensitive young man.

When a parent turns to a child for support, the child is expected to take on an adult's suffering, long before he is emotionally mature. It generally prevents him from focussing on his own growth and development. Siegel says that it is natural for a child to offer support and comfort to a parent but there are inherent problems 'The child ceases to be a child, and is given responsibilities he should be protected from for many years. Some children appear to do well in this situation and become 'little adults' who seem to be perfect ... [but] ultimately, being responsible for a parent's happiness demands that they sacrifice their own needs' (Siegel, 2000, p.55).

Chris was able to recognise in counselling sessions that he had 'parented' his mother when he was still a young boy. When his mother remarried, she had no further need for his support. Chris's stepfather had two sons. Following the marriage, there was considerable conflict between Chris's older brother and his two stepbrothers. Chris, the youngest of the boys, took on the responsibility for the entire family in the ensuing years, trying to be a go-between and to keep the peace with everyone.

Chris recognised that he needed to understand why he felt lost in his own life. He applied himself with great determination to the counselling process, exploring his feelings and his inner world. After some months, during which time he became stronger and clearer about what he wanted for himself in life, Chris took part in a weekend group. He decided to address his inability to move forward, and he told the group of the episode from his childhood involving the babysitter. He did a role-play with others in the group playing the various parts. The day after the weekend group, Chris phoned me to say he wanted to see me for one final session and also to tell me that he felt like a new person as a result of the weekend. In our last session, he described his experience in the role-play: 'Something weird happened that weekend. It was surreal. Once I started role-playing, I had no control over what I did or said. I started to think about my life and it just poured out of me, all the pressure of those years, trying to look after my mother and everyone in the family, trying to be reliable and dependable for all of them, never feeling carefree, never feeling like a child. Once I started letting go, I couldn't stop. I could see my life so clearly, and when I left that afternoon, I felt healed.'

I contacted Chris a few years after he finished counselling to find out how he was getting on, and I asked how he thought his life had changed as a result of having counselling. What I discovered was that Chris had remarried, was the proud father of two little girls and his career had blossomed:

'That's easy!' he replied. 'Absolutely everything about my life changed. I have a great marriage; my wife is extremely supportive and loves me unquestionably. My children are growing fast. I thought I was destined to work in overalls for the rest of my life but I am now operations manager for a company that builds equipment and sells it both domestically amd internationally. I am responsible for approximately twenty people and a very large financial turnover. I never imagined life could be so good'.

Chris no longer involved himself in issues concerning his family of origin. 'I don't need to be part of the family chaos any more. I can focus on my own life at last. This is who I would have been, I believe, if my family hadn't disintegrated. Now everything about my life has fallen into place. I know I would not be where I am if it weren't for finally acknowledging the truth to myself — that I needed help.'

What role did you play in your family?

Many of us choose to play a role in our lives. Gender, birth order and personality all contribute to deciding what role we will play. Chris's decision to be the reliable and dependable leaning post gave him a meaningful role in his chaotic family, but in choosing to do so he was denying himself the opportunity to pursue the things he wanted in life. Once he recognised his part, he was able to step outside the role and begin to live for himself, true to his own wants and feelings.

Chris was fortunate in having experienced a close relationship with his mother, and over time he also developed a good relationship with his stepfather. This gave him a solid base for addressing his difficulties in life. Many people are not so lucky. Without a supportive parent who is able to understand what their child is experiencing, young people are forced to fend for themselves and to make the best of their situation.

Case study: the absent father

Most of my clients come to me by word of mouth. A client I met under unusual circumstances was a twenty-three year old man, the barista in a café where I was having a coffee (and babycino) with my two year old granddaughter. He started playing with her and when he brought my coffee I commented that he must have a child as he was clearly very comfortable playing with my granddaughter. His eyes filled with tears. We began to talk and he told me he had decided that day to hand over custody of his three year old son to his ex-partner because he felt the hostility between them was too damaging. Michael had fallen behind with child support payments and had been denied access for many months. He had also had his son's name tattooed on his chest that day. I was shocked at what he was planning to do and told him it was crucial that he maintain contact with his son. His son needed to know him and to believe his father wanted him in his life. Michael understood. I had a new client.

Michael grew up without his own father as his parents separated when he was just six months old and his father moved interstate. Michael was told that his father had decided, after separating from his mother, that 'I should walk away, as otherwise it would affect Michael'. Twenty-three years later Michael came close to making the same mistake as his father.

Michael lived with his mother and her second husband. When he was sixteen, Michael was told to leave by his stepfather, following some fairly typical teenage defiance. At the time his mother was at work. Michael left, regretting it later but too proud to ask to go back. He felt betrayed by his mother (as well as his stepfather) as she made no attempt to get him to come home.

The pattern had been established. The idea of moving away from his son was one that fitted with Michael's own previous experience. At an unconscious level he could go along with the idea that 'fathers leave their sons'. Michael's stepfather, by his actions, had also left him.

Michael responded very readily when I told him, quite forcibly, that he must not walk away from his son (one of the rare occasions I felt it was right to tell someone what to do or not do).

Over the next two years, Michael put all his energy into forming a close relationship with his little boy. He would see me for counselling whenever his work schedule permitted. In our sessions he addressed how to become a good father as he had no personal experience of what it meant to be fathered in a loving manner. I recall many discussions with Michael about how to care for his son, how to occupy and nurture a young boy and even what to feed him.

On one occasion he brought his son to meet me. I was impressed by their close relationship. Relations with Michael's ex-partner were volatile. He would be turned away at times when he went to collect his son. He was forced to go to court time after time in an attempt to resolve access rights. This was at a high cost to a young man without family support and on a low income. The pressure he was under made it difficult to form another relationship.

In the time that he worked with me, Michael also addressed the issue of his employment as his low wage prevented him from setting up a comfortable home for his son. Through a friend he was able to obtain an apprenticeship as a plasterer. His other challenge was that for many years he had been addicted to marijuana. Once he began to take his duties as a father seriously, Michael had the incentive he needed to address his addiction. He was able to replace marijuana with becoming an effective and loving father. The two could not mix.

When I spoke to Michael recently, he told me that he is doing well, running his own plastering business. He has an excellent relationship with his son who is now twelve years old and achieving well at school. Michael also made contact with his own father after a long break but was disappointed in him as a person and didn't feel his father was a good role model for him or for his son.

Michael is one of those young people who simply needed some positive guidance, as he had been denied solid parenting in his teens. It would obviously have been quite easy for Michael to follow the fathering model of his family and to deprive his own son of a father. Fortunately for Michael and his son, a new pattern has been laid down. Men also return and stay to be fathers to their sons.

Feeling good about being a man

The men who commit to the process of counselling all yearn for a loving relationship but may have little idea of how to achieve this. If they are able to look honestly at the way they treat others, especially female partners (or male) and to understand the reasons for their behaviour, they are generally able to change their lives. Fundamentally they want to feel good about themselves.

A client in his mid thirties revealed he was at a loss to know how to make decisions in terms of his relationship and would simply avoid making any. He was aware that he was easily influenced by the wants of other people, particularly female partners, and would generally go along with their decisions so as to avoid conflict. (Needless to say, conflict was avoided in his family.) When he and his partner had an argument he would feel completely overwhelmed and would withdraw from her, sometimes for several days.

Ending a relationship seems to be extremely confronting for many men. One man worked with me in counselling sessions to address how to do this with greater style. Usually he would end a relationship via a text message (not uncommon practice). Then he would switch off his phone for a few days. He felt badly at the way he had parted company with a particular girlfriend.

'I just said I wasn't attracted to her any more, and in fact I wasn't *really* attracted to her at the start of the relationship.'

To be fair to him, he quickly understood how hurtful his behaviour had been and arranged to meet with her to apologise. A few months later he came to see me with his new partner, aware that unless he was able to learn how to address his feelings, the relationship would fail.

When a man has had the experience of being hurt by a partner ending a relationship, he will go to great lengths at times to avoid causing hurt. What he is avoiding, in fact, is honesty. Often the lack of honesty proves to be even more painful than knowing the truth. Conversely, a man who has been hurt may set about trying to hurt others.

Many of the articles in the news, day after day, concern 'men behaving badly'. Sporting heroes appear in the newspapers on the front pages as well as the back, charged with assault, possession of drugs, or alcohol-related driving offences. Their sexual misdemeanours, which seem to fascinate the public at large, make regular headlines. Alcohol and drug-fuelled violence on Melbourne streets is now a common theme in the media. It is invariably men acting up, hitting out at the world.

From female clients I regularly hear accounts of fairly shabby treatment meted out by men they become involved with, men who fail to reveal they have a wife or girlfriend tucked away, men who are verbally abusive and those who get drunk and are unfaithful, particularly when out with 'the boys'.

Having worked with many men, I believe that sometimes they have simply been hurt deeply in their lives and have learnt to act out of their suppressed pain. Hurt, unaddressed, turns to anger. Many men know where they stand with anger. Women are more likely to turn their anger inwards, becoming depressed and anxious or developing eating disorders.

What do you want out of life?

In addition to being able to get in touch with feelings, clients are encouraged to consider the question: 'What do you want for yourself?'

Many people have never thought about this question. They have no sense that they even have the right to consider what it is that they want out of life. What our parents want for us governs most of childhood and we often allow this to continue to control our lives into adulthood instead of pursuing our own dreams. Many young people in their thirties are still locked in a struggle with parents and resort to evasive tactics instead of saying to parents what they want, or don't want, in relation to them. The same applies, of course, in reverse. How many parents are afraid of their adult children's rejection? How many grandparents are denied access to their grandchildren?

Case study: handle snakes with care

I cannot know what is right for my clients or what direction they will take but it is usually obvious what some of the crucial factors might be when a client tells me of his life experience. In addition, it is clear what has not worked for the client, what patterns of behaviour have developed over time that are unhelpful for growth and maturity. It is the disowned parts, however, the unacknowledged aspects of the self that continue to control and prevent a client from knowing who he could be. Until an individual begins to change, to re-own parts of his true self abandoned along the way, it is almost impossible to explain the transformation. Nor is it possible to preempt the change he will go through or to tell him what to expect. This period of transformation can create considerable anxiety. Who will I be? Will people like the new me?

Barry came to counselling on the recommendation of a work colleague. He was in a very distressed state, having recently left his marriage: 'When I came to counselling I was terribly unhappy and full of guilt, having cheated on my wife and walked away from her. I wanted to be happy, but I didn't know what would make me happy. I was afraid of what others would think of me and I was unsure of how to act. If I were to change, I had no idea what my new life would be like, and if I didn't feel the same as I did now, how would I feel? Who would I be?'

I am always excited by the mystery of who will emerge as the authentic person. It is not something I can ever predict. What I observe is that clients who are brave enough to confront their inner hurt are able to form good relationships. Often they also change careers, once they realise what kind of work would offer them real fulfilment.

Barry's image of himself when he first came to counselling was one that reflected his feelings of shame: 'My image of myself at that time was a direct copy of the image that my wife portrayed to me, one of an unreliable, cheating, lecherous, lust filled man. She knew my family and her knowledge of the family history made me feel I came from tainted stock and that I had nothing to offer of any value to anybody. I pretty much believed her view of me.

'I wanted the normal things that a single man wants, including sex, but every time I found it, it was in the wrong places which only compounded my shame and guilt. I was feeling so low and I would grab sex wherever I could because it would make me feel better for a time. In fact it usually made me feel much worse afterwards. I got involved with a married woman and I knew it was the wrong thing to do. I felt deeply ashamed of my behaviour.

'I also had a close core of friends who had an opinion of me which was much better than my own opinion of myself, so I wouldn't tell them the things that I was thinking or doing because I was afraid that their image of me would shatter. On the one hand their opinion of me gave me a goal to work towards, but at the same time I didn't know how to get there because I'd dug a bit of a hole for myself.

'That's where the counselling sessions came in. Through talking about what I was doing and how it made me feel, and then looking at how I wanted to be perceived by others and by myself, I came to understand what I needed to do to achieve that end. But it took a while; change wasn't immediate.'

I describe myself as a counsellor, but in fact that description fails to give credit to the hard work that a client needs to do for change to occur. I do not see my role as giving advice (except very rarely). It is uncommon for just a few sessions to be sufficient to enable a client to change, particularly when addressing feelings and behaviours that are entrenched. People act out of their pain and it takes time to let go of old ways of being in the world, once the patterns are established.

For Barry, dreams were one of the most important elements in understanding how he needed to change: 'Initially I took the themes and images of the dreams to be demonstrating everything that was bad about me. My unconscious would throw up situations in which I was faced with temptation and I did behave badly. I took it to be confirmation that I was a terrible person, but as we worked through my dreams in the sessions, breaking down the images and picking little situations out of the dreams, it became obvious that the images, an animal or a person in the dream, was an aspect of myself. I could see that the animal being hurt was me, so instead of seeing myself as the destructor, I was able to see myself as a victim too. It helped me to understand that I needed to care for myself in order to like myself.

'One of the other themes that came through in several dreams was confrontation — anger and violence. Again I would see my actions as confirmation of my poor character, but by talking about the dreams, I could see it so differently. One that I remember clearly was about a lion that I confronted violently with a sword. My counsellor asked what I think of lions and I see them as the personification of selfish men. They have a den of lionesses who hunt for them and bear their children and basically look after the male — the ultimate egotist — and so when I confronted that image in the dream, I realised I was behaving exactly like that. The message was clear: if I don't like it, don't behave like that and my unconscious will leave me alone and let me have some sleep!

'I remember that three nights in a row I had a vivid dream about animals, or about myself! They became affirmations that I still carry around in my wallet: "I must not handle any snakes, I must keep the torrent at bay and I must behave like a good sportsperson." I remember being a little embarrassed when we explored what the snake represented!'

Barry's dreams are explored in greater detail in Chapter 6: *Trust your dreams.*

'A big part of my internal struggle, which I now understand so clearly, is the beast that lies within versus the caring feminine soul that I treasure, because it's what makes me a little different. It makes me me. During my marriage, the beast was dormant. Now it's a part of me, but I have learned how to tame it and use it only for good. I know now that what women want is a man they can respect, who also respects himself.'

At the end of a weekend group he took part in, Barry asked if he could say something to the other nine participants. This is what he said: 'As a result of the weekend I feel ashamed at the way I have treated and used many women in my life, and seeing the depth of pain and suffering the women in this room have endured from fathers, brothers, lovers and husbands, I have understood for the first time what women have to offer and what they want from men. From today, I will consider it an honour and a privilege to earn a woman's love. I now have a much better idea of how to love a woman.'

The women were astounded! Barry is now enjoying a loving and fulfilling relationship.

Shame on you!

One of the most crippling emotions, which many men experience, is shame. It is a difficult emotion to address without help from a professional with experience in this area. In my experience how to deal with shame is seldom addressed in training for therapists. Its effect on an individual can be highly destructive. Shame prevents you from feeling you belong, from believing that you are a likeable person, shame makes you feel like an outsider and prevents you from acting for yourself and pursuing goals. Most of the people I have worked with, male and female, who suffer from shame have a deep need to be liked by everyone. This overwhelming need colours all relationships and prevents them from being true to themselves. For many people it is even shameful to begin to admit to feelings of shame.

Many of the men I have worked with have experienced deep shame for many years, even for decades. For some, it is as though a tape-recording plays in their brain, chastising, criticising, judging their every decision and action. They have done nothing shameful. The crippling feelings of shame nearly always stem from the treatment they received as children and from the flawed relationships in the families they grew up in. Many of these men have told me they fantasise about being dead, so as to ease the pain. It is hardly surprising that the suicide rate among young men is so high.

A client told me of the torment he suffered on a daily basis, until he understood in counselling sessions that shame was controlling everything about his life. He described what it felt like to be in the grip of shame: 'I feel totally alone and while I hate being alone, I am most comfortable when I'm by myself. I want to feel connected to others, but I withdraw and feel distant. I feel I need to hide from the world and from other people. I'm very good at keeping people away. I avoid eye contact, look unapproachable, act as though I'm not interested. I know that when I'm being honest with myself I don't want to be this awkward, withdrawn person. I can't show affection because it feels fake. Inside I know I want to hug and be hugged by people I care about, but it is too uncomfortable. I feel like a little boy who is in trouble for something, but I don't know what I've done wrong. I am being punished, so I become defiant and distance myself again. If I think I've made a mistake I call myself an idiot and for weeks and months afterwards, I recall what I did and feel disgusted with myself, criticise, attack, and abuse myself. I expect people to think I'm stupid and look down on me. Deep down I hate myself. This is the normal feeling I have every day, unless something happens to distract and interest me.'

In their book *Letting go of shame*, Potter-Efron define shame as follows:

'What is shame? It is more than a feeling. It is a set of physical responses, (such as looking down or blushing), combined with predictable actions (such as hiding or withdrawing from others), uncomfortable thoughts (such as 'I am a failure in life'), and spiritual despair. Our definition of *shame* is that it is *a painful belief in one's basic defectiveness as a human being'*. (Potter-Efron, 1989).

I have used this book, more than any other, in working with clients as they recognise themselves in its pages.

Brutalised sons

Many boys are treated brutally, particularly by their fathers, when they are very young. As I write, I recall some of the stories of mothers who were pretty savage too.

As little boys, from as young as two years old, several clients received regular beatings from the people supposed to be their protectors. One client was physically abused by not one but two stepfathers from a very young age, another tried to intervene when his sister was being assaulted and then received a beating himself, and a third could only look on as his father kicked his puppy down the stairs. For several weeks that young boy had been making a model for his father's birthday, in secret. When he saw his father kick his puppy in an uncontrollable rage, he went to his room and smashed the model. A number of male clients were beaten by their mothers. Several were shut in a room and told to await their father's return from work, at which point the father carried out the punishment under instruction from his wife. In every case, the young boy had done nothing to deserve the violent treatment but of course was made to believe that he had. One man remembered arriving home from school, bruised, after being punched by another boy. His grandmother, 'a tough old bird', chastised him for being weak and sent him off to find the other boy and 'give him a good thrashing', which he did. My client still felt guilty, thirty years later, at having harmed the other child.

For these boys growing up, the violence experienced as a child controlled their behaviour and prevented them from feeling strong about who they were. How can you know how to become a confident, loving man when your role model, the man you want to look up to, behaves in a savage and cruel manner towards you and those you love? The young man growing up internalises the anger and violence and fears his own rage, or acts out of it. A brutalised boy may grow up to be a brute, or he may become passive, unable to pursue his goals in life because he is afraid of acting assertively:

'What do you think would happen if you were to stop behaving like 'Mr Nice Guy' all the time?' I asked a young man in his thirties who spent his life pleasing everyone around him — family, friends and colleagues.

'I would turn into the biggest arsehole and not give a shit about anyone,' was his reply.

The physical abuse experienced as a child also leads to deep feelings of shame.

Case study: hiding from the world

Austin came to counselling in his mid thirties. His mother was just fifteen when she gave birth to him. She had little understanding of how to nurture a child. He could not recall being parented by anyone as a child. In his early years his mother had a number of relationships, but none of these men offered Austin support or affection.

Much later in life he was told of an incident by his mother when he was just two years old. Austin had intervened when his mother was being assaulted by her partner at the time. It was also much later in his life that he learned that the man he thought was his uncle was in fact his biological father.

Austin described a time in early primary school when he found some soft toys in the park on the way home and ripped them up. Later that evening there was a knock at the front door:

'A little while later John, my mother's boyfriend, came bursting into my bedroom and yelled at me: "Did you rip up these toys?"

'I was terrified. I said yes. He said: "Right, I'm giving you the belt." I panicked, saying no, begging, trying to get away. I didn't think I deserved the belt. It felt wrong. I tried to get him to listen, but he belted me again and again. From that day I hated him. I don't know why my mother didn't do anything. I remember telling her it was wrong that he belted me like that and she said "I know". But she never did anything. I remember running away all the time, hiding out, staying on my own. Every time I got into trouble and thought it was unfair, I would run away. I became very good at it. Mostly I would hide in the bush and if I was planning to stay away for a long time I would build an inconspicuous shelter. I wanted to show them that I didn't need anyone.

'I remember once when I was in grade 3, a teacher caught me tripping up a boy in my class. I just put out my leg as he walked past. The teacher grabbed me from behind, dragged me down the corridor. He made me sit on the floor against the wall and yelled and screamed at me. I was so shocked and scared that I wet my pants. He tapered off when he noticed I had wet myself. Other people were looking at me and I felt terribly ashamed.

'I was in my late thirties when I decided I had to have counselling. I realised I was still hiding out in a way, keeping my distance from everyone. I felt most comfortable when I was by myself. I was extremely critical of myself, would call myself stupid, an idiot, or tell myself I was disgusting. No one knew how I felt inside.

'Growing up I had to look after my sisters. I learned to become the carer, a nice guy, always doing the right thing and minding others. What I realised in counselling was that I had lost all sense of my true self. I had suffocated myself. I felt shy and introverted, but I would play the extrovert. In my relationships with women, including my ten year marriage, I played a number of supportive roles: guide and mentor, provider, carer, teacher and even chef. It felt good because I had a very definite role to play, but it wasn't the real me. No one saw or knew the real me.

'It took nine months in counselling before I came out of hiding and could begin to like myself and I felt I could start to reveal to others who I was. I remember being lent a book on shame by my counsellor and crying when I started to read it. It may as well have been written about me. I realised I felt ashamed about absolutely everything in my life: my family, my relationships and my work.'

Understanding the effect of the treatment received in childhood enables the client to begin to heal deep wounds. If one considers Austin's account of his childhood, the absence of any nurturing adult, the bleakness and loneliness when there is nobody to confide in, it is obvious how crucial it is to heal the suppressed pain before attempting to form a long-term relationship or become a parent. It is not surprising that for people treated so badly in childhood, relationships are very challenging; giving and receiving love is totally unfamiliar. Even being hugged is quite foreign. Most physical contact in Austin's childhood involved punishment.

I remember a weekend group in which roughly half the group hugged one another happily while the others looked on, obviously uncomfortable at being touched. We discussed it as a group. The non-huggers were uncomfortable with being hugged either because it was totally unfamiliar or because it triggered for them the fear of being beaten as a child. By the end of the weekend, several non-huggers decided they were now huggers! Simply learning to trust was sufficient to bring about the change.

When I read accounts of men who beat their wives and children, sometimes to their death, I wonder what happened to these men when they were growing up, what violence did they witness, what beltings did they endure? No doubt they still have the rage, suppressed all those years ago. They may have no memory of the violence, but the body and the unconscious mind cannot forget.

In Melbourne the public was shocked when a man threw his four year old daughter off the Westgate Bridge. I thought a lot about that man (and his daughter, and his two sons who witnessed the tragedy). What kind of childhood did he experience? And how will his two sons who saw what happened contain the horror of their father's actions? What kind of men will they grow up to be? I sincerely hope they get the help they need.

In order to come out of hiding, Austin had to confront the loneliness, the isolation and the enormous fear that he experienced as a child. He also had to get in touch with his anger at the way he had been treated by the adults in his life. For nearly forty years he had continued to feel like a lost boy, barely alive, in his words 'a ghost'. Men were to be feared and avoided, so how do you become a man?

Why would you want to be a man? Austin had no example of how to live or how to form a good relationship.

'I can't remember ever being shown affection by a man. Sometimes I don't even know what it means to be a man.'

Once he was able to get in touch with the shame of his early life, Austin could begin the slow process of coming out into the world, recognising his value and strengths and developing his creative side. He was aware that he had worn a mask for most of his life in an attempt to hide all the things he believed were bad about himself, that he was of no value in the world, that people would despise him if they knew the truth about him, that he was defective in some way. Once he found the courage to face his shameful feelings, to monitor and then challenge the way he attacked himself daily, change began to occur. Austin was able to let go of the shame, to approach people for friendship and to see that they liked who he was. He started to achieve success in his career. He also took up playing the guitar and writing songs. He joined a band and within a few months found himself on stage, playing guitar and singing. He started living in the world, aware of his real worth for the first time in his life. When I asked where he learnt to play the guitar, Austin replied: 'On my own, in my bedroom, for the past twenty years.' He had never allowed anyone to hear him play. Austin once told me he had googled how to commit suicide although he assured me he wouldn't act on the advice. A year later he was googling how to perform as a rock star.

The men I have discussed in this chapter had all experienced at least one failed marriage or long-term relationship before counselling. When one considers the suppressed wounding from early years that underpinned their emotional state, it is hardly surprising the relationships ended. Their first task was to examine painful feelings that controlled them, in order to value themselves, to find their true self and then to explore what they wanted from a good relationship.

Often men come and go in counselling, looking for a reason to escape; invariably a new relationship with a partner is the trigger. The men whose stories are told in this chapter shared an understanding that they needed help and that it would take time to bring about the change they were looking for. They were prepared to stay in counselling until comfortable with themselves and able to express their feelings in relationships.

In recent years, it has thankfully become more acceptable for men to seek emotional help although I am sure many still believe it is not manly. A client who has served in Iraq told me that if you speak to a counsellor in the army, it is just a formality. You would not reveal your feelings, particularly in relation to fear or vulnerability. It certainly would not be considered manly for a soldier to need psychological help. Soldiers, surely, must need it more than most.

Chapter 5

The couple — the impossibility of a good relationship

Love one another and you will be happy. It's as easy and as difficult as that. There is no other way.
—**Michael Leunig**

Simply and powerfully, and in just a few words, Leunig expresses what is needed to make a relationship work. There is nothing more satisfying than a good relationship. It is, however, something that is not easy to achieve. In Australia around 40% of first marriages fail. This figure does not include de facto or gay relationships. In second marriages, where there are children from a previous marriage, the percentage jumps to 65%.

While many couples are electing not to marry (or, in some cases, one person is choosing not to), I do see the ceremony of marriage, making a public commitment in front of friends and family, as being somewhat different from a de facto relationship. In this chapter, however, rather than making a distinction between the two I will focus my discussion on significant relationships of some years' duration, whether married or not.

When couples who have enjoyed a long and happy marriage are asked how they have succeeded when so many fail, they invariably give a reply that sounds well rehearsed, (or perhaps is their official statement when asked). John Mills, the actor, was married for more than sixty years. When asked his secret, he claimed: 'If we had a disagreement I always said it was my fault, even when it wasn't.' This hardly describes an equal relationship. Maybe that was why it was so successful!

My uncle warned me, when I got married at the age of twenty (first time around) that divorce was hereditary. Going back three generations on my mother's side of the family, not one marriage lasted 'until death', apart from my great-grandfather's first marriage. His wife died in childbirth at the age of thirty. He subsequently remarried, but that marriage ended after a few years. Looking back at the person I must have been at that time, it is clear to me that I knew very little about myself or what I wanted from life, and I knew even less about the man I was marrying.

If one considers the diverse history of two people attempting to make a life together under one roof, the statistics around failed marriages are hardly surprising. Often the partners have emerged from different parenting styles, and possibly diverse cultures, as illustrated in previous chapters. A couple may have very different expectations in terms of what they hope for in a relationship or marriage. What does 'a happy marriage' actually mean to each one? Clearly the clients whose lives are discussed in the previous chapters had not observed a close and trusting relationship in their formative years. Many of their parents' marriages ended in divorce. The parents who remained together rarely enjoyed an intimate relationship and it is not surprising if the next generation found it hard to make a relationship work, without an adequate role model. Many people look to their partner to provide the love, support and the feeling of being connected to another that they yearned for, and may have been denied, growing up. Relationships invariably struggle if both people are hoping a partner will heal their emotional wounds and make them happy.

The perfect couple?

No one knows what a couple is really like. It is quite easy to present to the world a picture of the perfect couple, while one or both parties may be feeling desperately lonely or miserable. Society doesn't question couples in the way that single people are exposed to scrutiny. It is generally assumed that couples have their ups and downs, but fundamentally they are just that — a couple. Only when I started working as a counsellor did I realise just how unhappy many marriages are, how lonely and depressing, how common the infidelity, how violent and destructive the fights and for many how infrequent the sexual intimacy, even amongst the young. I am always saddened when it's apparent that a couple isn't going to be able to do the work needed to make their relationship thrive, particularly when children are involved or when only one partner wants the relationship to end.

When a couple arrives for their first session, I ask them what they hope to achieve from counselling. By the time they have decided to seek help, many couples are in a fairly desperate state. Sometimes one person has already decided to leave the relationship and is hoping a counsellor will facilitate the separation. Quite often there has been an affair (which one partner may not be aware of). In the first session I aim to demonstrate to a couple that they can turn their relationship around if they want, but there is always a risk. I warn both partners that while having counselling will certainly strengthen them as individuals, the relationship may not survive because one or both may decide they do not want to stay once they have done the necessary work on themselves.

Working with a couple can be like dealing with warring siblings. Some begin by blaming, exchanging insults and making generalised criticisms: 'You never ...', and the inevitable response: 'Well, that's because you always ...' Most couples arrive claiming they cannot communicate. The simple truth is that many people do not know how to relate closely to a partner. The most crucial factor, in my view, is how each one treats his or her partner. Some have little idea of how to value, appreciate or even respect a partner, particularly if their parents' marriage was not a happy one. We live in a throw-away society and some people see marriage as something that can be dispensed with easily if it does not live up to expectation. A number of my clients, mostly women, decided to leave the marriage without so much as an explanation as to how their partner had failed. They certainly did not want to have counselling or to explore ways of preserving the relationship. My understanding was that resolving conflict in an intimate relationship was completely foreign to them. Sadly, we cannot make someone love us or want to be with us. Once upon a time it was difficult for a woman to support herself, and maybe her children, if she wanted to leave. Nowadays this is no longer the case.

In my experience a new romantic interest is commonly the trigger that prompts men to leave a marriage. I always advise clients against leaving one relationship to go straight into another. This does not mean they necessarily follow the advice! It's impossible to predict how you will feel once you have left a relationship, particularly if children are involved. A relationship, like a death, has to be grieved. I have been told by several clients, who chose to leave one relationship to embark on another: 'If I knew then, what I know now ...'

For better, for worse ...

I have always liked the old description for the solemnisation of marriage, which dates back to medieval days. It contrasts starkly with the current ideal of 'romantic love'. Marriage was ordained for the procreation of children, and as a remedy against sin and fornication (I'm not sure it prevents either). '[And]... thirdly, it was ordained for the mutual society, help, and comfort, that the one ought to have of the other, both in prosperity and adversity'.

Couples who have survived happily for decades would, I'm sure, agree with this basis for marriage, but I suspect that few couples marrying today would settle for 'mutual society, help and comfort'. There is no mention of romantic love. It is, however, in times of adversity, whether it be illness, death, poverty, unemployment or any crisis, that couples need to be resilient. A young couple starting out has no understanding of the kind of adversity that might lie ahead, if the relationship lasts long-term.

What brings a couple to counselling?

Typically the most common issues that couples raise involve sex, money, in-laws and ex-partners, though not necessarily in that order. Frequently the couple is engaged in a power struggle over who does what in the relationship, particularly who shops, cooks, cleans and takes care of social engagements. Germaine Greer commented on 'Men's greater tolerance for filth'. In my experience, women are sometimes the ones who are allergic to domestic duties. I have spent many hours working with couples to improve their relationship in terms of the division of labour. Some men have managed to avoid cooking and cleaning for most of their life and fundamentally believe it is woman's work. Women often complain that male partners have to be asked to help them with domestic duties and then expect to be thanked. Men, on the other hand, complain that their partner finds fault with their domestic efforts. Perhaps the most significant factor two people should consider before marrying is compatibility in terms of tidiness and cleanliness. When working with gay couples, who attends to domestic duties (and how well they do so) is just as likely to be a source of conflict.

Domestic bliss?

Sometimes a seemingly trivial issue is a source of great anxiety and tension between a pair, as a result of earlier experience. Take a hypothetical couple, John and Jane. John grew up in a rigid household ruled by a domineering mother who forced him to do the dishes after meals, clean his room, put out the bins etc. Jane on the other hand grew up in a chaotic home where no one did much in the domestic line. Dishes sat in the sink for days, the house was always untidy and meal times were erratic. Being reminded to do the dishes/put out the bins/clean up will sometimes trigger memories for John of his mother's controlling ways when he was a boy. For Jane, John's unwillingness to help in the home may lead to heightened anxiety and to feeling she is alone in her struggle to maintain some kind of order, a reminder of the chaos of her childhood. For both people, the other's apparently uncooperative behaviour can develop into feelings of resentment and a withdrawal of affection. It's hard to feel intimate with a partner who is driving you mad. I expect John Mills did as he was told!

One man I worked with would aim his underpants at the laundry basket and not worry if they missed. Beer bottles and newspapers would accumulate in the kitchen until the next rubbish collection. While I aim to be non-judgemental, in the case of this young man I found it hard to be objective and on occasion I felt like strangling him. It took him a long while to understand that his behaviour demonstrated a lack of respect for his partner. One couple announced they had come to counselling 'to deal with piles of paper and junk taking over the house' — in this case the woman's detritus.

A couple can turn their relationship around in a relatively short time (even when dealing with really serious issues) if they are both committed to working hard and taking responsibility for their own behaviour. This is not an easy task. Admitting to your own faults is far more challenging than pointing out a partner's. I believe any two people can make a relationship work, if they both want it to. Honesty is crucial. Sometimes, however, only one person is committed to changing his or her behaviour or one partner may have agreed to counselling expecting the therapist to 'fix' the other.

Sex and the couple

Each couple's sexual relationship is unique and is subject to change over time. As a counsellor I have observed a vast range of sexual relationships within my client base. Many couples are influenced by past experience and by the attitude shown towards sex in their respective families. Some couples have sex daily, others hardly ever. Some share an enjoyment of pornography while for others it is a major source of conflict. Most of the men I have worked with who were addicted to pornography had had violent childhoods and found intimacy difficult. One man I worked with told me he only felt truly alive when he was having sex. I have worked with many women who endured violence or abuse in their early years and found it hard to enjoy sexual intimacy, as intimate contact was often associated with the fear of the abusive treatment.

At times, once the initial stage of passion and lust waned, it was the men who avoided sex with their partner, as they felt inadequate or vulnerable in terms of sexual performance. This may come as a surprise to women as their expectations are of a man to demonstrate greater confidence in this area. I have been amazed at the honesty and willingness of both men and women to discuss their difficulties in relation to their bodies and sexuality, in the safety of the counselling room. Generally, as a couple addresses other issues including childhood and adolescent experience, and their depth of understanding of each other grows, a significant improvement is seen in their sexual intimacy.

Attraction — both positive and negative

What is it that attracts two people to one another? In my experience there is an obvious surface 'positive attraction' which in general terms relates to some or all of the following: looks, age, intelligence, education, interests and social background. Sadly many men (and a smaller percentage of women) state that looks are their first (and main) consideration. Many men have a very clear idea of the looks they want a partner to have. More often than not (in Australia) it is 'tall, slim and blonde.' Discussing significant relationships, men often focus on appearance, describing their female partners according to body type, hair colour, style of dress. Some admit they want a 'trophy wife', one who other men will admire, because that will help them to feel more confident. When I ask them to describe what kind of person they are looking for, the answer is frequently 'someone who is fun'. It's a fairly sad commentary on society's values. I feel tempted to ask if they know any tall, slim, blonde fifty year olds who are fun. In Chapter 4, I explored the way men are often denied the opportunity to negotiate the transition to confident, adult male. The desire for a trophy wife is clearly a reflection of immaturity.

Geographical proximity was once a significant factor and thirty years ago it was common for couples to live, or have grown up, close to one another. I know several couples who met at high school and are still happily married. It is different today, in 2011, where couples are more likely to meet in the work place and via dating sites on the Internet, now considered a normal way of meeting a prospective partner.

It is well known that 'opposites attract'. Sometimes, unfortunately, opposites end up driving one another insane, once the romantic stage has passed.

More significant, however, for couples who seek counselling, is what lies buried inside the two people, which I describe as the 'negative attraction', the impact of the failures each one has experienced in life which may include significant deaths, a controlling parent, an absent parent (including emotionally absent), abuse in the family, an addiction, or severe depression of one or both parents. These experiences may lead to emotional need (usually unconscious), the need to feel supported or wanted, the need to be the carer, the need to be able to control a partner, or to be offered a submissive role with no responsibility, and in other words to reproduce one or more relationships observed or experienced in formative years. Few people are aware of the 'negative attraction'. Their unconscious mind, however, knows it well. The relationship that we observe most closely is that of our parents and it is inevitable that we will emulate their behaviour at times. That is why many first marriages fail. If we don't value or understand ourselves, we may marry someone who fits our emotional wounds. The relationship can work extremely well until one or other chooses to become more independent. If a couple seeks help from a professional and both parties are willing to explore their feelings and behaviour honestly, they can heal past wounds together and as a result a strong and healthy relationship can develop. Sometimes, sadly, this is not possible.

Not surprisingly, many clients find it too confronting to explore the buried emotions they would prefer to keep hidden, particularly if this involves revealing vulnerability to a partner.

Couple counselling is very different from working with an individual. If I were to rate my competence as a couple or marriage counsellor based on the number of couples that have stayed together, I would give up. Having said that, I know of several who stopped attending therapy sessions before achieving a harmonious relationship but, having understood their respective emotional blocks, went on to address their relationship conflicts on their own.

A gay couple with whom I worked found counselling sessions too confronting. Both women, however, were able to reveal the trauma of their early years at the hands of their stepfathers in our sessions and as a result understood one another (and themselves) far better. Working on their issues on their own, they were able to achieve the relationship they both longed for.

Brutal husbands

The difficulty some men experience in controlling their anger, when in conflict with partners, is often a severe impediment in a relationship. In every case that I have been involved with, the man had been exposed to anger in his formative years — a mother or father given to outbursts of rage directed at their partner or children (or both), an overbearing, controlling parent, beatings in childhood or some other early wounding. Often the man is not acting in a conscious or even rational manner. He simply reacts from the inherited pattern and loses control. What emerges, if he gets in touch with these early experiences, is that his anger at the treatment he received as a child has been triggered in the conflict with his partner. Once he is able to remember the trauma and to bring these experiences to consciousness, he is more able to change his behaviour.

It is sad that so few men will seek help. Often nowadays a female partner will leave the relationship. For the man this often comes as a shock. He may be unaware of just how frightening his anger is to his partner and have no idea he is risking his relationship.

I have often puzzled about men and anger. Surely the way they are raised and disciplined must play a significant role. I wonder how much of their anger is related to the resentment they felt as young boys, if their mothers were intrusive and/or controlling. Unable to behave in a confident and mature way once they are in a relationship, do they resent the control exerted by wives and partners?

One has to consider, at the same time, why women are drawn to men with an anger problem. Why are so many willing to walk on eggshells around explosive men? Is it what they are used to? Have they been terrified when they were younger by raging fathers and angry brothers? At times, needless to say, a woman may be goading her partner because that level of violence is what she is accustomed to as a result of her past experience. I have worked with several couples where the man's overt rage and aggression were mirrored by his partner's masked but savage (and at times manipulative) anger.

What's love got to do with it?

From a young age, girls in particular still fantasise about falling in love, getting married and living happily ever after. When couples fight about their relationship in the consulting room, love is rarely mentioned. On occasion a partner will profess: 'I love you,' to his or her mate while behaving in a decidedly unloving manner. If one person decides to leave a relationship he or she often attempts to explain the decision by way of 'I love you, but I'm not in love with you.' In truth, only a few long-term married people would claim they felt 'in love' with their partner on a daily basis.

A poem that I cut out of the newspaper about twenty years ago sums up for me the kind of love that is needed to survive (and thrive) long-term as a couple:

LOVE'S WEEDS
You think love is
a flower, as touchy
as a bruise, changing
its colours day by day,
as fragile as a crush.
I know love is a
weed, thick-stemmed,
springing from the
gutter, calling
through the dark
'alive, alive O'.
Margaret Barbalet

Case study: the pain of love

Recently I found myself encouraging a couple to separate at their first session. I shocked even myself. In their early thirties when they first came to counselling, Alice and Ted got together when she was not quite seventeen and he was just two years older. They had been together for sixteen years and married for four. Alice admitted she was at a low point in her life when she and Ted met and was aware she was looking for love. She had been severely bullied throughout her school years and left in year 10 as a result. The treatment she was subjected to at school left her feeling vulnerable. From their first meeting Ted offered her the support and affection she craved.

When Ted was young, he had a very close relationship with his father, but following the collapse of the marriage, Ted's father had a breakdown. A few years later he was diagnosed as manic depressive. He committed suicide when Ted was twenty-one. Neither Alice's experience of being bullied, nor the tragedy of Ted's father's death had been addressed before and neither had sought counselling previously. Like so many men, Ted felt ashamed of his past and believed he had to deal with his problems alone.

Alice had been unhappy in the marriage for some years. At the same time she felt guilty at the thought of hurting Ted if she were to leave as she cared for him and knew he had suffered greatly. Fear that he would commit suicide, as his father had done, was terrifying to her. Both Ted and Alice had been led to believe, by a psychiatrist, that his father's mental illness was hereditary and they concluded it was just a matter of time before Ted became ill.

As we explored their history in the first session, it was clear that both had work to do to heal old wounds. It was past experience that had in many ways attracted them to one another in the first place. Rather than address- ing their own issues, they had both acted out of buried pain and as a result put great pressure on the relationship. Over the years a lot of damage had been done. The way they treated each other had led to resentment and hurt. I thought how sad that they had not sought help years before. It was apparent that Alice needed to leave. It is the first time I have told someone in a counselling session, 'You need to let her go.' Alice obviously felt a sense of relief. I suspect that, in emotional terms, she had already left the relationship.

A week later when I saw Ted by himself, he told me that it came as a shock initially, but he recognised very quickly the inevitability of the situation. (Needless to say, if either had disagreed with me, they would not have separated so readily). Over the following weeks it was clear that separa- tion was the right decision for both of them.

What I have learned over the years and say to couples

is that a marriage is not over until it is really over. When a relationship ends, we can see more clearly what it meant to us. This is also true if someone dies. Sometimes time apart helps both people to recognise what they really feel about one other. Having looked at their respective emotional blocks, a couple may well decide they want to start again in a different, more satisfying relationship.

At times a couple presents as very unbalanced in terms of emotional strength. For example one may appear depressed and lacking in confidence while the other appears to cope well. Often what transpires is that as the depressed partner gains in strength, the initially 'stronger' partner is able to reveal areas of depression or weakness. In my experience, most couples that have been together for a considerable length of time are fairly evenly matched in terms of emotional adjustment although this may not be apparent on first meeting.

The process of working with a couple is to excavate, to explore the layers of emotional experience, both positive and negative, and to enable both parties to understand themselves and each other better, to be responsible for healing their own wounds and as a result to grow stronger. Ironically it is through exposing our vulnerability to a partner that we can develop a greater intimacy. In the counselling situation, it is possible for a therapist to reveal a great deal to both people about what lies behind their own and their partner's behaviour. What is it in their past, what insecurities and fears make them act in this way? Understanding a partner's vulnerability generally leads to much greater closeness.

Case study: A betrayed man

Recently a young couple, came to see me. Essentially they have a good relationship and are at a point in life where they want to make plans for the future, including overseas travel and buying a property in the country. I'll call them Mr Betrayed and Miss Guilty.

At the start of their relationship after just two dates (and living in different states), Miss Guilty slept with her ex-boyfriend. She chose to tell Mr Betrayed four months later. Two years down the track, her infidelity would be referred to every time even a minor argument arose, and it would escalate into a fight lasting days. How could she have done such a thing? Mr Betrayed wanted answers. He needed to understand. What else had she done, or might she do, in terms of unfaithful behaviour? How could he ever trust her again? They had reached a stalemate, and it was obvious they were both suffering.

An interesting point is that in this case it was the woman who had transgressed and it was clear her partner could not accept such behaviour in a woman he wanted as a life partner. By contrast, no one is shocked if men are unfaithful, particularly in the early stages of a relationship. On a weekly basis in counselling sessions I hear accounts of men's infidelity. Furthermore, Miss Guilty's crime would be considered insignificant in some relationships, given that it occurred two years earlier and after seeing each other twice.

In asking about their families and early years, it was apparent that neither had grown up in an environment where feelings were discussed, or where members of the family could address anger and hurt. Life was very black and white, according to Mr Betrayed, and he wanted his partner to redeem herself in some way.

In their first counselling session it came to light that Mr Betrayed felt betrayed by his mother, who spoilt and favoured his younger brother, 'Mummy's little soldier'. He also resented his older sister who had suffered ill health since birth and dominated the family, in particular his parents. Betrayal was a sore point, one that had never been addressed openly.

In the same session it was revealed that Miss Guilty had had very sad experiences with men prior to meeting Mr Betrayed. She expected all men to take what they wanted (i.e. sex) and move on. She didn't have a boyfriend for a number of years and her experiences with men had left her wondering if there was something wrong with her. She was unaware, initially, that she had met someone with a greater depth of feeling and sounder values, who felt serious about her.

Going on her own experiences, what Miss Guilty did was what every partner had done to her. Having sex with her ex-boyfriend, in fact, meant very little. When fights erupted over the next two years, she would tell Mr Betrayed to, 'Just get over it.' It came across as though she were minimising her actions and dismissing his pain. When I asked her what she was feeling when she tried to silence his interrogations, Miss Guilty became upset and replied: 'I feel bad. I feel guilty about what I did. I just don't know what to say. Every time he brings it up I feel terrible.'

It was obvious that Mr Betrayed was moved by her distress. He was beginning to understand her better.

A further shift came about as both partners recognised they played a part in maintaining the impasse. Miss Guilty *felt* guilty and was willing to remain in the role of the one who had transgressed. It came as a surprise to discover that she could contribute to healing the rift by standing up for herself and forgiving herself. She had, after all, been honest and apologised.

Prior to that insight, Miss Guilty believed she had to wait for her partner to change his attitude and forgive her. She revealed she was afraid he would leave her, as her previous boyfriends had done. Mr Betrayed, by contrast, was assuming the high moral ground, wanting some kind of penitence from his partner. He had failed to see that his past experience in his family was continuing to control him.

In the third session, further exploration of their early years revealed that under the anger at his treatment as a child, Mr Betrayed felt deeply hurt. It takes a while in counselling before a client is prepared to reveal the pain that lies under the anger. Anger is so much more acceptable, particularly for a man. Mr Betrayed didn't have the skills (or the desire) to address his hurt with his parents. He didn't want to admit to them that he felt hurt. There was an obvious parallel in the way he viewed the betrayal in his childhood, and the fact that he was unable to move on and forgive his partner. He described an apology by his mother as, 'Too little, too late. The damage is done.' His reaction to the conflict with his sister had been to avoid all contact: 'I just cut and run.'

For her part, Miss Guilty was able to be far more confident and to let go her feelings of guilt, while Mr Betrayed continued to struggle. We explored again the betrayals of his childhood. His mother and sister, the two females in his family, could not be trusted to care for his feelings. His sister had treated him badly. He felt neglected by his mother. Like many young boys, he had been hit regularly by his mother for fairly trivial reasons. It was apparent he was still controlled by wounds inflicted on him decades earlier, before Miss Guilty appeared in his life.

By their sixth (and last) session, they both looked and sounded far happier and were looking forward to their move to the country. I suspect that without counselling Mr Betrayed and Miss Guilty would have clung to their learned expectations which came from past experience: women betray and men take what they want and leave. They would also, unconsciously, be responsible for maintaining the status quo.

Both partners were interested to hear that I believe in general each person is 50% responsible for resolving conflict. A couple has a much better chance of surviving together (happily) if each takes responsibility and learns how to resolve conflict. Conflict is inevitable and a part of any relationship. Many clients I have worked with avoid conflict at all costs.

Case study: who says I'm crazy?

While the most effective way to help a couple with relationship difficulties is to see them together, seeing just one partner can make a huge difference to a marriage without the other partner attending counselling sessions. Needless to say, the other partner has to want the relationship. Priscilla came to counselling believing she was mentally ill and her marriage was in serious trouble. For the next few years, she worked hard to heal herself and her relationship.

It is not uncommon for a client to come to see me having been diagnosed with some form of mental illness. A client may already be taking medication. Most commonly a general practitioner has prescribed antidepressants, but on occasion a psychiatrist has prescribed heavier drugs.

In her first session, Priscilla told me she was concerned

about her weight. She had been married for four years and following the marriage she and her husband Sam had moved to Melbourne for his work. Priscilla found the adjustment difficult. She missed her job, her friends and family and became angry. She told me that she had been violent towards her husband, smashed crockery and damaged his property.

Priscilla's doctor referred her to a psychiatrist who diagnosed her as manic depressive. He prescribed lithium which she had continued to take for two years. As the psychiatrist behaved in an inappropriate way towards her, Priscilla stopped seeing him. She went back to her doctor. She was referred to a female psychiatrist, who prescribed a variety of drugs, finally settling on Epilim, a drug prescribed as a mood stabiliser.

By the time she came to see me, Priscilla had been taking Epilim for three years, a total of five years on medication. While she believed she could get off all medication, her husband, family and friends wanted her to stay on it. Priscilla's other concern was that she wanted to start a family and needed to be free of medication in order to do so.

Priscilla's husband had been diagnosed with Attention Deficit Disorder when he was young. He would have angry outbursts when they fought. When Priscilla became explosive, he would tell her she was crazy. There were times when she believed this to be the case. She understood that she was suffering from manic depression. Being labelled as having a mental illness was a major source of anger.

Priscilla was also the oldest of three girls. She had always had a difficult relationship with her mother, who had never praised Priscilla, was critical of her weight and told her that she would never amount to anything. She favoured a younger sister. Priscilla was close to her father, describing him as loving and kind. She told me her father was addicted to speed when he was younger. Priscilla said that for a time she had used speed in her teens.

When she came to her second session, Priscilla told me that the previous week, after seeing me, she had woken in the morning early, choking and overwhelmed with feelings that she had pushed down for years. She was in touch with extreme anger at her treatment at the hands of doctors and psychiatrists. She said that I had learnt more about her in one hour than they did in five years. The psychiatrists would ask her about her medication, her levels of suicide ideation and promiscuity. She was furious at the way she had accepted the diagnosis of manic depression (bipolar).

She also told me that three years earlier, while taking lithium, she had tried to commit suicide. She had gone to a hardware store, bought a rope, tied one end around her neck and the other around the bedpost and started climbing out of the window. Fortunately, she was observed by a neighbour who screamed loudly, attracting attention, and the police were called.

When I first saw Priscilla, I had been working as a counsellor for less than a year. I wondered if I would be able to help her (given my lack of experience and the fact that two psychiatrists had clearly failed). I wondered if I were out of my depth.

In the second session I stressed that I was not a doctor or a psychiatrist and that I was not qualified to diagnose mental illness or to prescribe drugs. I told Priscilla that I wanted to see if she would make progress with psychotherapy. In time I hoped she could discontinue medication, but it would need to be withdrawn slowly. I told her that I saw her as someone who was struggling to deal with the effects of having grown up with a volatile mother who favoured her sister. I believed she had sustained many losses in her life, including the difficulties she experienced in moving to Melbourne.

Priscilla's husband could also be described as volatile, but she was the one identified as the problem. It was clear she was angry that she had a label, 'bipolar', which everyone in her circle seemed to want to keep in place. I raised the question of whether drug-taking as a teenager had had some effect on her moods. Priscilla thought it had.

I also told Priscilla that I wanted to see her husband, if he was willing to come, as she was bearing 100% of the responsibility for the violence occurring between them. He had to be playing his part. Priscilla was pleased because she was always identified as the problem, her husband an innocent party in their conflicts.

In Priscilla's words: 'My original reason for going to counselling was that I was overweight and I couldn't seem to find the willpower to lose it. At that stage my life was a complete mess. My marriage was a volatile disaster. My relationships with my family and with my husband's parents were very unhealthy. My mental state was unstable. I was taking lots of different medication for manic depression and also for just being me. I wasn't doing anything in life that I wanted and to say that I was unhappy would be a complete understatement.

'In counselling sessions I started to see things about myself, and the people in my life, that I could never have seen before. Through trusting another person, I found the strength to face fears that I didn't want to face. I would never have done so on my own. I suspect that by now I would have ended up in a very horrible place, without somewhere safe where I could talk, cry and scream my deepest, darkest feelings.'

When Sam came to a counselling session (on his own, in order to meet me), he admitted that they were both responsible for the violence that took place between them. I saw this as a very positive beginning for them as a couple. He also described his mother as volatile.

When Sam was a teenager, his father suffered some financial setbacks. As a result, Sam often worried about money and wanted to feel in control of his own finances. He told me later that after his first session with me, he sat in his car and cried for half an hour. He had never cried like that before.

I remember commenting one day in a joint session that what we were dealing with was their respective mothers, both volatile women. Perhaps we needed to have the two of them in a counselling session! Both fathers, on the other hand, were mild-mannered. (The negative attraction between Sam and Priscilla was clear).

Not surprisingly, money was a major issue for the couple. Priscilla was used to being given whatever money she wanted by her father and expected to have whatever she needed in the marriage. Sam resented having to hand over money he had earned. He was in fact quite extravagant in the things he bought for himself from time to time and admitted: 'I do go overboard sometimes spending money ... it makes me feel good ... I've got a lot of toys (sporting equipment etc.).' He was able to concede that he was 'a bit stingy'. Priscilla, on the other hand, believed strongly that the day she married Sam, the money should be considered as joint. I recall several sessions, from that time, in which the couple displayed their inherited volatility!

Many couples fight about money. Working with Sam and Priscilla together, getting to the bottom of their respective attitudes to money, helped them to reach an understanding. It also became apparent, over time, that Sam was the better money manager.

Three months into counselling, Priscilla came off medication and was pregnant soon afterwards. I remember many sessions with Priscilla during the pregnancy as she adjusted to what would be a major life change. I saw her a few times after the baby, a little girl, was born. I recall the first time she brought the baby with her. As soon as I began to speak, the baby turned her head towards me with a look of recognition. She had been hearing my voice for several months in the womb.

It took a considerable while for Priscilla and Sam to resolve the conflict in their relationship and to learn how to handle disputes without resorting to violence. Priscilla worked hard at balancing her own emotions, without medication.

It is to Priscilla's credit, I believe, that the marriage thrived. She demonstrated clearly for me the way one person is able to bring about change in a relationship. While Sam came to counselling sessions from time to time, Priscilla was committed from the first session.

I contacted Priscilla recently via email and was pleased to learn that the family is doing very well: 'My marriage is now a normal marriage. I don't think it is right to say it is perfect, but we certainly have learned how to be patient, to listen to each other and as a result we are able to understand each other. We just couldn't do either of these things before having counselling.

'I am happy to say that I now know I don't have a mental illness. I freely admit I am quite an emotional person and I don't mind that about myself.

'I am the mother of two very beautiful, clever little girls. I live in the USA with my husband. I am content and very happy with my life. I love my family more than words can say. I learnt to accept that you cannot choose your biological family; you just have to make the most of what you've got. It takes a lot of courage to go through with counselling, but I am living proof that it's worth it!'

I also contacted Sam to discuss the possibility of including their story in this book. We spoke on the phone about the progress they had made and he later emailed me: 'We always had, and still have a strong love for one another, and now we are older and hopefully a little bit wiser, our relationship is better than ever'.

Sam also told me that he believed: 'You taught us better conflict resolution skills...you also taught us to see our own faults from within, as opposed to concentrating on the other's faults'.

It is rare to receive feedback from a couple, in terms of how they are years after their time in counselling.

Case study: the carer and her patient

After puzzling for quite a while over how to illustrate the way a couple can heal and change, I have decided to describe in detail the way one couple addressed their relationship difficulties in counselling, over a three year period. I believe they have demonstrated what is possible if each person takes responsibility for his or her own part, and equally importantly, works hard to bring about change in the way they interact with each other.

Sophie and Mark were prepared to acknowledge their own emotional difficulties and to work at resolving the problems in their relationship. To spend so long in counselling and to devote so much time to making a marriage work is unusual in my experience.

Sophie had been separated from her husband, Mark,

for six months when she first came to see me: 'I came to counselling in response to a crisis in my life. I was thirty-one years old and had recently separated from my husband. I loved him deeply, but his long-term struggles with depression and anxiety placed a huge pressure on our relationship. After many years together, I couldn't cope any more and I left.

'I was a real mess. I was grieving for the breakdown of our marriage, missing him terribly and also recovering from years of stress and heartache that comes with an unhealthy relationship. I felt like my whole world had been turned upside down. I had come from a stable home and loving family. This wasn't supposed to happen to me. I sought counselling to help me work through what happened, how I had got myself into this situation and what was going on in me that contributed to the breakdown of our relationship.

'My husband and I were separated for about nine months. I had regular counselling for six months before feeling strong enough to give things another chance.'

Since separating, Mark had returned to the UK where he grew up with his family. Sophie and Mark had remained in contact via phone and email. One day in a counselling session I had asked Sophie what Mark was like, apart from being deeply depressed. She replied, 'He's kind, intelligent, sensitive, intuitive, clever, funny.' Soon after our discussion, Sophie asked Mark to come back to Australia, to see if they could repair the relationship.

About three months later, with considerable trepidation on both sides, Mark came back to Australia and began counselling. In the twenty or so years that he had been in and out of depression, he had sought professional help at times and had read every self-help book he could lay his hands on. Nothing had changed his feelings of despair.

Mark committed himself readily to counselling. Working with both parties together is generally the most effective way to bring about change. The interaction between the two reveals aspects of each person that would not necessarily come to the surface otherwise. At times I also arrange individual sessions.

Mark was forty when he first came to see me, the age at which many men decide to change their lives. While he felt despair about his depression, he knew he wanted to move forward and make his marriage work.

Mark's story

Mark was the only boy, the second child in the family. He had three sisters. From a very early age, from as far back as he could remember, Mark's father drank heavily. Mark recalled the violence that would erupt when his father came home from the pub. Sometimes he was the target of that violence. When he was nineteen, Mark's mother left his father, taking all the children with her. A few weeks later, his father committed suicide.

It was more than twenty years since the tragedy, but in the ensuing years his father was not discussed in the family. Mark's mother and younger sister had decided that his father was to blame for all the family's difficulties. Years later when he had first sought therapy in the UK, the impact of his father's suicide was not addressed. Death is handled very poorly in our society (see Chapter 9) and in Mark's family no one spoke of his father. Mark could not allow himself to think about him or the state he must have been in when he killed himself. The emotions trapped inside Mark for several decades were a confusion of sadness, anger and guilt, and an overwhelming feeling of shame.

On first meeting, Mark and Sophie appeared to be a
fairly unbalanced couple in terms of emotional strength.
Sophie came across as capable, warm and caring. She
revealed no obvious weaknesses while Mark presented
as highly anxious and depressed. My experience told me
Sophie must also be carrying depressed or anxious feelings but at this stage could not reveal them because Mark's
need for support was so great. Sophie had slotted into the
role of carer.

Mark described his emotional state prior to having
counselling with me: 'I had tried everything — seen a psychiatrist, changed my diet, started meditating and regular
exercise. All these things helped me to feel relatively more
whole, but my life was still governed by severe anxiety
and depression. My marriage was failing and I continued
to struggle to find a meaningful occupation. I see now
that suicidal thoughts were never too far away.

'I felt I had to defend myself from the world, which I
saw as treacherous. This entailed shutting myself off from
life and meant that any relationships were extremely difficult. I kept people at arm's length and could not allow
myself to be authentic. I was barely surviving and I experienced the continuous, painful conflict of wanting to be
close to others, yet needing to keep them as far away as
possible. In short, I saw myself as a failure, and at forty, I
was rapidly approaching the age at which my father had
committed suicide. There appeared to be too many parallels between my life and his and it seemed that I was out
of control, hurtling down the same path. It is quite shocking to me to see clearly the truth of this. It is terrifying to
contemplate where I would be now had I not been given
the opportunity of questioning those beliefs about who I
saw myself to be. I remember being asked to describe my
father. What kind of man was he? I was able to see, after a

considerable period, that I was not the same as my father. It had never occurred to me before. I felt I was destined to follow in his footsteps.'

I have worked with several people whose parent committed suicide. In every case the child believes he or she will inevitably follow the same path, particularly if the parent suffered a mental illness.

I remember Mark's first session with me when he returned to Australia. I was aware that it was crucial to bring about change quickly. If Mark withdrew into depression again, Sophie would feel despair about a future together. Under normal circumstances I would take considerably more time to earn a client's trust before asking about painful experiences, but in this case I felt it was important to act quickly. Both needed to feel hope for the future. Mark needed to see that I could handle his wounds and help him.

When I told Mark, in that first session, that I believed it was necessary for us to discuss his father's suicide, he admitted he was terrified at the prospect but was prepared to do so. There are times as a counsellor when, to help a client move forward, it is necessary to confront extremely distressing feelings. There is a temptation to avoid doing so because witnessing another's pain (provoking it even) is never comfortable. It was apparent, however, that Mark could not progress unless he faced the feelings associated with his father's death. For twenty years he had avoided doing so. It was impacting on his emotional state, on his inability to pursue work and particularly on his marriage.

In counselling sessions, Mark responded readily to the exploration of his wounds and was able to contact his emotions easily. Over several months, Mark worked at excavating the painful feelings about his father's death. As he did so, he began to feel lighter in himself.

As with several of the men I discussed earlier, Mark suffered from deep shame, which went hand in hand with his depression and this was one of the first issues we confronted: 'One of the major revelations in counselling sessions was to see how feelings of shame had controlled my thoughts and the view that I had of myself. Taking ownership of those repressed feelings has been a painful but essential process. It is clear to me now that I could not have come up with the insights to do this on my own.

'There has been a long process of finding out that feelings such as shame arose at a very early age. They then became habitual and just an automatic response. I have come to understand that the shame was instigated by the actions of my earliest carers and had nothing to do with my own behaviour. My parents regularly acted in what were to me, as a small child, shameful ways. I was ashamed of their behaviour, but I internalised it and carried that shame with me into adulthood.'

I remember asking Mark to tell me all the shameful things he had done in his life. He couldn't come up with any. He could recall, however, numerous episodes when his parents fought, on one occasion in full view of the neighbours. It was his first realisation that the crippling feeling of shame emanated from the way his parents behaved. He had done nothing shameful. He could see that as a very young boy his parents were unable to nurture him or protect him from their own problems. Mark was a highly intelligent child who achieved well in school in his early years. He liked doing well and coming close to the top of the class. As the years of emotional neglect continued, he lost the motivation for study and his increased anxiety made concentration impossible. When he began to fail in school, he saw himself as a failure. He could no longer fit in with his friends. This is the destructive effect of shame. It silences a child and isolates him from his peers. How many children fail at school because of emotional difficulties?

Confronting the painful experiences of his early years began the long road to recovery. Around this time Mark did an extraordinary drawing — the first of many — depicting 'shame' being extracted from his chest.

'Shame was an insidious, extremely powerful force. It steered me deeply into withdrawal and isolation. Over time I came to understand why this was occurring. I have increasingly been able to say: "This is my feeling of shame at work", and as a result I can interact in a healthier way. This has worked especially well in the improvement of my relationship with Sophie, my wife.'

Having confronted his feelings of shame, Mark was ready to contact his anger. I often observe, when working with men, that many are terrified of their own anger if they have grown up with violence. Children often feel they are to blame when parents fight. If the hostility and conflict persist, the child takes it inside himself. The anger lives on inside the child. Later in life it will find a way of revealing itself. Some men become violent and take it out on those around them, including loved ones. Others turn it inwards, becoming depressed and powerless.

'As a child, anger was always terrifying. Verbal abuse was common in my early home life. Vicious, drunken screaming matches were a weekly occurrence at one point and physical violence was fairly common. I have the palpable memory now of a constant, seething undercurrent of anger and resentment. Even when things were going well, for me there was always a trepidation about doing the 'wrong' thing. I became super watchful and cautious, a strict sensor of all my words and actions. The exhausting work of pre-empting the potentially angry reactions of others became crucial. It often reached the now laughable point where, if anyone in my vicinity was enraged, it was my fault.

'At all costs I avoided provoking the anger of others or looking at the real reasons for the presence of the anger that was boiling away inside me. If it had been suggested, I would have vehemently denied that I was even angry. But there was, in retrospect, a fury in me. Toxic and directed inwardly, it was eating away at my life energy. It left me exhausted and with a feeling of never standing on solid ground. I can describe it now as wandering through life as a ghost, feeling totally separate and isolated from what I looked out on as the "real world".'

In a letter to his mother, Mark attempted to explain what he was going through and to tell her of the painful feelings he had experienced growing up. His letter was free of blame, but his mother and sister took it as an attack. His sister told him she believed he was suffering from a mental illness and advised him to see a psychiatrist and get treatment. For Mark, their response was shattering.

One of the ways in which Mark revealed hidden strength was that at no time had he turned to alcohol or drugs to ease his pain, knowing full well that this was not an answer, however tempting. Many clients, male and female, struggle with an addiction, the only way they have been able to keep at bay their deeply destructive feelings.

For a time Mark took antidepressants, but found that while they dulled his pain, it was in fact harder to work on his emotional state. He suffered very debilitating withdrawal symptoms for several months when he came off the medication.

A counsellor's main role is to accompany a client on his journey as he faces and confronts his buried pain. It is challenging to remain optimistic when clearly the client feels hopeless. It is hard, too, to witness a human being in pain. All I have to rely on at times like these is the conviction that the process works. Clients heal if they are prepared to confront painful, buried feelings. The process is slow. If a client has lived with feelings of depression and hurt for decades, it cannot be resolved in a few sessions.

There are days when we appear to be going over the same ground and making little progress, but I have learnt that this is sometimes necessary. I cannot speed up the process, I can only be there, supporting, reflecting to the client his feelings, observing body language, challenging erroneous thinking and identifying any change or break-through. In my experience the client has to work through the layers of pain in his own time. The importance of the relationship between therapist and client while he does the work cannot be overestimated.

I often refer to the process of counselling as 'peeling another layer of the onion'. As the client gains in strength, he is able to confront the next layer. Needless to say, many clients do not continue with therapy when it becomes too confronting and painful or when they feel they are not progressing.

Talking is just one way of working with a client. I always ask about a client's dreams, encouraging them to write them down and bring the dreams in to our sessions. Dreams are pearls of wisdom from our unconscious. Often it is through the exploration of a client's dreams that real progress is made. (Chapter 6 explores in greater detail the way clients have been helped by their dreams.) From the first session I also encourage clients to keep a journal as a way of getting out of their heads and hearts some of their feelings. Some clients find that through drawing or painting they are able to produce images and expression that help to identify the elusive feelings they are grappling with. I could see that through his drawings and paintings, Mark was able to contact his anger, which had previously terrified him to such an extent that he needed to deny its existence. It was apparent that he was a highly skilled artist though unaware of his own talent. This gift became a safe-enough container through which to work with his rage.

'The counselling process, talking, drawing, writing and exploring dreams has helped me to accept my anger and express it in what I feel are healthy ways. Left to myself I would never have realised that I had anything to be justifiably angry about. It is definitely not judged accept-able to feel angry with one's parents, let alone to express that anger. I have come to learn that when I was growing up I blamed myself for the hateful circumstances of my home life. No one ever explained to me that it was not my fault and it was not an option for me to express my own anger and frustration. To compound this, any anger directed towards me was seen as deserved. It must have come because I was a bad person.

'To be able to understand and act upon all that I have learned fills me with gratitude and relief. There are occa-sions when unconscious thought/feeling patterns take over and I am again temporarily seized with anxiety. But those times are occurring less and less frequently. When they do occur, I feel that I now have the ability to observe them with a real curiosity as to what is happening. This allows me to recognise that they are just feelings. They then lose any power that they would have had over me. I still interact meaningfully with only a few people, but the relationships that I do have are more authentic. I am less vigilant in the monitoring of what I do and say and that has brought about a greater sense of ease, and a more fulfilling way of being in the world. The belief in my own convictions and my intuition is getting stronger all the time. There is far less need to look to the world to tell me what I should be doing and how I should be acting. It feels like a reclaiming of what was always mine, a return to living as that which I always knew deep down to be the truth of who I am.

'For me, the process of counselling was life changing. I actually believe the term life-saving to be no exaggeration. What more could anyone want from life than to discover the answer to the question: "Who am I?" I know that the full answer will always be a mystery, but now I know that I am not the faulty goods that I had previously allowed myself to believe.'

For many months the focus of the work was primarily about Mark. His need was great and as a couple they could not progress while he felt so debilitated. While many of the sessions involved both Mark and Sophie, there were times when they would see me on their own. Many therapists do not believe that a couple should be seen separately and together by the one counsellor. In certain situations I find it invaluable. Therapists work in very different ways. Involving other professionals would, in my opinion, have complicated the process.

Sophie's story

Gradually, as Mark began to look and sound better, as he spoke of times when he felt good about himself, Sophie came forward, wanting her feelings to be addressed too, even though she still felt worried about Mark. She had had the opportunity to reflect on her experience of childhood, recognising some of the ways it had impacted on her relationship: 'One of the first things that came out of counselling was that my childhood wasn't as perfect as I had always believed. When I was ten years old, my dad had a nervous breakdown and suffered severe depression for a number of years. His illness was hidden from my two older brothers and me, in a misguided attempt to "protect us". I had never really thought that this had affected me much until I started to explore my memories of this period when things were not quite right in our house. I also began to see similar patterns in the way I coped with and responded to my husband's depression — namely avoid talking about it, pretend everything is fine and just soldier on. I hid our struggles from friends and family. I had no idea how to help or relate to Mark and had even less idea how to voice my own suffering.

'As a child during Dad's illness, I was directed to stay away from him, not bother him and basically be a good girl. I didn't understand why my usually affectionate father was sullen and withdrawn, and I somehow assumed it was my fault. This is certainly how I felt when my husband was depressed, that his mood was my doing, that if I could only be a better wife or try harder, he would be happy again. His withdrawal was devastating to me. I would feel utterly abandoned, rejected and worthless. Through counselling I came to realise that these were old feelings, triggered from childhood, as much as a response to the current situation.

'As well as Dad's depression, I have had to face that Mum was not available emotionally while I was growing up. Although a loving parent and capable home maker, there has always been a lack of real intimacy and emotional connection in our relationship. I could never go to her with issues or problems, so that from an early age I learned I just had to deal with things on my own. My traumas included school bullying, friendship issues, adolescent anxiety and body issues, all of which would have been much less painful if there had been an adult in my life with whom I felt able to share things.'

Although on the surface the two families were very different, there were patterns that were very similar. Mark's family would reveal no change in their emotions, regardless what was going on in the household. In Sophie's family everything was swept under the carpet. Feelings were simply not addressed. Even when the family went through major upheaval, nothing was discussed openly. The 'negative attraction' I always look for was very apparent. Mark and Sophie had both experienced deep fear and loneliness as young children, with no one to go to for support. Taking on the responsibility for a depressed male was also, of course, a familiar path for Sophie.

They were both working hard to address their personal difficulties as well as what was occurring in their relationship. After a while I could see the balance between them had started to shift. Sophie had recognised the value in getting in touch with her feelings: 'I always thought that my husband's problems were worse than mine. He had a brutal childhood and survived the suicide of a parent. There was nothing in my story comparable to this, but I have realised through counselling that everyone has their "shit" to deal with. No one's "shit" is more important than someone else's. Suffering is a part of life, but the real damage comes when people are not prepared to look at it and to see how it affects their lives and relationships. I now see that becoming aware of old feelings, unhelpful patterns and behaviours is the key to not repeating them again and again.

'A huge lesson for me has been in becoming more aware of my feelings and being able to share them. It sounds so basic, but it was so foreign to me. In our family, feelings were not talked about unless they were pleasant. Anger, hurt, upset, sadness, etc. were not expressed or shared in a constructive way. I learnt from an early age to hide those feelings, which became a huge handicap in trying to build a close and honest relationship.'

Sophie remembered feeling terrified as a young girl when her brother was in trouble with their father. The sound of her father's gruff voice was enough to make her disintegrate. She felt wary around her father, never really understanding why and, from a very young age, worried about doing the wrong thing and getting into trouble. She took on the role of the helper.

If Sophie had not agreed to have counselling with Mark as a result of their breakup, she would probably never have needed to explore her early years or the way she felt she had to act in the world, always doing the right thing by everyone else and silencing her true feelings. The counselling could be seen as a blessing as it opened up a new understanding for her of the world of feelings and gave her the opportunity to grow as a woman.

It was clear that Sophie had elected to join her husband in the pit of depression at times. The wounded part of her, the hurt young child, not seen or heard by her parents, had identified with the damaged, frightened boy who was also left on his own to deal with a chaotic family, a family whose members were disconnected from one another, suffering alone. For the first time Mark and Sophie had someone who valued them and saw them for the sensitive, loving people they were. Their love was strong enough to withstand the agony of the relationship when times were tough, as was often the case, because they both wanted to make it work. It would not have come as a surprise if either had thrown up their hands in despair and announced: 'Enough! I can't do this any more!' I felt for both of them.

Working with a couple, exploring the way each one relives the experience of childhood is a fascinating process. It can be the source of deep healing for both parties. Many therapies only address present-day issues, rather than exploring early life experience and some are designed to be brief, approximately six sessions in total. In my view a couple with early wounding such as that experienced by Mark and Sophie could not move forward without first addressing the buried hurt. There is simply too much controlling their emotional state.

Mark and Sophie

After working hard at their individual issues, Mark and Sophie reached a point where they understood why they behaved in certain ways and what was being triggered when they experienced conflicts. They started to recognise what they needed from the other in the relationship, rather then focussing all their energy on past damage. It was an exciting shift.

The relationship began to change rapidly once Sophie wanted to have a more equal relationship and to abandon being the carer. I remember saying to her that it was time to let Mark stand on his own two feet. It was apparent she needed to relinquish her role so that she could also live her life to the full. Needless to say, this was not an easy task. While she wanted to get out of the pit and let go of minding Mark, she worried that he might become depressed again or take his own life. For a long time this fear had prevented her from asking for her needs to be met.

She started telling Mark how she felt when he withdrew into depression, which related directly to her early years: 'I feel I'm not seen by you. I feel lonely, desolate and rejected.'

Expressing her feelings openly was a significant change. It was also a risk. She had no idea how Mark would react to her. Would he be angry? Would he retreat into depression? It was not easy for her to change. Sophie always felt it was up to her to do something, if anyone was upset: 'I find it very hard. I feel tight in my chest and afraid of letting go, afraid you might fall in a heap.'

Mark's reply was very clear: 'I can look after myself.'

For Mark, it was in fact easier to hear Sophie's feelings, expressed openly. What he was aware of was his fear when he sensed that Sophie was upset with him but was not expressing her feelings (in just the same way that he had assumed he was the cause of the anger when any of his family exploded in his childhood). Mark had gained in strength to a point where he could see that shutting down got him nowhere.

In joint counselling sessions there were many moments of insight for both Sophie and Mark, which heralded change. I think of all those moments, the most significant was when they were able to express their anger to one another, particularly when it was about the other. Few couples can do this effectively, taking responsibility for their emotions. It was particularly challenging for them because anger had been so terrifying as a child and in their families negative feelings were never expressed in an honest way.

It must be noted, too, that expressing anger, taking responsibility for one's true feelings is not the same as venting fury on another person, attacking and abusing.

Sophie told me one day that she had managed to

express anger to Mark for the very first time: 'Although I said it very meekly!' She was finding her voice.

Sophie, however, was still not being offered the things she wanted from Mark and she was understandably impatient. She had hung in for a long time, shouldering most of the responsibility for them as a couple. She was sick of it.

In her family there were very clear roles: Sophie, as a female, modelled herself on her mother — be good, keep quiet, ignore distress, contain all feelings. One day I suggested she would have to try being a bad girl for a change since being a good girl no longer served her in the way it had in childhood.

'But I don't know how to be bad!' she replied.

For several weeks Sophie was unwell and couldn't recover her health. Her illness forced her to confront her feelings and to recognise she needed to abandon the way she had learnt to act as a child. It was a necessary collapse.

It became apparent that Sophie was now someone who could speak up for herself when, in the following session, she was able to tell me she was angry that I was putting Mark's needs above hers. She wanted her feelings heard equally. Expressing anger clearly to a therapist is a sign of obvious strength. Sophie and I both knew she could not have done so a few months earlier. I felt pleased that she was able to reveal herself. It was an important turning point. This came at a crucial time for Mark. He was rapidly approaching the exact age his father was when he took his own life and Mark felt very vulnerable leading up to that time. This made it even more significant that Sophie wanted her feelings heard regardless of the timing. For too long she had had to take second place.

Like many men I have worked with, Mark had told me he often thought how much easier it would be to give up the struggle and end his life as his father had done. I was concerned about the risk of suicide. One day I asked why he needed to hold on to depressed feelings. What was the gain? What he recognised was that his depression was the one thing he still had in common with his father. 'If I let go of that, I'll have nothing to keep me connected to him.'

In a joint counselling session, Mark was able to get in touch with the anger he felt, deep down, towards his father for abandoning him and taking what seemed, to him, like an easier path. It is very hard to admit to feelings of anger towards a father who was so disturbed that he killed himself. Sophie was clearly moved by Mark's distress. At the same time, she needed to hold on to her own wants and feelings. For Mark, this period presented an obvious challenge: 'Do I choose to live life, or opt out of it like my father?'

It was a confronting time for all three of us. When working with a couple, needless to say I always aim to be even-handed, but I was acutely aware of the timing. How would Mark negotiate this critical period? Would he be able to choose life where his father had chosen death? Would Sophie throw in the towel at this point? Couple counselling has its own particular challenge!

It was clear that Sophie had abandoned being the good girl and was prepared to put herself on an equal footing in her marriage. I pointed out to her one day that she could leave Mark, if she decided she needed to. It wasn't up to me to make her stay (although obviously I wanted them to come through together). Sophie appeared shocked at the idea, but it gave her strength. She was able to explain to Mark what she now needed. She certainly didn't want to be his carer any longer: 'I need to let go of being your helper and minder. I don't want to be solely responsibility for our life together. I need to start putting myself first.'

Sophie was now ready to live her own life, regardless

of the consequences. Fortunately she could achieve this without leaving the marriage. She enrolled in a number of courses in yoga and meditation, reducing her anxiety and gaining considerable strength as a result.

Around this time I commented to Mark that 'You seem to be coming alive. Maybe half of you is now fully in the world, the other half still choosing between life and death.' My comment came from an intuitive sense of Mark that day. He replied that he had just finished a painting at home of 'half of myself drowning in water.' He believed this was the part of him that still wanted to stay connected to his father who had drowned himself in the river, alone.

Over the time that I worked with them, Sophie and Mark were able to transform their relationship.

In Sophie's words: 'Mark and I have been together again for three years. We have had lots of counselling during this period, both together and separately. We have learned so much about ourselves and one another. Things are still hard. Long-term depression and anxiety don't just disappear. We are getting much better at dealing with it. We communicate better and much more honestly. There is less of me looking after him. We take care of each other. I am able to be more honest with him than anyone else in my life, and I have come to value emotional honesty above all else in relationships.

'We are now considering starting a family. We don't have a lot of money, and I worry about how we'll cope financially. One thing I do know is that we'll be emotionally present for our kids. They'll be allowed to share their feelings and feel heard. We'll be able to take the good things we've learnt from our parents and discard the 'shit'.

'Counselling has been life changing for me. It certainly saved our marriage. It has been a real roller-coaster, some periods intensely painful. What I have learnt so far will help me with whatever life brings, and I feel immensely grateful.'

Postscript

I consider it one of my duties as a counsellor to tell women who want a child to 'get a move on' when they are in their mid thirties, particularly if they have the right relationship in place. I had encouraged Mark and Sophie, when they told me they were considering having a child, even though financially they were struggling.

Approximately six weeks later, Mark and Sophie arrived looking very excited and told me they were expecting a baby. I felt thrilled for them. When they worked out the probable date of conception, Mark was exactly the same age as his father when he committed suicide. Mark had chosen (unconsciously) at that crucial time, when his father ended his life, to create new life.

Mark and Sophie were able to make a real and a rare commitment to one another, to settle for far less than 'mutual society, help and comfort' at times and to survive long periods of extreme adversity. In the time that I have known them, they have both grown and become more confident and assertive people while still retaining their sensitivity and their love for one another.

Mark and Sophie's daughter has enriched their lives. They are both very loving parents.

Sophie believes that as a result of having counselling: 'I am a much better parent than I would otherwise have been'.

For couples who come to see me when their relationship is in trouble, the counselling process helps to take the heat out of areas of conflict, through an exploration of the traumas and losses experienced in the family of origin. As a result, both partners are given the opportunity to understand themselves and the other better, and to learn how to resolve conflicts for themselves.

Once this stage has been reached, every couple still needs to negotiate their way through the maze of their relationship. As a result of the work in counselling, however, they are usually more tolerant and accepting of their own and the other's imperfections and vulnerability. This provides the opportunity for the couple to develop a deeper, stronger and more loving relationship.

Chapter 6

Trust your dreams

I have dreamt in my life dreams that have stayed with me ever after, and changed my ideas; they've gone through and through me, like wine through water, and altered the colour of my mind.
—**Emily Bronte** *(Wuthering Heights)*

began to have a recurring nightmare in my early teens, around the time that my parents' relationship was falling apart. It was so frightening I would force myself to stay awake for fear of going back into the nightmare. That was what usually happened as soon as I went back to sleep. Thirty years passed before the essence of the nightmare became clear to me, and before I told anyone about it. In the dream I am standing on a small piece of land, surrounded by water. The water begins to rise and to cover my feet. Terrified, I jump onto another piece of land, and again the water rises up over my feet. All the while, I hear a menacing sound. Looking back now, I can see that at that time in my life, when my parents were in turmoil, there was nowhere I could go where I felt safe.

As soon as I began to see Sid (a psychologist), I started remembering my dreams. He encouraged me to write them down, bring them in to the sessions and discuss them as important material from my unconscious. The first dream that I told him seemed insignificant because it was so brief: A penguin was lying on its back in a box, with no room to move, its flippers pressed to its side. The penguin was looking out and I can still recall the sadness in its eyes.

I had no idea what the dream might mean, but once Sid had asked me what I thought and felt about penguins, and how the penguin of my dream might relate to me and to my life at the time, it was clear. It connected me to the realisation that I wasn't living a life that was true to my real nature or to what I wanted for myself. There was a vitality missing. I was fascinated and from that day I have used my dreams to help me to understand myself better.

Why had I dreamt of a penguin? What is it about penguins? Sea birds that live in the Southern Hemisphere and travel vast distances by sea, they are unable to fly but are expert at diving. I grew up in the Northern Hemisphere but migrated to Australia. I have always felt a particular affinity with the clients whose families came from Europe, who had to begin a new life in this remote land. It was a huge adjustment for me when I first settled in Australia, without family support, cut off from my roots. I still remember the shock of realising, when I was about to set sail from Southampton, the enormity of my decision at leaving England and my family and friends. Communication in the 1960s was very limited. The cost of an overseas phone call was exorbitant. This was decades before email and text messaging. Months would go by between letters from my family.

I have always felt at home by the sea. I feel more alive, more at peace with the world, whenever I am near the ocean. I am still enchanted by penguins, and since the time of the dream, have moved to a home that is close to the ocean. I have even seen the occasional penguin. Recently during a holiday in Phillip Island with my grand-daughters, I had the delightful experience of watching the fairy penguin parade as hundreds of penguins ventured ashore at dusk on a beautiful, moonlit night.

My penguin dream was a very long time ago, and yet when I recall it now I can see other meanings in the dream. I have kept journals and old letters from my family in a box in a cupboard and when I read through some of those letters a few months ago — hunting for an old pho-tograph — I understood a lot about my life in a different way. A part of me was lying dormant in the box. A year ago my sister produced a large box full of letters written by my parents to one another in their early years, dating back to 1939. Just reading a handful of letters, written when I was an infant, gave me greater insight into how I came to be the person I am.

In my work with clients, dreams offer the most pow-erful way into the psyche, to what is going on for the client. I think of dreams as a gift from the unconscious. It is through working with dreams that we can under-stand our feelings and relationships better and we can see what action to take in life. Healing can take place through exploration of the images in our dreams.

There is an honesty in dreams that we may not acknowledge in our conscious way of talking about our-selves. Since paying close attention to my dreams, I find it impossible to ignore the messages they contain. In 2006 I had a dream. On a blank page the word 'BOOKS' was writ-ten in capital letters. That was all there was to the dream.

Pondering the dream's message, the first book that came to mind was a contribution for one entitled *Ten Pound Poms*. I had responded to an advertisement in the newspaper and, following a couple of phone calls, had agreed to write my story of having come to Australia in the sixties as a ten pound migrant. Nearly a year had passed since then, but for some reason I hadn't put pen to paper. Believing I needed to honour the message of my dream, I contacted the author, Jim Hammerton, a historian, straight away. He told me he would like me to send in my story, but I had only two weeks in which to do so. I started immediately.

Some months later, the author interviewed me as he planned to include my story. What I now realise is that writing about my experience of being an English migrant, and one who remained in Australia while thousands (including my brother) returned to England, had inspired me, at an unconscious level, to write a book of my own.

For some time I had been thinking about writing, but I didn't even know whether I wanted to write fiction or non-fiction. Waking up that morning having dreamt the word 'books', I knew what I wanted to write: an account of my clients' courageous journeys and my involvement with them along the way. It was as though my contribution for *Ten Pound Poms*, the telling of people's stories of migration (and my own) had seeped into my unconscious. It occurred to me when I considered the two books that had I returned to England to live, I doubt whether I would have followed the path of first seeking counselling and later opting for a career in this field. My unconscious had alerted me to the fact that there was a connection between the two books.

The morning after my dream, I awoke with the chapter headings in my mind. Over the years, the headings have changed very little. It seemed as though the book had been planned. My task was to follow the pattern already established in my unconscious.

We dream every night, but many clients assure me they

never dream. I look into their eyes and tell them that now that I have asked their unconscious, I am sure they will remember a dream. They invariably do. It often comes as a shock, especially to male clients, because their dreams may reveal to them inner feelings and aspects of themselves that surprise them. On reflection, of course, they recognise the authentic feelings presented by the dreams. It can be difficult to understand dreams without the help of an expert because dreams present stories to us in an almost forgotten language, via image and metaphor. Sadly in our society we are no longer accustomed to tuning in to our inner world.

Mary Symes (dream counsellor and author of *Grief and Dreams*) suffered profound grief when her husband was lost at sea. At the time, she was the mother of two young daughters. After a long period of depression and despair, Mary had a number of dreams that set her on a new path of understanding: 'I found that grief had led me to the beginnings of a journey, via my dreams into my unconscious. My dreams opened the door into my other, unknown self and I became aware that I had made contact with the incredible stores of knowledge, understanding and healing that lay waiting to be used on the other side of consciousness.'

It was through dreams that Mary was able to gain a new understanding of what she needed to do to heal herself after the tragedy of her loss: 'During that first year of recorded dreaming, I grew up. I left behind childhood dependency and parental values. I grew through the experience of grief to a new understanding about life. To do that I had to be able to value what I had experienced, but not only intellectually. I had to be able to see it and feel it and know it in an intimate way.'

For a number of years, I have consulted with Mary

to understand my dreams, which seem to have become more elusive and complex over time.

Trusting psyche

Individual clients will often dismiss a dream in the early stages of therapy: 'I don't think it meant anything', 'it was just a weird dream' or 'it was very short.' In time they are able to recognise that all their dreams are significant and are invaluable as they reveal the inner landscape of their being. If a client is prepared to trust his or her dreams and to spend time working with the dreaming process, important images and experience unfold, opening up a dialogue with the unconscious.

Something to hide

Sophie and Mark, whose relationship, 'The carer and her patient', was explored in Chapter 5, both regularly brought in dreams to their sessions and found they illuminated previously hidden aspects of themselves. Sophie arrived for her second appointment, having been encouraged to remember a dream: 'In the dream I am going on a school camp and just before going I get my first period. I am sleeping in a very large, white dormitory, with lots of girls. Mine is the last bed in the row and next to my bed on the wall is a mirror, which reflects the whole room. When I get out of bed I see bloodstains on my pyjamas and on the sheets, reflected in the mirror. I feel anxious. Can I get to the bathroom without being seen and can I wash the sheets and pyjamas without anyone knowing?'

There is a great deal to explore in this dream. When I

asked Sophie what she thought about blood, she replied: 'it's what you're made of', 'your insides.' In the dream it is the blood of her first period, the moving into womanhood from being a child. She is embarrassed and feels the need to hide the bloodstains. The room is very white and clinical. The atmosphere is not conducive to confiding and sharing the intimacy of 'secret women's business'. Sophie feels she has to conceal the blood and get to the bathroom without being seen. In therapy sessions, particularly when we were working on issues to do with her marriage, Sophie's belief that she was 'not seen', first in her family and later by her husband, was a recurring theme. Was she also choosing to keep some part of herself hidden?

The events that take place in the dream are reflected in the mirror. On one occasion the mirror reflects the room, later the bloodstains are reflected in the mirror.

Counselling was Sophie's first opportunity to explore the inner world of her feelings. It was also the first time someone had reflected back to her the effect of growing up in her family where feelings were not discussed and in particular where all negative emotion was swept under the carpet.

Sophie had a second dream before her next session (which she was sure meant nothing). She dreamt of several huge piles of mulch. When I asked her to tell me what association mulch holds for her, she replied: 'Well, it's earthy and it's decomposing, but then later it nourishes and gives life.'

It wasn't hard to make the link to the fact that in coming to counselling Sophie was 'decomposing' as we explored numerous aspects of her life that she wanted to change. At the same time she could feel that the work she was doing in therapy was nourishing her and offering her new life. Mulch is earthy, real matter and not necessarily 'nice'. I remember Sophie telling me how strange it felt to be talking about herself and her feelings. At the start she found the process exhausting.

Dreams work on many levels and what they symbolise only the dreamer can 'know'. The dreamer comes up with the images and the narrative and I always ask a client if he or she is able to get inside the dream and understand its significance. Sometimes re-telling a dream helps the dreamer to gain some insight. I encourage clients to record their dreams, to reflect on the images contained in them and to write about their dreams in a journal. Several clients also draw the images of their dreams.

Hungry Jack's or McDonalds?

Some of the briefest dreams offer great insight. Charlene, a client in her thirties, had just spent a week in the country for her work and found she was able to slow down and care for herself better than she would normally. She dreamt that 'Hungry Jack's changed to McDonalds.' I was particularly interested in this dream as it was one of the first dreams she brought in to our sessions. It helped us to find a way in to what she needed to explore.

Again my client thought this dream held no meaning. When I asked the obvious questions she replied that generally, when she wasn't caring for herself, she would go to Hungry Jack's and 'grab fries, hash browns, onion rings.' Consciously taking the trouble to look after herself, she avoided buying fried food while away in the country and instead would go to McDonalds, buy a pre-packaged salad and a coffee and enjoy her lunch in a beautiful spot in the heart of nature. 'It was lovely being out in the country and I felt so much better.'

The dream highlighted, in just five words, the change in the way she was nurturing herself by simply presenting the two images of food outlets. Interestingly, caring for herself was the major focus of counselling over the next two years and led to a far healthier life in many ways. I doubt whether either McDonalds or Hungry Jack's would feature today in a dream for her. One of her concerns was her weight. I remember saying to Charlene one day that once she was able to free herself of her 'congealed feelings', I was sure the weight would drop off. This is precisely what took place. Following a number of significant emotional breakthroughs, Charlene succeeded in losing twenty kilograms. Charlene's story is told in detail in Chapter 7: *Start loving, stop punishing your body.*

The dream: whittling a stick

Patrick, whose story in counselling is told in Chapter 4: *The boy becomes a man*, brought in his first dream after seeing me for several months.

'In the dream I am whittling a stick. I feel calm and happy and deeply grounded.' (This is not at all how Patrick felt normally, when anxiety controlled him on a daily basis).

Patrick believed the dream to be highly significant because it felt like a new beginning, starting to live again, with just the basics. He drew a picture of himself whittling the stick and wrote next to the picture all the feelings and ideas the action brought to mind: 'basic, relaxed, calm, purposeful, timeless, clearing away the rough outer layer, no anxiety, satisfied, sitting, comfortable, fundamental, natural — *real*'.

Patrick had often whittled sticks. He was aware that it was something he enjoyed doing, and something he never did when around his mother. Usually he would be away from home, camping or on holiday.

In the dream Patrick feels at peace. Whittling is normally an action undertaken by men, a primitive act, and I had the feeling that Patrick was choosing to harness his masculine energy in a new, pure way. In clearing away the rough outer layer (he was a man given to explosive rage like his mother), Patrick dreams of getting underneath the outer layer (the bark) to reveal his true, innocent self.

A year after having this dream, Patrick told me that he had come to understand just how significant his dream of whittling was. He realised that since the dream he had whittled away at everything in his life. Everything was changed — his career, his relationship with his parents and with his wife and children.

Three months after the whittling dream, Patrick took part in a weekend personal development group with six others. The following night, he had a second dream.

'A group of people are going on a horse ride and just about to head off. There is another horse with no rider, which will have to go on a different ride. The rider-less horse is called Ben. He was a little dark horse with a brown nose, nondescript in appearance, but he looked sad. If he had longer ears, he would look more like a donkey — not a pretty horse.'

Patrick said that he felt sorry for the poor horse, as without a rider it will miss out this time. One of the other group members had spoken the previous day of her ex-partner, whose name was Ben, 'a caring, patient, lovely man.' She was aware that during their relationship, she had drawn him in at times, but also pushed him away.

Patrick likened this to the way his mother regularly drew him in, only to reject him later.

When asked what he feels about horses, Patrick said that humans have an illusion of control over a horse, but in fact a horse is extremely powerful. It weighs half a ton and could easily kill a human being.

My sense was that Patrick's dream was revealing to him that he is possessed of a great deal of personal power, but so far he has not 'mounted' that power or climbed into the saddle of his own life. In the dream he is in touch with his caring, patient, loving side, which to date has not been allowed to 'go for a ride'.

When we discussed Patrick's description of the horse, I asked him if Ben might be an inner representation of how he felt about himself. The words of the dream 'dark horse', 'nondescript' and 'sad' all seemed pertinent. I was curious about 'brown nose'. Patrick instantly replied that when he was at school, his mother made him 'brown-nose' teachers, taking them presents. This made him feel extremely uncomfortable. His mother was anxious when he hit puberty and had commented to him that they needed to make sure he came through puberty 'handsome.' In the dream, Ben is obviously not a handsome horse. Patrick was also made to feel foolish, 'useless', as a child, like a donkey, an ass.

The language of dreams always fascinates and often amuses me. Patrick dreams of 'a dark horse, brown nose, sad, etc.' It is always helpful to pay attention to the words in dreams. The unconscious seems to love puns and, reading a dream aloud, we often 'hear' other, sometimes more subtle, interpretations.

Animal guardians and protectors

Some months after beginning counselling, feeling lonely and in despair about her gambling (see Chapter 8: *Change your addiction*), Shirley, a client who had been raped some years earlier, had a series of powerful dreams of animals. The images of the turtle, albatross and seal (all animals intimately connected to the ocean) have remained with her in the years since. She referred to the animals as her guardians and protectors.

Shirley recounted her first dream: 'A huge albatross was caught up in a (beer) 6-pack plastic holder, and the albatross was holding on to a big turtle. It was trying to fly away and take the turtle with it, but it was caught in the plastic. I pulled the turtle down and it landed on its back. I was struggling to turn it over and to get it back in the water, heaving and shoving and cajoling. Then I turned to the albatross. It was exhausted and fearful but beyond trying to flee, waiting for the inevitable.'

When I asked her what she thought and felt about the albatross, Shirley said: 'They are beautiful, large, graceful birds, free-wheeling. They relax me. I love watching them,' and she added: 'They have to survive.'

It is not hard to see how the image of the albatross would relate to Shirley's sense of herself. She felt it was the spiritual side of her, which needed protection from the world. As a result of her unhappiness, Shirley often felt like flying away, fleeing this world. The turtle 'travels long distances. There is grace in its size,' and to Shirley represented 'civilisation destroying something very beautiful.' The turtle reflected the earthly side of herself, which she felt had been damaged as a result of the rape.

A few months later, Shirley had to attend a wedding that she was dreading but felt she could not avoid. All her extended family would be present. As the day grew closer, she became anxious and fearful. She drew a picture of the huge albatross of her dream and began to sense the powerful bird as a protective presence in her life.

The day before the wedding, Shirley drew another large picture of her albatross, its wings enveloping and protecting her, its head strong and powerful, looking out for her and not allowing her to be subjected to attack.

Shirley was aware that since the rape she had never allowed anyone to get close enough to her to offer her protection. For the week leading up to the wedding, the albatross stayed by her side. On the day of the wedding, as she set off in a taxi: 'I could feel the albatross's wings around me, guarding me and protecting me, giving me the courage I needed. It looked after me at the wedding.'

Two months later, Shirley dreamt of the seal: 'I am looking for a tram with some other people and then a cab pulls up, driven by a stunning Hawaiian who has been told to pick us up. There is a seal sitting up in the front of the cab with the driver. We are driving through scrub alongside a river. We arrive at a huge expanse of water. I have to get out and swim with the seal and the driver. It's a beautiful sensation, the water on my body — free, light, sensual. The cab driver and the seal are swimming around my body, playing, ducking, diving, rolling around me. We travel a long way and then have to swim back. The river has started to dry up, so I have to give the seal water in the puddles. There is lush green grass everywhere. I still have a long way to go, but I know I will get there. I am carrying the seal. The cab driver wants me to let the seal walk, but I say no and continue on. I keep hold of the seal, taking it from waterhole to waterhole, until we see the cab in the distance. My eyes are opened.'

Shirley described the seal as 'a free spirited animal,

which needs to be in its natural habitat.' She was aware that she wasn't living in an environment that felt right for her. She wasn't caring for herself enough or working in a field that gave her a sense of fulfilment. Shirley drew a picture of her seal and brought it in to her next session.

Just a few weeks later Shirley dreamt about her seal again: 'In the dream, the feel of water gliding over my body, gently, sensually and caressing, and I am enjoying the touch, revelling in the sweetness, the warmth. Then the touch turns to torment and skin comes away. It's not bleeding, but the gentle protective layer is gone and I am exposed. More and more skin is wiped away, leaving extreme tenderness, rawness, but no pain.'

Shirley understood the dream, which brought to mind a seal shedding its skin, to be a reflection of how she felt inside, under her skin, and it made her wonder what it was that held her together if she no longer had a protective layer. She was looking at her own wounding in life, feeling too exposed for the world's judgement. She had been violated in her life, by the rape and by other people, and she hadn't been able to protect herself.

Shirley did another drawing of the seal, its body pink and raw. Initially it appeared trapped, rigid, unable to move forward, but over time she saw the seal differently. She sensed more hope in the body, some lightness and a sense of freedom, no longer the same rawness. She also felt a sense of newness, a new beginning in her own life. She was allowing herself to be healed by the image of the seal.

Shirley's dreams of the seal bring to mind the story Sealskin, Soulskin, by Clarissa Pinkola Estes, (*Women who run with the wolves*, 1992, p.255).

The animals of Shirley's dreams seemed like an offering from the dream world. Like her dreams, the large drawings she did of the animals appeared to have come from her unconscious and to be there to help her get in touch with the painful events of her life. In immersing herself with the oceanic animals of her dreams, Shirley was able to connect to inner mother figures that would begin the process of healing and learning to trust again.

Years later, when I contacted Shirley and asked her about the animals of her dreams when she was in counselling, she sent me a number of poems she had written about her seal. She also told me she got 'goose bumps' when I mentioned her animals.

A little over a year later, Shirley had her most graphic dream: 'In the dream I had to drink my own blood. I knew that if I didn't drink it, someone else would, so I drank it. I remember how it looked — bright red, thick, rich and velvety, not gushing.'

Shirley said that the dream felt like: 'Just life, taking in life, taking it into myself.' She was deeply affected by the dream and the following week stated that she felt 'renewed and much more hopeful.'

The dream brings to mind the blood of the communion service. In drinking her own blood, Shirley is communing with herself and taking into herself her own vitality, her life blood.

'I'm getting married in the morning, Ding dong the bells are going to chime ...'

Several of my clients have dreamt of being at their own wedding. Women who dream of getting married are often dealing with issues related to identity. Marriage is celebrated as a positive new beginning in our society and carries with it enormous expectations, sometimes impossible to fulfil in the real world. Couples who have lived together for some time assume that they know what life will be like when they marry. Often relationship difficulties emerge once the ceremony is over and they have made a public commitment to one another. There is no longer the sense: 'I can just walk away.'

A number of clients have seen me in the weeks leading up to their wedding, at times having serious doubts about the step they are about to take, wondering even if this is the right partner. Weddings have become such big business. Huge sums of money are spent on having a grand occasion with all the trimmings and the pressure in the lead-up to the 'perfect' day can be overwhelming. Recently a couple told me their wedding is likely to cost in the region of $50,000 and is causing great tension between them. I asked if they had considered eloping and spending the money on the deposit for a house!

Milly, an English client, dreamt of getting dressed for her own wedding, waking in the middle of the night crying, hitting her partner Carl: 'I was in the UK, getting married. Mum, Carl and others were there, forcing me to wear a dress I didn't want to wear. I said 'No, it's my special day.' I had a meltdown, ran out on everyone, but they talked me 'round and made me change my mind. The one I wanted was silk, elegant, beautiful and strapless. The one they chose was a baby doll dress, chiffon, a 'flicky' style. It was okay but not what I wanted to wear.'

When we discussed her dream, Milly said it made her aware that people often make her feel silly and not good enough. She frequently asks others for their advice because she doesn't trust her own judgement. In the dream Milly was adamant that she knew which dress was right for her, which one she wanted to put on. The dream helped her to see that in understanding and accepting her own feelings and wants, she could trust her ability to make decisions because she knew what was right for her. This dream marked a significant turning point for Milly as she began to develop a clearer sense of her own identity. She was also able to stand up for herself with regard to an issue which had concerned her in her relationship with Carl. The dream also highlighted for Milly her desire to pursue a career which would offer her greater fulfilment. Milly was interested in fashion design and since the dream had started to explore the possibility of moving into that field. She had already begun classes in designing and making clothes.

(A year after she had the dream, Milly broke up with Carl.)

In a second wedding dream, Carrie was getting married: 'But I was a guest at someone else's wedding. The guests were just ordinary people, not anyone I recognised. I thought there were cannibals at the wedding feast. Soup had been served to all the guests in elegant china bowls, a casual meal. In each bowl of soup, my hands and feet were sticking up.'

Carrie told me that her hands and feet are her favourite parts of her body. Her hands are often busy, working, studying and typing and her feet are always on the go with activities such as walking, travelling and moving about. The presence of the cannibals, a group of savage people who might even devour her, indicates some kind of disturbance for Carrie. Was it possible she was in part devouring herself by getting married?

At the time Carrie was in the process of planning her wedding and was worried by comments from friends which implied that her life, as she knows it, will end following her marriage because she and her partner will have to buy a house and settle down. She may also need to discontinue her PhD studies. She identified the presence of the cannibals to be highlighting the way she felt she was being 'eaten up' by the pressure leading up to her wedding. As well as being a positive celebration of new life, marriage for a young woman implies the end of her single life, the death of her freedom to choose her identity and how she lives her life. Many young women still take their husband's name when they marry. In the dream Carrie has cut herself into pieces in order to serve others (with the best of her) and this was how she perceived her situation at the time.

I dreamt I had a baby

Clients sometimes tell me, in a concerned tone, that they dreamt of being pregnant or having a baby. I begin by reassuring them that the dream does not have to be taken literally. I always view such dreams as being significant in terms of the client's growth and development. In response to the question 'Are you aware of some change in you, or some new aspect of you in the world?' a client is often able to identify the emergence of new and positive aspects of the self.

In working with my clients and these dreams, a considerable amount of time was spent in exploring the messages and the layers of meaning that each dream contained for the dreamer. I have generally highlighted the main and generally the most obvious significance of the dreams for the client.

It is possible to formulate many interpretations from any one dream. I always ask the client (who, after all, wrote the script) to tell me their immediate associations and feelings. Between us we invariably succeed in reaching a level of understanding that is helpful to the client.

Donna's grandmother — the witch

Donna made an appointment to see me after carrying my card around for a long time. She told me at our first meeting: 'I carried your card around for over a year. I'd even moved during that time and your card was still there. It wasn't even in my wallet but in amongst a whole lot of things I needed to sort out, so you were still there after the move. One day I talked to Mum as I was becoming increasingly tearful and she suggested that I see a counsellor. I said I had already decided to, that I had your phone number. I rang to arrange a time straight away.'

In her early thirties, Donna had no idea why she felt so miserable, as early in her life she had been happy. In the first session I said that I was interested in hearing clients' dreams and Donna mentioned that since childhood she had had a recurring dream: 'I am trying to run up the driveway at my grandparents' home in Tasmania, but the drive is very steep. I can never get up the drive as it seems to be moving downwards and I cannot get a foothold in the moving gravel.'

Recurring dreams are always important; a message is trying to get through from the unconscious. What is important is to observe whether anything has changed the next time the dream is dreamt. Being pursued by someone menacing, appearing naked in public, having one's teeth fall out or being unprepared for an important exam or performance are all recurring dreams clients have explored with me. Donna's dream, recounted at her first counselling session, led us straight to the heart of what lay behind her distress.

The dream was located in Donna's grandparents' home, and I asked her to tell me what came to mind when she thought about that house. Donna's grandmother had died a few years earlier and when she talked about her, Donna started to cry. My first thought was that she felt grief at the loss of her grandmother, but in fact Donna had no cause to mourn this old lady. Initially it was difficult for her to talk about her grandmother in honest terms as she was controlled by the need to show respect towards her deceased grandparent. Aren't all grandmothers kind and loving? Not this one! Donna described her grandmother's treatment of her: 'I would go to see her on weekends at the same time as my cousins, two girls the same age as me. Whenever she saw me she commented on my hair, and I felt she didn't really see me as a person. She treated me differently from my cousins. She always had a little present for them, which they would show me when we went into the garden. I would wonder if she had something for me, but she never did.'

From an early age, Donna's grandmother had treated her differently from her cousins. When they were alone, her grandmother would criticise her son, Donna's father, to her, adding, 'And you're just like him!'

The pattern began early in childhood and Donna assumed that it was her fault. Her grandmother was clearly loving and generous towards her cousins. Somehow she alone was unacceptable to her, so there must be something wrong with her. After hearing Donna's account of her grandmother, I referred to her as 'a witch'. From that moment Donna was able to face the way she had been wounded by her grandmother as a young child and to recognise that she had done nothing to deserve her treatment.

Donna had another dream, immediately after her first counselling session: 'I was in a restaurant and I was carrying a bag of snakes. I dropped the bag and all the snakes slithered out. One was a rattlesnake. The snakes were moving in between the legs of the tables and it was hard to avoid them, so I ran out of the restaurant. Someone re-bagged the snakes.'

In the counselling session our exploration of the snake dream didn't progress very far beyond Donna's conviction that the rattlesnake represented her grandmother. Since that time I have immersed myself more in working with dreams, both my own and those of my clients. Why a rattlesnake? Rattlesnakes are not found in Australia but live in dry, arid areas in Arizona and California. At the time, I recall, we discussed whether the rattlesnake placed the timing of her grandmother's wounding back to when Donna was still an infant, playing with a rattle.

The impact of the wounding by her grandmother had affected Donna profoundly for over twenty years. As well as the emotional pain she had suffered, Donna had taken the hurt into her body and described the feeling 'like a stone' in the pit of her stomach. When I asked her to elaborate on 'the stone', she told me she thought everyone had that feeling inside them. She described it as cold, hard and immovable.

Later Donna found out from her father that her grand-mother had died of cancer: 'She had a large tumour that started in her ovaries and spread to her stomach. It was the size of a dinner plate. She apparently knew she had a tumour, but chose to ignore it.'

It is hard to ignore the possible connection between the stone in Donna's stomach and her grandmother's tumour, which had spread to her stomach.

I remember feeling a little shocked that I was refer-ring to a client's grandmother as a witch. This was not my usual response when hearing of abusive treatment (a fairly common occurrence in counselling). It was, however, something that I felt I knew intuitively about her grandmother. Interestingly Donna was no longer tearful. It was clear that having her grandmother's venomous treatment acknowledged by an outsider had led to renewed energy and a sense of optimism.

What still remained, however, was the physical embodiment of Donna's grandmother — 'the stone' was still lodged inside her. Some action was needed. I asked what she would like to say or do to her grandmother if she were in the room with us. Donna replied, quite meekly: 'I'd like to slap her.'

I put to her that perhaps something a little more potent was required: 'I'd like to chop her head off,' Donna announced with relish. She looked excited at the idea.

This took place early in my years as a counsellor. Again, my suggestion that Donna take some action to kill off her grandmother was something quite out of the ordinary for how I normally work. Mostly I rely on language to help a client move forward. In this case, action seemed crucial. I suggested Donna draw a picture of her grandmother on a large sheet of paper and I offered her the choice of scissors or a knife for the beheading. She chose scissors. I was quite surprised to find the ideal pair of scissors (more like shears, in fact) in the kitchen where I had my practice. Donna drew her grandmother and with a look of delight, proceeded to chop her head off and then cut it into small pieces. For both of us, this felt like the appropriate course of action. In performing this ritual, Donna was able to free herself from the pain she had internalised. The 'stone' in her stomach disappeared immediately.

As discussed earlier, Donna had red hair, which was curly and striking. It was her hair that her grandmother would comment on whenever she saw her, rather than acknowledge her granddaughter as a person.

Growing up, Donna's hair had proved both a blessing and a curse. She was accustomed to hearing people say: 'Oh what gorgeous hair you've got.'

On the one hand, Donna felt consoled that her sadness and hurt were not apparent to others and that she was seen as someone without emotional difficulties: 'Oh you can't have any problems in life. You've got nice hair.'

While the positive attention enabled her to feign confidence, Donna was left feeling bewildered: 'What I really felt was frustration because these comments about me and my hair made absolutely no sense and I would just think 'you must be kidding'.'

Donna's grandmother had established the pattern of focussing on Donna's hair and in so doing had made her feel invisible as a person. At school there were times she was teased for having red hair and freckles. The focus of attention was continually on her hair and this reinforced her sense that she was not seen by others for who she was, for her true self.

Donna's own relationship with her hair became confusing too, as a result of others' obsession: 'Because everyone always said, 'Oh what gorgeous hair you've got,' I used to go through the same scenario all the time where I'd grow my hair long, but whenever a relationship with a partner ended, I'd cut my hair off as a release. Then I would grow it again. I used to say to myself: I don't want to go out with another guy, so I'm going to make myself unattractive and cut my hair off and then I'll be left alone.'

I put it to Donna that maybe she felt her hair had let her down when a relationship ended, that it hadn't been sufficiently powerful after all. Donna agreed.

Donna came to view the elimination of her grandmother as marking a new beginning. In her words: 'When I was six I got given a certain level to play on. Perhaps a better way to describe it would be a faulty foundation. (The moving driveway of Donna's dream comes to mind). That's what I was given by my grandmother, and I had to learn a number of things. I lived a very faulty life as a result of her treatment and then when I came and saw you I got rid of all that. It was a new foundation, a new beginning. I felt I could start again.'

Donna came to appreciate that she had been subjected to abusive treatment by her grandmother and that no one else appeared to have noticed. She remembered a photograph of herself with her grandmother and in the photo: 'My grandmother has her hands around my neck. It was supposed to be a cuddle, but at the time it didn't feel like it.'

Two years later, when I contacted her, Donna still recalled the day she dealt with her grandmother: 'Chopping up the picture of my grandmother. That was fantastic! And there was something that you said to me that made me change completely. You referred to her as a witch and she was. And that was the first time I'd been given permission to actually refer to her how I felt, and after that it was — poof! All the hurt, the pain, the stone, it was all gone, amazing!

'I don't know whether it's because I'm artistic that it had a big impact on me or whether it relates to what I used to do as a child. I used to draw and cut things up, as you normally do as little children. It was quite a child-like opportunity, cutting up my grandmother. Maybe it was connecting me to the time when all my pain and hurt started with her cruel treatment ...'

(Over the next five years, a number of clients came to see me, referred by Donna. They had all heard the story of 'chopping up the witch'.)

Following the beheading of her grandmother, Donna

spoke to her parents about the way she had been treated and was able to discuss with them the resentment she felt because they hadn't protected her from her grandmother. Her parents assured her they were oblivious as to what was taking place. Donna's father had kept from her the fact that his relationship with his mother was conflicted because he felt it was better for her and he wanted her to know her grandmother. Maybe he hoped that magically his daughter would be spared his mother's savage treatment. He had in fact withdrawn from his mother. Unable to wound her son any further, the grandmother made Donna, his daughter, the target of her hostility.

In confronting her grandmother's unresolved, poisonous treatment handed down through the generations, Donna was able to free herself of her hurt and sadness and to change a destructive family pattern.

When Donna first came to see me, I was alerted by her first dream. The first dream often reveals an unmasked view of a client's core issues. It was also a recurring dream of her grandparents' driveway leading downwards, implying a descent into her unconscious. While we didn't explore in detail the dream she had immediately following her first meeting with me, Donna was certain the rattlesnake represented her grandmother. In my mind lingered the phrase 'let the cat out of the bag' or, in this dream, the rattlesnake. In telling me her dream, Donna revealed the source of all her discomfort. Neither of us forgot the dream in the five years that followed.

Having explored dreams with greater understanding and depth in recent years, I became aware of obvious parallels between Donna's two dreams and the story of Medusa in Greek mythology.

Briefly, the relevant parts of the myth, for those who are interested, are as follows: Medusa was one of the

Gorgons, a female monster, sometimes referred to as a witch. Her home was inaccessible to all but those who knew her. Medusa had been a female of absolute beauty, mostly because of her long, silky hair. She boasted that she was more beautiful than the Goddess Athene. One day, she was ravished by Poseidon in Athene's temple. Athene was so outraged that she transformed Medusa into a hideous creature with snakes instead of hair. Medusa was so ugly that anyone who looked at her was turned to stone, literally petrified.

Perseus, son of Zeus, is invited to a feast by Polydektes, king of the island of Seriphos, along with all the other men of the island. They are told to bring with them the gift of a horse. Perseus, being penniless, offers to bring the head of the Gorgon Medusa instead.

Perseus is helped in his task by Athene who gives him a shield in which he can see Medusa reflected and as a result does not need to look at her directly (and be turned to stone). She also guided him to the nymphs who lent him winged sandals, the helmet of invisibility and a bag in which to transport Medusa's head. Hermes, messenger of the gods, gives him a sickle with which to cut off the head.

When Medusa is decapitated, her two children, fathered by Poseidon, sprang from her severed neck (revealing the help needed by Medusa's children to be free of their mother).

In Donna's dream, she is carrying a bag containing the rattlesnake as well as other snakes. In our first two sessions, Donna's grandmother's venomous, witch-like treatment is reflected to her, honestly, for the first time in her thirty odd years. Donna reveals she has 'a stone' in the pit of her stomach. I offered her a pair of scissors (not a sickle) with which to chop off her grandmother's head.

Donna's father was clearly incapable of freeing himself from his mother, other than by distancing himself. He was unable to confront her wounding ways. That task was left to his daughter (whom he failed to warn about his mother's venom), a daughter whose hair had invited great admiration, but admiration that came at a high cost as she was not seen for her true self. Donna, the person, was invisible. I felt that my part in enabling Donna to free herself of her grandmother's influence was determined for me. I simply had to follow my intuition.

When I explored the Medusa myth, I found myself reflecting on some other venomous, toxic mothers who had wounded their children (my clients) in their early years. While men are known to be aggressive and violent towards partners and children, on occasion women are capable of a level of extreme savagery, often masked and unseen. They behave in a manner that is completely devoid of feminine principles.

In the days following my writing about Medusa, I was surprised when several clients, all female, revealed they were feeling stuck. The first of these was Annabel, a lawyer, a client in her forties who has achieved considerable success in her career. She grew up with an alcoholic mother and a father who at best was limited emotionally and lacking in concern for her welfare. She had been struggling for some months with depressed feelings and these were exacerbated following a weekend personal development group she took part in. Curiously, each member of the group was addressing the effects of living with a difficult and at times 'witch-like' mother.

Annabel had shown great empathy for the other participants. It was clear she felt extreme indignation and anger at the way they had been treated in childhood, but she was incapable of expressing the same anger for her own lack of nurturing by her parents. Annabel didn't understand why she couldn't 'put the shit where it belongs' and reveal the anger she felt towards her alcoholic mother in particular, whom she had had to parent from the age of twelve.

It was clear Annabel was afraid to reveal her anger. I asked what would happen to her, what would she look like if she were to do so. She replied, 'I would look just like my mother.'

I asked her to describe her mother when she was drunk: 'At five o'clock most days she would be angry, yelling, crying, ranting, mad, pulling her hair out of her bun so it stuck out of her head.'

When I asked her what her mother reminded her of at these times, she replied: 'A witch.'

At my suggestion, Annabel drew a large picture of her mother, wrote a description of her when she was out of control, her hair standing on end, looking quite deranged. She looked hard at her picture and then with great determination, she screwed it up into a tight ball. I pointed out there was one word she had omitted: 'terrifying'. I wondered if the thought of turning into her mother was so terrifying it had prevented her from expressing her anger. It had paralysed her. Annabel agreed.

Six years had elapsed since Donna had worked with me to confront her grandmother's treatment. One after the other my 'stuck' clients succeeded in contacting their anger towards their witch-like mothers which they had avoided doing previously. For most, this involved quashing uncomfortable feelings of guilt. What kind of daughter is it that calls her mother a witch and wants to kill her? But as I asked each of them: what kind of mother treats her child this way?

Jemma, whose story is told in Chapter 3, drew not

only her mother but also her maternal grandmother, telling me: 'Now, she was a real witch, a nasty, vicious, cold woman.'

For a week it seemed that Medusa was everywhere. I wondered if I had unleashed her in some way. What was apparent was that releasing their anger, their totally justifiable anger, these women had freed themselves of their depressed and anxious feelings.

Around the same time that Medusa was exerting her influence in my therapy room, a client brought in a dream. She is someone who only remembers dreams occasionally and this dream upset her. 'I go into the laundry and look in the mirror. There is mascara running down my face. I start chopping at my hair violently. Then I see my mother, reflected in the mirror, standing behind me. I cry out 'Mum, mum...' wanting her to help me. When I turn round, she's not there. When I look in the mirror once more, she is behind me but she's not really there'.

My client believes her hair is her 'crowning glory' so in the dream she is attacking what she considers her most attractive self. When we discussed the dream, she said that her mother is physically present in her life but is not nurturing and does not help her emotionally. She feels her mother is not 'behind her' or 'there for her'.

The dream helped my client to see that she needs to care for herself, rather than attack herself. She recognised that she cannot look to her mother for emotional support.

My feeling is that writing about Medusa in my book gave me an understanding of the savage witch, alive in some women. This enabled me to provide a container (a bag), so that clients felt they could risk looking at the significant Medusa figure in their own lives, who had wounded them at a very deep level.

Confronting the inner beast

When Barry, who had been seeing me for a little over a year, came for his last session of counselling, he told me that it was the dreams that we worked on for many hours that had led to the greatest insights in his therapy.

Barry's story 'Handle snakes with care' is explored in Chapter 4. When he initially came to counselling he had left his marriage and was feeling ashamed and guilty at his behaviour.

'One of the themes that came through in several of my dreams was confrontation — anger and violence. I would see my actions as confirmation of my poor character and shameful behaviour, but by discussing the dreams in counselling sessions, I was able to understand the messages contained in the dreams and to have a different view of myself as a result.'

The following is part of a dream in which Barry seems to be a heroic quest: 'I was in some kind of patrol. A lion came up out of a stairwell to face me. I was told that I had to get rid of it. I was armed with a samurai sword and as it approached to face me, I was extremely confident that I would kill it easily with one sweep of the sword, as if I had done this in the past. I had a bench between myself and the lion and I slashed and missed. This aggravated the lion and it slashed at me. My blows with the sword were ineffectual, glancing off its paws. I whacked it fair on the nose two or three times again with no effect. I said to my comrade, "I think it's going to get me." I then realised I had the sword the wrong way round so I was hitting with the back of the blade.

'I turned the sword around and cut off its right paw. I then attacked its other paw and although I inflicted a really nasty wound, the lion continued to advance. No matter how I tried I could not get close enough to cut off its head. It leaped at me and I hit it in the middle of the face, cutting deep into its bottom jaw and nose, straight up the middle of its head. It couldn't bite me but was still pushing forward and I realised that to kill it I would have to push the sword through its head until I cut out the brain.

'I pushed harder, gripping the top of the blade and the handle and it cut slightly deeper. The lion was still straining to get at me and I pushed harder again and in a rush the sword cut deep up the middle of its head, deep enough to be lodged against the skull where the left eyeball used to be but now was a bloody pulp. The gore was extremely vivid: I had warm blood spurting onto me, the colours of flesh, bone and severed tendons was vivid. I felt disgusted but kept pushing, trying to put the lion down. It wouldn't quit and I couldn't get through the skull to the brain. The lion was on its hind legs trying to get on top of me and I was pushing up and back. This gave me a really clear view of the wound. I woke up, making a kind of frightened, disgusted whimpering sound.

'My counsellor asked me what I think of lions and I see them as the personification of selfish men. They have a den of lionesses who hunt for them and bear their children and basically look after the male — the ultimate egotist — and so when I confronted that image in the dream, I realised I was behaving exactly like that. The message was clear: if I don't like it, don't behave like that and my unconscious will leave me alone and let me have some sleep!'

It was clear that Barry's dream had alerted him to the way he was behaving like a beast in his treatment of women, assuming they were there for his pleasure. When he takes on the lion in the dream, he almost gets inside the lion, in particular the lion's head, reaching to its brain, the nerve centre perhaps. As a result Barry was able to appreciate how the 'lion' part of him operates in the world. It was around this time that, in order to raise money for a charity, Barry volunteered to have his head shaved. Prior to this he had long hair (a mane?).

Barry brought in two dreams one week that he knew were significant. In the first dream: 'The taps in a shower were running and I couldn't turn them off. The water was flooding out and I remember a feeling of despair that I couldn't contain the flood.'

In the second dream: 'I dreamt about a snake that bit me hard and pumped a lot of poison. I remember you helping me to see that the snake was me (or a particular part of me!) and what I was up to at the time. I was sleeping with a married woman even though I felt it was wrong to do so.

'This was a pivotal counselling session because I first came to see you feeling total despair. To me the dreams were symbols of how the world saw me — poisoned and inadequate — but you turned that around and showed me that the dreams represented how I was feeling and how I saw myself.'

It is unusual for a male client to value dreams to this degree and to want to explore their meaning. It is also rare for a man to admit to himself so readily the way he needs to change in his treatment of others.

When he came to his last session Barry gave me a card, thanking me: '… for your support, guidance and your humour. I shall always try to handle snakes with care, keep the torrent at bay and walk comfortably (but cautiously) beside my inner lion!'

This became Barry's mantra. He also carried a card

around in his pocket for months on which were written these words, just as a reminder.

I find that working with clients and their dreams is always rewarding. Recently a young client and I struggled for a considerable time in a session to understand why she was feeling very flat. We were able to uncover the reason after some effort. I then inquired about any dreams she might have had. She told me about a dream whereupon we both laughed because it revealed very simply what we had puzzled to comprehend in the session.

I began this chapter on dreams with one of my own dreams and thought I should end with two dreams I had late in 2010. Both dreams, I am sure, relate to writing this book, which can feel like hard work and at times is quite confronting.

In the first dream: 'I was in my car, driving endlessly up hills, approximately thirty hills in all. It seemed to go on forever and it was a huge effort. I got a little help along the way, I think from a man.

'Then I was going into something like a shower block and there were some other women, also showering. I was holding my clothes against my front (so as not to be totally naked).'

'Driving uphill' needs no explanation. Why thirty hills? I think I have included the stories of around thirty of my clients. Covering my nakedness in the shower block I am certain relates to my fear of being exposed, in a number of ways, when my book becomes public.

The following dream was two months later: 'I wanted to discuss my dilemma re my pregnancy. A young woman was laughing at what I was going to say because of a previous saga that was made into a TV series. I was pregnant and the doctor wanted me to have a caesarian. I said I didn't want one. I said my stomach wasn't yet big enough.

I didn't look pregnant enough. I suggested my chiropractor be at the birth as I know he is opposed to caesarian births. They didn't want me to have him there.

'I saw the man who made the TV series. I said a lot of people were changed as a result of corrupt dealings. I thought about whether the baby might die.'

Again it isn't difficult to understand what the dream is revealing: I am concerned that my book will not be taken seriously and may be viewed like some kind of television melodrama. The clients' stories might not be respected, as I would want. They may not even be believed. I don't feel ready to 'give birth' to the book as yet and am worried at the prospect of an intervention (a caesarian). I know my chiropractor (in real life) would insist on a natural birth. Finally, I am concerned the book might just die, or be stillborn.

Several months have passed since I dreamt these dreams. Reflecting on them now, I can see I have moved beyond the anxious stage and am anticipating with excitement 'the birth' of this book. I have begun to discuss with clients their stories as they will appear in the finished book; their response has been enthusiastic. They have been able to see just how much they changed as a result of the work we did together. I have also shown the manuscript to a few people and each one has taken the book and the stories it contains seriously. I do not need to worry. The clients' stories will be respected.

Nowadays I cannot imagine counselling clients without including discussion of their dreams in our sessions. It is through dialogue and engagement with their dreams that many clients have been able to gain a deeper and richer understanding of their inner world, and have been directed to a path of greater insight, knowledge and healing.

Chapter 7

Start loving, stop punishing your body

Healing
I am ill because of wounds to the soul, to the deep emotional self
And the wounds to the soul take a long, long time — only time can help
and patience...
—DH Lawrence

Counselling has provided me with a totally unexpected education. I have benefited enormously from the deep well of experience clients have shared with me. In particular this led me to an appreciation of the way our physical body, through illness and dis-ease, reflects our emotional life. I have also come to recognise that our bodies store the memory of all experience, as well as our emotional response to that experience. I had no idea this was the case before working as a counsellor.

Case study: holding on to pain

Early in my career, one client in particular demonstrated the truth of this premise. A woman in her late fifties came to see me, understandably grief-stricken a year after her youngest son died of a heroin overdose. She had two other adult children. For some time we addressed the death of her son, and then a number of other issues came to the surface.

One day I noticed Katherine was sitting awkwardly in her chair and I asked if she was uncomfortable. She replied: 'Oh it's just my back. I've had it for years.'

She told me she had seen numerous practitioners over several decades, but in spite of various forms of treatment, she still suffered back pain on a regular basis. I asked a number of questions: Where was the pain? When did she experience it most? Could she remember when the pain first started?

Katherine told me the pain was in her back and she had had the pain for about thirty-five years. She was a little dismissive of my exploration, no doubt having discussed her problem with professionals far more qualified than I am with regard to backs. She believed this was simply pain that she had to contend with. I asked if she could recall what was happening in her life around that time, thirty-five years ago?

I was amazed at her reply, and so was she. Her face changed colour and her eyes filled with tears as she told me: 'I gave up a child for adoption.'

Katherine hadn't discussed with anyone what she revealed that day. The only person who knew of the adoption was her baby's father. Part of her distress stemmed from the fact that some time later they had married, and he was also father to her other three children. The relationship didn't last, however, and they divorced. The two surviving children didn't know they had an older brother.

Later in the session Katherine told me, in near disbelief, that the pain had gone from her back: 'But I'm sure it will come back.' It didn't. A week later she was astounded that her back was still free of pain. It was, of course, the loss of another son, her youngest, that had prompted her to see me, and no doubt part of her grief related to the loss of her first child. The pain had remained in her body for thirty-five years; simply telling me was enough to release it. I remember vividly Katherine's deep sorrow that day as she contacted the pain she had stored inside her as a result of that sad decision. She subsequently told her two children that they have a brother and was considering whether to try to contact her firstborn.

In her own words: 'I initially sought counselling following the death and funeral of my youngest son who died of a heroin overdose — one of a mother's worst nightmares.

'In counselling I was able to express my hurt without feeling I was being judged. As the sessions progressed, a number of other issues were addressed and I realised I had had many losses in my life that I had not spoken about to anyone. I had repressed the feelings (sadness, grief, pain, hurt, etc.), thereby causing me to lose my sense of self-esteem. This I had covered over for such a long time by working extremely hard and being available to do anything asked of me by anyone. I always found it extremely difficult to say no, especially to loved ones. It was quite a revelation to realise that a lot of my suffering was caused by what I had lost or what had been taken away from me.

'After many months of counselling, I found that I was slowly gaining an inner strength that has allowed me to make better decisions regarding my life. I no longer let people take advantage of my naturally forgiving nature (which was always to their advantage and my detriment).

'I came to recognise that health issues can be caused by repressing emotional experience. This became extremely obvious to me when the back pain that I had suffered for much of my life dissipated after just a few sessions. I found this extraordinary.

'Once I was able to realise the correlation between mental and physical health, I changed the way I dealt with conflict and issues that arise. To this day I process them and acknowledge my feelings instead of internalising them. As a result my health and feeling of wellbeing are generally excellent.'

When I contacted Katherine, several years after her time in counselling, she told me that she subsequently made contact with her first son and they have established a close relationship. She now has three more grandchildren too. She was delighted that her son felt no bitterness towards her but was pleased to know his birth mother finally. Indirectly, Katherine's back pain had led her to reunite with her oldest son.

Case study: confronting 'it'

A client whose father had died a few years earlier in their home in France came to see me because she was very distressed. Since her father's death she had developed severe pain in her insides.

In Antoinette's words: 'When my Dad died, I thought I had to be strong. He was a really strong man. He would tell me often that I was like him. I believed that this meant I should be strong, just like him. "Being strong" I thought meant not crying in public and not discussing it. I didn't really understand what the "it" was that I shouldn't be discussing — was "it" my father's death? The cancer? My pain? My fear? All I did know was that I was feeling lost and lonely. I felt as though I had been stabbed in my heart, as if the knife was still hanging there. Everyone could see it, but nobody would do anything to help me. I had a big lump in my throat all the time and my head felt like it was about to explode.

'I would tell myself that losing a father wasn't such a big deal. If you think about it there are always other people in much more difficult and painful situations. But it was a big deal for me. I didn't understand that at the time and I started keeping everything in.

'I developed a terrible pain in my insides, at times so painful I would be bent in half. The only way I could get rid of the pain was when I finally managed to get to sleep. The pain was worse when I was my most vulnerable — when I was tired and upset, stressed or angry about something. The pain became a big problem because I could no longer get through the day.

'I was feeling very anxious and unhappy with where my life was heading. At twenty-five I thought I'd feel more settled in my life. I was stressed and angry, angry at the whole world. I felt shaky.

'I decided to see a counsellor to help me. It seemed such a bizarre thing to do. I thought counselling was only for weak people. It's funny to think I believed such nonsense.

'I started seeing the counsellor on a regular basis. She told me early on that she was running a weekend group in a few months' time and she thought it would be very good for me. I decided to do it. I had nothing to lose.

'The group was amazing. It was as if we had been put on stage. The story line was ours — our pain, our difficulties, our relationships. But it was no performance. It was real. It was us, confronting our lives, our hurt and pain. It was such a strong experience. I spat "it" out. I talked out loud about "it". In the end I learned that "it" was my father's death, and loss, pain, my fear and worries.

'As strange as it sounds, I felt I would be fine after that weekend and I truly believe I am. I've grieved now. And I learnt that time eases pain if, and only if, you are willing to confront it and deal with it, if you let yourself explore what's inside you. In the three years since that time, I've only had the pain once. Just once.'

Where is the pain in your body?

Over the years, numerous clients have been helped to resolve their emotional stress by tuning in to their body's intelligence. When I run groups I always ask those taking part where they store pain in their body. Every client can give an answer without having to think too hard: 'in my head/chest/stomach/shoulders/back/throat etc.'

Clients begin by thinking I am a little strange when I ask the question, but over time they learn to tune in to their body, and to where they feel pain. When men are struggling to contact their feelings in a session, asking them to locate where they experience pain in their body invariably helps to reveal hidden feelings.

Patrick, whose journey in counselling was discussed in Chapter 4: *A mother's love*, was helped to understand the reason behind his outbursts of rage by discussion of the physical changes he experienced when he felt out of control. This often occurred when he was feeling controlled (however subtly) by his partner. He would feel powerless and out of control as the rage built up inside him. This is how Patrick described the physical symptoms he experienced: 'I can't breathe … my breath just goes … I feel terrible pain in my stomach, as though someone is cutting me open with a knife and spilling my guts. If I can't escape from whatever is making me angry, it feels like I'm treading water. I have no resources left to keep my head up, to stop myself from drowning. I feel I have no relevance. I am nobody and nothing. I'm terrified that I'm going to cease to exist.'

Once Patrick had identified his internal struggle, he was able to address the source of his agony: the years of being afraid of his mother, terrified that he would be annihilated by her.

In the previous chapter, Donna's stone (which she thought everyone had in their stomach) alerted me to the fact that Donna had taken into her own body her grandmother's poison and that she needed to take some action to free herself. The stone led us to the source of her wound.

Generally speaking, people think about their bodies or speak about them when there is something wrong — a headache, stomach ache or something more serious like high blood pressure, asthma, a stroke. Most of us resent being ill and seek to hasten our recovery. Learning to understand why we feel unwell can be beneficial in many ways. It may point to action that we might take or changes we could make that would help us to feel better emotionally as well as physically. I always suggest to clients that they think about the questions 'What is my body trying to tell me? Why these symptoms?' What we don't do in general is value our body, enjoy it, admire it and care for it on a daily basis. I am not suggesting, of course, that there is no such thing as physical illness without an emotional base. Bodies do get sick.

Some cocktail!

I always ask clients about their drug and alcohol use, including prescription drugs, and I assure them this is not a judgment on their lifestyle, but it is useful information for the client as well as for me. What is apparent is that many people have no understanding of the effect on their system of combining alcohol, drugs (prescription or recreational) and, where women are concerned, the contraceptive pill. Several women I have worked with discovered that their feelings of depression stemmed from taking the pill.

A young woman who saw me for a few months, told me in her first session that she was taking antidepressants and also the contraceptive pill. In addition she was drinking quite heavily and using marijuana on a daily basis. She told me she was concerned that she perspired constantly (even in winter) and was surprised when I suggested her body was struggling to deal with her cocktail of drugs. She decided to stop taking the pill, since she wasn't in a relationship and would not consider engaging in casual sex. The sweating ceased almost immediately. My client began making other positive decisions regarding her body and health. She began to know her body a little better.

The perfect body

In 2011, perhaps more than any other time in our history, women feel under pressure to have the perfect body. In our society this means being slim because to carry any weight, to be shapely, with natural female bulges (breasts, tummies, hips and thighs), all normal for the female body, is not considered the ideal of what is attractive.

Rubens, the artist, would not be impressed. The stereotype of the ideal body is reflected constantly in the media. Skeletally thin models still appear in fashion pages of women's magazines. Television reality programs compound the problem with intense scrutiny and criticism about appearance. Tragically very young girls are being sexualised and encouraged to dress like adults, complete with bare midriffs, high heels, hair styling and make-up. An article in the *Herald Sun* (31 March 2011) reported that girls as young as seven are being seen in hospitals, suffering from anorexia.

Not all men like their women skinny, but the majority of the men I see (between the ages of thirty and forty) assume that other men do. I have been told that in some male-dominated work places, it is common for men to compare notes, rating female employees out of ten. Men often compete with other men and will bow to the pressure of peers, believing they will be admired and therefore feel more confident if their wife or girlfriend fits the stereotype of attractive — invariably tall, blonde and skinny (in Australia at least). I have worked in counselling sessions with men who struggle to commit to a partner even if they like her as a person, admire her values and are attracted to her, if she doesn't conform to society's (and their peers') view of what is attractive. On occasion it is a man's family that exerts pressure over a partner's desirable appearance.

There has been a large increase in the number of women prepared to undergo cosmetic surgery, as new treatments emerge. Women as young as eighteen are choosing to have surgery because they are uncomfortable with their appearance. I was shocked to learn from a female client in her forties (who was a normal, healthy weight, with no excess body fat) that her ex-partner had urged her to have liposuction 'so that I can't even get hold of your flesh with my fingers', and in addition to paying for the procedure had offered her the sum of $10,000 as a bribe. I am pleased to say she ended the relationship.

It is rare for me to work with a woman who is happy with her body and this includes young women who come to me for counselling for any number of reasons, who look healthy and are perfectly normal in terms of weight. To me they exude vitality and because of this they look 'attractive'. Many feel uncomfortable with their appearance — too short, too tall, too fat, too thin. They refer to parts of their body in a disparaging way: my big bum, my flat chest, my fat thighs. Many young women dislike their body and speak of it as though it is not a part of them but something they own and have to contend with.

In addition to the influence of the media, much of the poor body image stems from teasing and bullying in school. If you are teased about your body as a child, your self-esteem is likely to be affected. One young woman was constantly teased at school for being *too* thin and for having 'a gap at the top of my thighs.'

By far the strongest influence for young women who are critical of their bodies is the attitude of parents and family when they are growing up. I have worked with several women who were made to feel shame when they were very young as a result of comments and criticism by a mother or father and sometimes both. A client's father, obsessed with his own physique, would comment frequently on her weight and tell her: 'Fat people are inefficient and lazy.'

Unhealthy advice

Linda, a young client, was in an anxious state when she first came to see me. At the age of nine, Linda's mother told her she was unattractive because she was too fat and 'your legs are too big.' Linda remembers being shocked because she was not aware that she was at all overweight. Her mother told her frequently, 'Linda, hold your tummy in.' She would bake cakes for the family but tell her daughter she shouldn't have any.

Linda described her mother as a bitter, judgemental woman. She always dressed Linda to look young and child-like. Linda believed it was because she didn't want her to grow up. By the age of twelve she remembers being a lonely and introverted child. She also became aware of her fear of putting on weight and began making herself sick once a day.

Some months later she spoke to a doctor. He didn't refer her for help but told her that vomiting once a day was 'really not bad', adding that 'the norm for vomiting was often six or seven times a day,' so Linda increased the frequency to that number.

Twenty-five years old when she came to counselling, Linda had suffered from bulimia from the age of thirteen.

A second client who studied ballet from the age of eight to fifteen was made to feel that she didn't fit in at the ballet school because her body was not the typical shape of a ballerina. Prior to this, she was not aware that there was anything "wrong" with her body. A mean-spirited ballet teacher instructed her to diet before the concert, adding: 'I'm not having those fat legs sticking out of one of my tutus.'

Cruel words such as these are rarely forgotten. The teacher taught the ballet students how to vomit and instructed them to use laxatives to shed kilos rapidly. By the time my client began university she was suffering from anorexia.

It seems quite possible that many of those commenting on the weight of these young people were in fact projecting their preoccupation with their own body or weight.

Case study: protection from bullies

Rosie, a young client, remembers her aunt telling her she was fat and had a belly. At school Rosie suffered at the hands of a group of vicious bullies in grade 6. One of the girls (supposedly her best friend), became leader of the class bullies and turned the group against Rosie. It was a long time before Rosie felt strong enough to tell me what took place when she was bullied in school. The teacher who became involved clearly mishandled the situation, making things far worse for her.

In her words: 'I know that it was being bullied in primary school that caused me to put on weight. By the time I went to high school I was chubby and I never had luck with boys. I felt ugly, fat and unattractive. In my twenties, in counselling sessions, I started working on myself and realised that it's about looking after myself and taking control of my body. As soon as I addressed my emotional issues, I started to lose the weight. I know that it's when I feel stressed or not good enough that I am tempted to overeat.

'I love been skinny now and I'm proud I have maintained my weight. To change your body dramatically is a huge thing. You can look good and feel good on the outside, but those issues are still there somewhere on the inside. I now know the warning signs and that I need to look at what is stressing me rather than eat for comfort.'

Case study: aiming for perfection

Jade came to counselling to address her anxiety. She told me that she was eating compulsively for emotional reasons. When Jade was growing up, her mother was obsessive about the state of the house: 'It was like a museum, not a home, always neat and tidy, the bin never full. My mother's entire focus was about the house looking perfect, so she couldn't allow for comfort or relaxation in the home.

'Mum was highly critical, quick to judge, to point out anything that was wrong in her eyes — quite literally a hair out of place. Even in public she would scrutinise my appearance. I had to be groomed at all times, my posture perfect, a smile on my face …'

Jade recalled that when she started school, a letter went home to her mother asking her not to dress her up so much as it was difficult for her to play easily.

Her mother's opinion was difficult to ignore when Jade was growing up. It was hard to trust her own judgement as she felt she needed her mother's approval in all things.

When Jade moved out of home in her early thirties, she found it a challenge to know what she wanted or even what she liked. She found herself judging everything as though through her mother's critical eye.

In counselling Jade addressed her anxiety and her uncomfortable relationship with food. It was not hard to understand why she was eating for comfort. In part it was a rebellion against her mother's control. Jade was single at the time. She was concerned that she wouldn't find the right partner and be able to settle down and have children. As with all major decisions, Jade found relationships were a challenge because her mother's judgement was impossible to ignore. Whose feelings and opinions about a potential partner should she consider? Her own or her mother's?

In our sessions I encouraged Jade to appreciate her body, to care for it and value it. I suggested she did some paintings. I was delighted when Jade brought in her artwork to our next session — a painting of herself naked. It was the first time she had attempted to paint. She had enjoyed doing the painting and the experience had made her feel more appreciative of her body. She told me she didn't think about food at all when she was doing her painting.

A little while later, Jade brought in a second painting, a repeat of the first picture of herself naked. She was very happy with the second version. Looking at the painting, she described it as: 'Softer, more sensuous, with no harsh lines.' She added, 'Painting is balancing me, helping me to appreciate myself in every way.'

When I contacted Jade earlier this year, I learnt that she is happily married and has a little girl. She loves being a mother.

Case study: healing from the inside

Beth was in primary school when she first started dieting. A memory from that time has stayed with her ever since: 'I remember a boy telling other kids in grade 5 that he would like to invite me to the dance, but I was too big to fit through the door. I wasn't that big in fact, but I'll never forget his words. Funnily enough he moved into my street when we were in high school and asked me to his year 11 formal. I asked him if he remembered what he had said in grade 5 and he did. He apologised, but the impact of his words had already affected me greatly.

'My mother would comment too, believing she had my best interests at heart. This was the beginning of my being a serial dieter. I would hardly eat any lunch at school but on my own, at home after school, I would consume a massive amount of food.

'I tried every diet under the sun. By the time I was twenty-five I had been to Weight Watchers three times. The first time I was nineteen years old and weighed 62 kg. I'm 163cm tall, so really my weight was fine. I got down to 52 kg, but the weight went back on. I've also done Lite 'n' Easy, the grape diet, the lemon diet and my own diet — "just don't eat."

'After my brother's death I wanted to have some control in my life and thought my weight was a good place to begin. I was smoking a lot of dope, eating too much and generally trying to destroy myself. I started attending a well-known naturopathic clinic. I knew several people who had been there and succeeded in losing weight. It was a high protein diet — 30 g of protein three times a day. I attended for several months. They would weigh me in weekly and test my blood and cells. I was incredibly loyal to the diet, but it made me sad and my weight climbed. The naturopath was puzzled and consulted other naturopaths. It was also costing me a huge amount of money.

'I decided to see a counsellor. Very quickly what came to the surface was that in addition to the grief of my brother's death, I hadn't really dealt with my father's death five years earlier. I was also hanging on to my long-term boyfriend for the wrong reasons. The loss of my father and brother made it hard for me to let him go and move on. I was terrified of losing another man in my life and being alone.

'At the first counselling session I was advised to give up attending the clinic and stop dieting. My counsellor told me I needed to heal from the inside, deal with my grief and the rest would follow. She explained that it was all the feelings I hadn't dealt with making me hold on to the weight. I needed to let go and face the pain of my brother's and father's deaths. As soon as I quit the clinic, I lost three kilograms very quickly.

'I remember my boyfriend would get upset with how I stressed about my weight. I never felt I looked good when we went out and I would often end up in tears. He would tell me that if I really wanted to lose weight I should eat well and exercise. I know now it is that simple, but only if you are ready to lose the weight.

'I broke up with my boyfriend and stopped counselling before reaching the stage I am at now. I felt sad for a long time but then decided to set myself a challenge: no dope, eat every four hours but smaller portions, exercise four times a week. I also resolved to keep a journal, detailing how I was feeling and how I was sleeping. It wasn't about my weight, it was a way of caring for myself and seeing if this made a difference. I lost 5 kg and I wasn't even dieting. I just kept going and got my weight down to what I was in primary school.

'I think I will always have to watch my weight. What I want most of all is to choose to like myself, and this means liking all of me and respecting myself enough to be aware of what I put into my body. I am choosing to eat well because it helps my brain, my mood and my self-esteem. I used to eat for so many reasons and none of them had anything to do with food. It was all about how I felt about myself. If I look back, I can see I didn't want to lose weight. I would tell myself that if I were thin, boys would like me and I would be happy. But what if I lost the weight, became thin and I still didn't feel happy? If I lost weight, I would lose all my excuses. I did have to heal from the inside. When I see very overweight people nowadays I wonder what it is they hate about themselves.'

There is invariably a gain for people when they choose to resist change, whatever form that change might take. I often ask individual clients what is the gain in remaining stuck? Frequently it is fear of the unknown. Beth had to reach a point where she felt she could risk letting go her weight, knowing that this might or might not make her feel happier. It might make her more attractive to men; was that what she wanted? Was she ready to get involved with a new partner? In Beth's case, losing weight led to many changes in her life. It was, however, risking a different way of being in the world that ultimately achieved a state of wellbeing and happiness. Losing weight was just the beginning.

Case study: a painful life

A client who had been seeing me for some time talked in every session of the chronic pain in her body. I came to the conclusion that if her pain had a physical basis, I was not the person she should be seeing. My instinct kept reassuring me that her pain was emotional. After asking her one day where the pain was located and hearing her describe pain in practically every part of her body, I inquired, very gently, if it were at all possible some of the pain she was experiencing might have an emotional basis. She was furious, so furious I thought she was about to storm out of the room. She managed to calm down but clearly resented my insinuation. Months later she would laugh with me about her reaction that day.

In Charlene's words: 'I first sought counselling because my friends were really worried about me. I had just had surgery and I was very down on myself. The recovery was taking a long time and I thought my body was holding me back. So I was going out drinking — drinking far too much and then crying. The crying turned into two suicide threats — an overdose of pills one time and cutting myself with a knife another. On both occasions I ended up in hospital. No one asked me what was wrong, and I wasn't willing to talk about it anyway because that was the way I was used to living my life. It was no life to be living.

'Two years later I had an operation on my back. I now know I hindered my recovery by eating badly and not looking after myself. I can see that I put my body through hell. The outcome of abusing my body for years was that I couldn't see how to repair it. I also put on a lot of weight around this time and I just couldn't lose it.

'When I first started counselling I was *very* reluctant to admit that my physical pain had anything to do with my emotional or mental pain. I remember going to see my counsellor and explaining all the physical ailments that I had at that moment or had experienced in my life. I got very angry when she tried to tie these ailments to a particular thing that was happening at the time. I would look at her as if to say, *"Are you listening to me?* I am talking about *physical* pain, not *emotional!"*

'I think it took me two years to understand that whenever my body was hurting, it was connected to what was happening in my life, i.e. my back was sore — what can't I stand? My throat was sore — what am I not saying? My tummy was sore — what is it that I can't stomach? And so the list went on. It reminded me of when I was younger, I *always* used to have a sore throat, especially when I was stressed or I had to go back to school after the holidays. It was a physical form of the pain that I was feeling about not being heard at home or at school. No one was listening to me, so what was the point in speaking!

'Under all the pain I believe was abuse that I suffered over many years, starting in my childhood. I think it began when my sister was born and I was taught to make tea and do laundry at the age of two. It was an abandonment and rejection issue — the Cinderella syndrome, as I like to call it. I was the oldest of four girls. Growing up my Mum very blatantly favoured my next sister (and admits it now). I got the blame for everything and was often punished for things that I didn't do. I think that this abuse then contributed to my lack of self-worth which once lost, is very hard to find again.

'My parents divorced when I was sixteen. My father remarried and had two sons. I always felt he treated them much better, with a lot more love and understanding, than he treated me.'

Charlene addressed her relationship with both parents around this time. She invited her mother to come to two counselling sessions and was able to improve their relationship significantly by telling her mother how she had felt as a child. She also wrote to her father and he began to make more effort with their relationship. There were other issues we needed to explore: 'When I was fifteen I got into a relationship with someone (the head boy of a nearby school) who abused me physically for four years. I think I was so used to abusive treatment that I stayed with him all that time. When I was twenty-one, I was raped by a friend's brother. It had a terrible effect on me and no one seemed to understand that once these things happen, they affect the rest of your life and the actions that you take in the future. There was very little understanding from the people around me, that even though it happened "so long ago", it still affected decisions and actions that I was taking — including abusing myself in any way that I saw fit, and not valuing myself.'

In our sessions, Charlene worked at getting in touch with the pain she had held in her body for several decades. In accepting the poor treatment of those years Charlene was denying her own wants and feelings. She had instead adopted the role of 'Miss Fixit' in everyone else's life, putting herself out for friends, solving their problems, helping them in whatever way they wanted.

She was part of a group that met with me on a monthly basis for three years and her role of 'group helper' was apparent. At times I felt I had an assistant. I decided to address her need to put everyone else first. At work she was taking on far more responsibility than she was required to do and was frequently subjected to abusive treatment.

Charlene was still experiencing back pain and told me one day that she was considering having another operation. I was alerted to the fact that I needed to work more deeply with her to see what was still causing the pain in her body. What other buried emotion was she holding inside, not wanting to face or reveal to me? I was determined she wouldn't agree to another back operation.

Charlene would happily discuss her boss's abusive treatment but always gave the impression that she was unaffected by how she was being treated. She later admitted to using defence mechanisms, including sarcasm and humour, to conceal the pain she felt.

I explored with her the possibility that shame at the treatment she had been subjected to in her early years was making her stay in her job, as the treatment she seemed to be inviting from her boss could only be described as shameful. By staying in an abusive work environment, she was shaming herself. It was a way of life that felt familiar.

Charlene was able to acknowledge the distress, the anger and hurt — the painful feelings she had tried to deny — but she found it very uncomfortable to discuss shame.

I decided to lend her a book that I believe addresses shame very effectively; I thought that once she had read about shame (and the way it is experienced by many), we would be able to discuss how these feelings were affecting her.

The next day I received an email: 'I thought that I would start reading "The Book" when I went to bed and almost immediately as I began to read, my heart started pounding, my head went all funny and my ears started gurgling! Then I found that as I was reading, my eyes were straying so that I wasn't reading what was on the page. This is going to be much harder than I thought!'

The issue of shame was so confronting, Charlene was not even willing to write the actual title of the book in an email to me. She referred to 'The Book'. It was too shameful for her to speak of shame.

I don't think she did ever read the book, but in our sessions she confronted the shame of her life and the treatment she was prepared to accept from her boss.

Once Charlene was able to recognise she was accepting abusive treatment and to see the connection between her pain and her emotional state, rapid progress followed. She bought a house, resigned from her job and took an extended period of leave.

'The turning point for me was leaving the job that had dominated my life for seven years. I remember my counsellor asking me from time to time why I chose to stay when I was treated so badly. It was a toxic environment. You were encouraged to get things wrong so that you could be berated. I realised today that since I quit my toxic job, my back has not been sore *at all*. This is so significant for me.

'As soon as I left, I started to lose weight. It was as though my body had been in survival mode for years, always waiting for the next attack and storing up fat to see me through the next day. Since leaving I have lost twenty kilograms — through thinking. I think about what I eat and whether it will affect me adversely. If it's a treat, I still consider the consequences. At last I am looking after myself.

'Looking back now, it is really strange to think about all the pain I put my body through, and all because I didn't know how else to handle my emotional and mental anguish. Now when I feel pain somewhere in my body, or I get sick — I know *why* it is and I can either address it or ignore it. It's all about knowing and understanding my body and myself.'

Case study: a journey of healing

In Chapter 2, I introduced Alex, who was sexually abused by her uncle at the age of fourteen, and I included her account of her dilemma in deciding to seek counselling and come to her first session. The reason that I have included Alex's story in this chapter is that it was her body, ultimately, that forced her to confront her wounding. Alex is a gymnast who has achieved great success in her field. She trained her body and relied on being able to control it at all times in order to be at the top of her field. She is someone who believed in 'going it alone'. Control became crucial in her life. Over a number of years, beginning with insomnia at the age of eighteen, her body forced her to undertake her healing journey, with a series of physical 'ailments' including, amongst other crises, a breakdown, a torn hamstring and most curious of all, a rare eye condition. It is hard to know whether she would have persisted in her goal had it not been for her body's insistence that she needed to face the truth. Alex gave me her 'journey of healing' and I have reproduced it here, almost word for word, for those who are interested in reading it. The account is detailed and comprehensive; I considered editing her story for the purpose of this book, but concluded there was nothing I could remove.

Alex's story demonstrates a number of important aspects of healing for anyone who has suffered sexual abuse: the temptation for a victim of abuse to avoid confronting the truth, the confusion as to who is the guilty party, the damaging effect of shame that continues to control until the feelings are explored, the length of time needed to gain sufficient strength to continue the journey, and most importantly, the reluctance to be alive, to remain in the world as a result of the abuse. Nearly every client I have worked with, who is a victim of sexual abuse, has suffered in a similar way. Each one has needed to take a break from counselling from time to time in order to allow healing to occur, to process what has been achieved at each step. And each one has felt suicidal at times.

When clients 'disappear' without explanation, I aim to keep in contact with them — a brief email or message — so that they know I am thinking of them and will welcome them back at any time. I know how tempting it is for clients to avoid counselling because they would like nothing more than to put all thoughts of the abuse out of mind. Sessions are often tough. I can think of several clients who found the journey too painful to continue.

What is different about Alex's journey is that it was her body that forced her to keep going, to keep facing the truth. I believe that Alex's story would be of huge benefit to anyone who has been sexually abused. I would like to think it would serve as encouragement to victims to find the help they need.

This is her story: 'I was sexually abused by my uncle when I was fourteen years old. The pain and suffering this caused in my life was almost unimaginable. My journey of healing and self discovery has been long and extremely difficult and still continues today. Although it has been tough, the rewards of choosing to begin and continue this journey have been greater than I could have imagined, let alone hoped for.

'The abuse started in a very subtle way and increased slowly so that I was groomed to believe that I had asked for it, deserved it, enjoyed it and was completely to blame. When the abuse finally stopped, I was left with overwhelming feelings of guilt and shame. I told no one of the abuse but with a deep self-loathing created an image of perfection. I maintained absolute control in my life and portrayed a confident, independent and happy person. I put the abuse completely out of my mind.

'At eighteen I moved away from my home town to go to university and developed severe insomnia. The university counsellor helped me to identify that I was pretending that nothing had happened and that this was contributing to my insomnia. I spent many sessions remembering what had happened between my uncle and myself. Over time I accepted what happened was real and was wrong. At this point I thought I was over the incident and got on with my perfect life.

'I met the love of my life at university and when the relationship got serious I mentioned what had happened when I was fourteen, reassuring him I was fine. We spoke very little about it over the next sixteen years. During this time we married and had two wonderful children. When pregnant with my first child I started to have dreams and flashbacks about what had happened when I was fourteen. Over the next seven years the dreams and flashbacks steadily increased and I thought about the sexual abuse more and more. I was living the perfect life. I was married to my best friend, had two amazing children, was working in a job I loved, competing successfully in one of my passions (gymnastics), was fit and healthy and surrounded by extended family and friends who loved me. To the outside world I am sure I appeared confident and happy and living the perfect life, but the truth was I wanted to be dead.

'My thoughts of wanting to be dead only reinforced the deep-seated feelings of guilt and shame. I started to avoid social situations with family and friends, worked and trained harder than ever and tried to be the perfect mother. It was only a matter of time before I fell apart. Two distinct incidents pushed me to open up and ask for help. First I had a severe panic attack at a shopping centre. It was terrifying. My heart raced, I couldn't breathe and I couldn't feel my body.

'It prompted me to tell my husband what I had been feeling. To be honest, I sugar-coated it a little (I certainly didn't tell him I wanted to be dead). He was wonderfully supportive and suggested I see a counsellor'.

Alex's reluctance to accept she needed counselling was described in Chapter 2. Her story continues with our first session:

'The session started with background information about my parents, my siblings, my husband and children and my work. I calmly and openly answered all her questions. This was not so bad. Then she said something like "Okay, now tell me, why are you here?" I was not prepared for that, lost my composure and blurted out the basics of the abuse and my inability to cope. It is all a bit of a blur to me even now. I talked and cried and walked out exhausted and in a haze, not even sure what I had said.

'After the appointment I managed to hold it together for a few hours until I saw my husband and then it all became very real. I lost it. I cried like I had never cried before. I could not speak and then I just shut down. I was numb. I could not think, I could not concentrate, I did not move or speak or see clearly for a few hours. My husband literally put me into bed. I lay awake most of the night and when I heard the kids in the morning I pretended to be asleep so I did not have to see them. My husband rushed them away so I could "sleep". As he closed the door I started to sob for what felt like hours.

'My husband came back to check on me and without saying a word he climbed into bed and held me until I stopped crying. I have never felt anything like I felt that day. I was numb, detached from my body and the world, anxious and paranoid. I could not follow conversations and I felt like I was moving in slow motion through a thick fog. As terrible as I felt I knew it was an important step and I was hopeful that this counsellor could help me. She asked me to keep a journal and in my first entry a few days later I wrote: "I feel like I have taken one step up Mount Everest and it would be easier to turn back than continue on the very difficult, painful and probably life threatening path that lays ahead". At the time I did not realise how true this was or how grateful I would be for that journey.

'The next few months of counselling were really tough. I was exhausted all the time. Mornings were the worst. The thought of the day ahead was just too much. Simply getting out of bed was hard work, but I had to get up, get the kids ready and off to school and go to work. I cried a lot and slept little. The pain, confusion and the flashbacks consumed me and I found it extremely difficult to function. I could not focus and just could not get everything done. My husband was picking up the slack at home and my friends were at work. It was hard on everyone.

'Healing for me had an ebb and flow quality. At times it was full steam ahead and healing would be a priority and I would work really hard. Then I would back off and let it slip to the background. Sometimes I would go back to old habits and use work, training, life or alcohol to avoid dealing with it. Sometimes I would just take a break and focus on my family and friends. Looking back this created distinct stages in my journey.

'During my first session my counsellor asked me to write down my feelings and any dreams I remembered having. Writing became an extremely powerful healing tool and I learnt how to utilise my dreams as a window to my thoughts and feelings. The first stage of the healing journey for me meant understanding what happened, talking about it, telling people about it and understanding the coping mechanisms I developed as a result of the abuse. Intellectually I also started to see how I did not deserve what happened to me. I was not to blame and should not feel shame or guilt.

'A dream I had gave me an insight into the impact the abuse had on my life: I was driving along happily on a freeway in a white 1980s car. A car came out of nowhere and crashed into me. I lost control and smashed into the wall. The car I was in was wrecked, but the other car was nowhere to be seen.

'I woke up from this dream angry. Anger was not a feeling I had or expressed very often. What was I angry at? It was clear to me that the freeway represented my life path, the white 1980s car me, an innocent girl in the 1980s. I was travelling along enjoying my life until my abuser crashed into my life, pushed me off my path, left me wrecked and then disappeared. This was the first time I felt anger towards my abuser.

'Understanding my fear of anger and how this held me back was an important part of my journey. My counsellor encouraged me to try painting what I had experienced in my early years. I discovered that through painting I could express my feelings, particularly about anger. I do not consider myself artistic and I certainly will never make a living from painting, but it was a safe physical way to express my feelings and thoughts. Unfortunately my anger at this stage was still mostly focused on me as I struggled to let go of the guilt I felt. My counsellor encouraged me to "put the shit where it belonged", but at this time I was unable to. I knew what she meant and was sure this applied to most people, but if she knew the whole truth she would understand that it did not apply to me. During this stage I felt like I was going in circles. I was working hard but thought I was achieving little. After six weeks of counselling I wrote in my journal: "I don't feel like I have achieved anything. I am so scared it will take so very long and I am sick of it already. I have had enough. I am anxious, depressed, tired and sad. Everyone is paying such a high price and it just does not seem worth it. I am not worth it".

'Looking back now I can see that I had achieved a lot since first opening up to my husband. I had accepted that it was sexual abuse, I had told more people about the abuse, had a clearer understanding of the impact the abuse had on my life and understood the coping mechanisms I had developed. But I felt as though I was getting nowhere. The healing process combined with a busy life had worn me down and I started to make excuses as to why I could not get to counselling sessions. I gave up temporarily and took a break. I still talked about what had happened and looking back I can see it was an important time of absorbing what I had learnt. It was a huge relief and for a while I was not consumed by it all. The only problem was that so many people knew about the abuse, but my parents and siblings didn't. I found it impossible to switch from being honest about the abuse one moment and then hiding it the next. I wanted people to know. I was sick of hiding and pretending.

'The second stage of my journey began. I booked another counselling session and began working on understanding how I felt about my parents. This was very difficult. My parents are wonderful people and it was extremely painful to admit that I was furious with them for letting me down, for not protecting me. Writing and painting helped me to let go of the guilt I felt for feeling this anger towards my parents. My counsellor also helped me to investigate how I ended up the target of my abuser and why I was vulnerable. Being free of feeling guilty for being angry at my parents and understanding the family dynamics that allowed the abuse to happen gave me the confidence to tell my parents and some of my siblings. This was a huge achievement and finally I felt like I was getting somewhere. Telling my parents was extremely difficult and did not go exactly to plan, but they believed me and I felt empowered. I felt good and took a break from counselling and spent much needed quality time with my family. I was a long way from healed, but I was no longer miserable all the time but rather I had good days and bad days.

'After a month or so the flashbacks and dreams began to increase. Songs from the eighties were unbearable as they reminded me of my abuser and I began to think I was seeing him everywhere. I was depressed again and desperately wanted it all to stop. I was full of self-loathing and felt no one would understand if they knew the whole truth. Although I had told a lot of people what had happened, I had not told anyone the whole truth. I would lose everything if they knew who I really was.

'I started counselling again and my counsellor kept pushing me to look at why I could not forgive myself and put the shit where it belongs. Eventually I told her the horrible truth, that he was my first love, that I knew it was wrong but went back for more, that I craved the attention and in the beginning I enjoyed his advances. The most shameful truth was that I physically enjoyed his touch. As the abuse got too much it all repulsed me, but that did not stop my body reacting to him. My counsellor was not shocked by what was, in my mind, a huge revelation. She reassured me that I had done nothing wrong. Many sessions were spent discussing this issue and working to accept that it was not my fault.

'Having a trained counsellor understand was one thing, but I still could not believe that everyone I loved and cared about would understand. I needed to tell my husband to know if he could love me after learning the truth. Nine months after I first confided in my husband about the impact the abuse was having on me, I told him my horrible truth. I could not believe his reaction. He did not skip a beat, he was not shocked and he simply said: "I don't care if you threw yourself at him naked, you were a child and he was an adult. He did this to you. It is not your fault."

'I was in shock. He was not disappointed in me and he did not blame me. He understood completely and loved me more than ever. He said he was proud of me and that

I was one of the strongest people he knew. I was ecstatic. I felt like the weight of the world had been lifted from my shoulders. I had one more counselling session as a kind of debrief, I took some time off work and we went on a family holiday.

'It was the happiest I had been in my entire life. I literally could not take the smile off my face. I distinctly remember one day while on holiday thinking I haven't thought about the abuse for days. At the end of this third stage I honestly believed I was home free. The hard work was done and I could get on with life.

'After a month or so I started to feel depressed again. I was finding it hard to sleep and was extremely emotional. I had accepted it was not my fault, had admitted the truth, was not hiding it anymore, but I could not stop thinking about sexual abuse. I was worried for my children. What if something like this happened to them? I would never forgive myself if I failed to protect them. I was desperate to stop child sexual abuse. When I saw children I wondered if they were victims and when I saw adults I wondered if they were perpetrators. I was angry and frustrated one minute, sad and depressed the next.

'Thus began the fourth stage of my journey. I will never forget the trigger that motivated me to go back to counselling. I had started to wish an end to my life, but I was completely unprepared for the sudden impulse to turn my car into a truck. It took all my strength not to end it all and instead to pull off the road. I made the call and went back to counselling. But it was no longer working. I was a mess again and I believed the pain would never end. I honestly thought it was impossible to get over it and just wanted to be dead. I wrote in my journal: "I wanted to crash into a truck again today. I do not want to kill myself. I do not want to do that to the people I love, but I cannot see another way out. I am tired, so very tired. Existing is too hard. I want to leave my body. I just do not want to be. I do not want to exist. But these feelings just make me feel so very guilty. I have so much. I am so pathetic and ungrateful and so self-involved".

'I felt it was hopeless and the counselling was not working so I stopped.

'After I stopped counselling, I thought things were better. My husband kept pulling me aside and asking if I was okay and if I should cut back the drinking. I reassured him I was fine. Friends kept asking if I was okay. "I am fine," I reassured everyone. The truth was I was acting crazy, but at the time I honestly thought I was okay. I was not consumed by the abuse and it felt good. I was drinking a lot, going out a lot, buying heaps of clothes I did not need and acting irrationally. I was angry at my husband for not making me feel good, for not looking after me well enough. I was angry at my counsellor for failing me, for not fixing me. I was over-emotional and behaving in destructive ways.

'The low point came at a staff function. I was excited about the function so I went out shopping to buy a whole new outfit and came home with three. I was as excited as a school girl. I got dressed up and went out without my husband. I drank so much that I remember little of the evening and literally could not stand up straight. I was told the next day that I yelled at a few of my colleagues and threw a drink over one of them. A friend took me outside for fresh air and offered me water. I accused her of putting alcohol in the water and refused to drink it. I started crying uncontrollably, vomited and passed out. I was taken to hospital where I woke up and begged to be taken home before I was admitted. A friend called my husband and took me home. My husband met the taxi in the front yard and helped me out of the car. I told him to leave me alone, accused him of not taking good care of me and told him that I did not want his help now. I lay on the front lawn vomiting, refusing to go inside and yelling that I wanted to be dead.

'The next day I felt terrible and apologised to everyone. I finally admitted I still had a problem and agreed to go back to counselling. My counsellor helped me understand that I was behaving like a fourteen year old. My life had been changed forever at fourteen by my abuser. As a result I felt as though I had skipped adolescence and gone from child to adult. I did not get the chance to grow up. Instead I just pretended to be grown up. My counsellor encouraged me to reconnect with the girl I was at fourteen. What did she need from me now?

'The fifth stage of my journey involved going back and feeling like I was fourteen years old again and growing up emotionally. I realised that the anger I directed at my counsellor was actually about my mother. The anger I directed at my husband was actually about my father. Working through these feelings and growing up emotionally was a slow but very important process.

'I avoided the next stage of my journey. I was starting to grow emotionally and seemed to be on top of things, but I was still confused about what I wanted. I was unsure about where I was headed and why. I no longer believed that one day I would simply get over the abuse and I was unsure what the alternative was. Lost and confused, I got on with life and tried to put it out of my mind.

'Once again my body did not allow me to simply give up. I partially lost sight in my right eye over a period of approximately twenty-four hours. I had tests and scans that revealed that I had swelling on the optical nerve at the brain end. This type of injury was often caused by whiplash in a car accident or a fall, but I had not been involved in any type of accident or fall. The doctors suggested it was probably caused by stress. So I was left with perfect vision in my left eye while everything I saw through my right eye was smaller, duller and blurry. The split vision gave me headaches and made me nauseous. I was unable to work or train. So reluctantly I agreed to take some time off work and address the internal conflict that resulted in a matching visual conflict.

'This was the sixth stage of my journey. I started counselling again, rested, looked after myself and slowly I got stronger and started looking at my journey. I realised that although part of me could see my abuser for who and what he really was, part of me wanted to hang on to the fantasy that I had created when I was fourteen. I believed he loved me and was an innocent man who had made a mistake. This was a very sensitive area for me and my counsellor guided me carefully as I addressed this conflict and began to see clearly through both eyes. Fifteen months after I first opened up to my husband I started to realise that I had come a very long way. I no longer felt fourteen. I had grown up emotionally. I realised that I had to accept that the sexual abuse is a part of my life, that I would never get over it, but it will hurt less and I will feel better. I had to stop fighting and start accepting. I understood that I wanted my parents to see how they had let me down and I wanted an apology from them. I decided I wanted to confront my abuser. I had a new understanding of my journey and new direction. I had finally let myself off the hook. I truly believed it was not my fault. I now knew what I wanted to do, but I was not ready to do it. So true to my pattern I took a break. I enjoyed some family time over summer and then threw myself into work and training again in an effort to avoid the scariest step of all: "putting the shit where it belonged."

'I entered the seventh stage of my journey as a result of three combining forces. First my daughter was due to go on school camp and I was terrified. Second, I saw a very moving piece on TV about a young girl who confronted her abuser. Third, my body once again forced me to stop working and training. This time I had severely torn my calf and was on crutches for three weeks unable to train or work.

'I went back to counselling and discovered that one of the fears holding me back was my feelings about my mother and father. When my daughter arrived home from camp I thought I would be relieved that she was home safe and sound. But I was not relieved; I was completely panicked. I realised I would never know for sure if anything had happened to her or not. My parents didn't know what my uncle was doing to me and I had hated them for it. How could I know for sure? The answer — I couldn't — and this terrified me. I needed to get to a place where I was truly okay with the abuse so that if the very worst ever happened to my kids, I would know they could get through it and be okay.

'The piece I saw on TV was inspirational. A young and obviously still very broken lady confronted her abuser, lay charges and told her story in court. She inspired me to take everything I had learnt on my journey and do what I believed to be right. Speaking up and telling the truth had become very important to me. The best way survivors can stop abusers is by speaking up and that was exactly what I was going to do. The injury gave me the time to do the work to prepare.

'Well, if I thought getting to this place was tough, it only got tougher. I was obsessed with finding my abuser's address and preparing for the confrontation. Counselling was crucial to my preparations and ensuring I had all the tools and information to allow a positive outcome for me. Almost two years after I first began this journey I found my abuser's address. I decided on a plan for the confrontation and finally decided to put the shit where it belonged.

'The eighth stage was one I was never sure I would reach. The thought of confronting my abuser was terrifying and the one-hour trip to his house was excruciating. After much procrastination and lots of support and nudging from my two friends who came with me, I got out of the car, knocked on the door and confronted my abuser. He used all the classic defence mechanisms that my counsellor said he might use. Being prepared for this meant he was unable to distract me or put me off course. First, he pretended he did not know me, then he said nothing happened, then that I had asked for it and enjoyed it, then that he was sorry and that he had suffered too. I said what I needed to and then all of a sudden, I knew I no longer needed or wanted anything from him. I had written a note detailing how I felt in case he was not there or I was unable to speak. I handed it to him, turned my back and walked away. It was one of the most amazing, exhilarating, powerful moments in my life. I will never forget it. In that single moment I saw everything differently. He was a pedophile, he sexually abused me and the blame lies squarely with him. Everything changed and I knew I had done the right thing.

'It has been over two years since I first opened up to my husband and twenty-two years since the sexual abuse. I am now in the ninth stage of my journey. I do not know how many more there will be, but I hope there are many. I am reflecting on the confrontation and on my journey so far and I am grateful. If I was told two years ago that I would be grateful I would have laughed, or cried, or both. I have accepted the sexual abuse as an important part of who I am. I love the person I am now and so I have to love that part of me too. I would never wish it on anyone, but I am grateful for all the ups and downs of my life and the lessons they have taught me. I recently had a dream that helped me reflect on how important it is to embrace every part of who I am.

'The dream begins with me running away from an unknown female. I am not scared, more annoyed. It is like we are playing a game of tag that I do not want to be a part of. First I run away as fast as I can. Initially I can get away from her, but then I get tired, she catches up with me, taps me on the shoulder and smiles calmly. So then I run away again, dodging and twisting in an attempt to get away. At first I can get away from her, but then I get tired, she catches up with me, taps me on the shoulder and smiles calmly. The next time I run up and down different alleyways trying to lose her. I run into a dead end and she catches up with me, taps me on the shoulder and smiles calmly. Then I get smart and decide to hide. I am all alone in my hiding spot for a while, then I turn around and she is right there standing next to me. She taps me on the shoulder and smiles. Next I try to hide in a crowd with the same result as before. Finally I push her to the ground and tell her to stay there. I run away again, but she catches up with me, taps me on the shoulder and smiles calmly. Then I stop running and stop fighting. We walk side-by-side, arm in arm, calm and happy.

'My journey continues. It is a life journey of self-discovery. I have more work to do, but I am doing great. Life is not perfect and neither am I, but I am really present in my life, feeling everything as it happens, not later. I am not scared of making mistakes or being wrong. I am comfortable with the truth about the sexual abuse and being honest about it. I no longer feel shameful or guilty about what happened. I am no longer angry with myself or with my parents. I have stopped punishing myself and have put the shit where it belongs. I am free to live life to the fullest'.

Some months into her counselling, Alex told me of an experience she had had one morning before a session with me: 'I arrived at my son's kindergarten and saw a little bird caught in some wire hanging from the guttering of one of the buildings. I could see the bird was struggling to breathe and I realised that if I did nothing the bird would die. I ran into the kindergarten and asked someone to help me. Grabbing a stool I ran back, climbed onto the stool and freed the little bird. When I put it down on the ground, the bird was momentarily stunned, then it fluffed its wings, gave a little shake and flew into the sky. I felt deeply moved by the experience. It struck me that like the little bird, I needed help to live, and to fly. It was very clear to me. I can't do this alone. I need help.'

Nine months after confronting her uncle, Alex reported him to the police. Members of Alex's family were told about the abuse. One morning she received a call from a close relative: 'Thank you for being so brave. He did the same to me when I was fourteen.' Alex's journey continues.

D.H. Lawrence's poem, quoted at the beginning of the chapter, describes clearly the way clients are able to benefit from an understanding of their wounds 'to the deep emotional self'. He reminds us, also, that these wounds may take a very long time to heal. A number of the clients who chose to explore the pain they had taken in to their body, needed years, decades even, before they were able to free themselves and to contact the source of their wound. In so doing, they were able to care for themselves far better and to change how they felt about themselves as a result.

Chapter 8

Change your addiction

That I might drink, and leave the world unseen,
And with thee fade away into the forest dim.
—John Keats *(Ode to a nightingale)*

My parents met in 1939, just before the Second World War began. My father was in the British army, so he was away for six years apart from the times he came home on leave. They married in 1942. My mother lived through the war on her own for the first four years and for the last two with my older brother, born in 1943. I was born two years later as the war was ending.

Which came first for them, I wonder, alcoholism or the collapse of their marriage? Certainly their relationship was put under enormous strain — four children (in the days before reliable contraception), my mother's deteriorating health, my father leaving the security and order of the army and huge financial worries. This was a time before the psychological impact of war was acknowledged. My father fought at Dunkirk and was clearly traumatised by his experiences. He would never talk to us children about his war experience, but once when we were playing a game involving racist abuse of Germans, my father burst into the room and shouted at us, 'You don't understand anything! We did as terrible things to them as they did to us!' He then stormed out and I remember feeling stunned. Surely my father was on the side of the good? Weren't the Germans our enemy and therefore 'bad'?

It is hard to imagine how any couple could come together again after such a disruption to their relationship and resume a normal domestic life. My father attempted numerous careers, without success, and returned to the Military Academy at Sandhurst to teach maths. As their relationship deteriorated, they both turned to alcohol to numb the pain and blot out the things they couldn't handle about their lives. My parents were very different people, from completely diverse backgrounds. I am not sure that I would have succeeded in working with them in marital therapy! It wouldn't be difficult, however, to understand the wounding of their early years. The most significant blow for both, I am sure, was the death of each of their fathers when they were still young, my mother twenty-one and my father twelve. I now understand a lot more about my mother's insecurity and sadness following her father's death. He died alone, without any of his family, in Canada. He and my grandmother had separated a few years earlier, but this was not discussed with the children and they believed they were living in England for reasons of education.

My mother drank gin and tonic as did so many English middle class, army wives. In the morning she got out of bed later and later during my teenage years. She was never up before we children left for school. We learned to write our own notes for school and forge her signature (luckily an illegible scrawl at best). I remember being sick and deciding to stay home from school on occasion. My mother would find out when she emerged from her bed, midmorning, but it was never a cause for concern because our education was not of great interest to her. Generally around ten-thirty she would reluctantly face the day, and straight away she needed a gin. I'm sure that staying in bed was a way of putting off that first drink and besides, there wasn't much to get up for. Quite apart from the effect on her mood, the cost of gin, which for some years amounted to a bottle a day, was crippling. I remember my father showing me, in despair, some figures on a sheet of paper. My mother's gin and cigarettes amounted to more than his salary.

My father drank too, but he made his own potato wine, always referred to as his 'brew'. Once a month the entire house would reek with the smell of it — potatoes, raisins, yeast and sugar, fermenting in a huge green plastic tub. As children it was fun to help him, using the primitive gadgets he found in second-hand shops, to slice the potatoes, mince the raisins and mix the sugar and yeast by hand till it became a sticky, slimy mess. He was proud of the fact that it cost one shilling a bottle (about twenty cents at that time), the only problem being that it was a highly potent concoction and a few unsuspecting visitors, who politely agreed to sample his brew, had been known to pass out after one glass.

There were times when my father would throw himself into a terrible rage, particularly Sunday lunch which usually took place around two o'clock when he and my mother returned from the pub. He would explode about things like modern sliced bread and the poor quality of sausages. On one occasion he threw his soup across the room because he objected to the bowl it had been served in. Thinking about it, his behaviour was not unlike a two year old's tantrums. John Cleese as Basil Fawlty comes to mind! It seems comical now. As a small child it was terrifying. What is clear now, of course, is that my father was behaving in this way because he was drunk. But in spite of his frightening behaviour on occasion, I felt sorry for my father. I suspect he was very lonely during those years.

When I was little I didn't question my parents' drinking. I remember we children were made to dig a large pit at the bottom of our garden to bury the huge number of gin bottles because my mother felt too ashamed to put them out with the garbage. It seemed like fun at the time. We four children formed an alliance over our parents' drinking in our teenage years. Rather than admit how their erratic emotional state upset us, we would dissolve into fits of laughter and mockery at their disordered behaviour. Decades later we would speak about those years honestly with one another. Only as I became more aware in my high school years did it dawn on me that my friends' parents didn't behave like mine. For a start, they didn't take to their beds each afternoon on weekends as mine did and they didn't drink with such determination.

I had started to notice the pattern of my mother's drinking and the effect it had on her moods. I dreaded friends coming to the house and remember feeling acutely embarrassed, particularly the times I was sent to the pub to buy a bottle of gin 'on the slate' (i.e. on credit). Who knows how long it took my mother to clear the slate? One such occasion is still a vivid memory, presumably because my emotions were so acute at the time: 'It's late in the evening and my mother is in a highly anxious state. She bribes me with a bar of chocolate, a rare treat in our family, if I will go to the pub. I hear the dreaded words: "put it on the slate". I cannot refuse. I know this after-dark errand to the pub is my fault because, earlier in the day, I poured some of her gin down the sink in the foolish hope that she would drink less. I can still recall setting off — the blackness of the night, the huge fat moon sitting above the outline of the trees, and the bitter cold. I have to walk down our long drive in total darkness and I am terrified that someone is going to jump out of the bushes and grab me. When I reach the road it feels safer. At least the streetlights will enable me to see my attacker. If it weren't for the daunting task ahead of me, walking down the hill to the pub would have been exhilarating. As it is, a feeling of dread accompanies me. I'm not even sure it's worth a bar of chocolate any more.

'It takes all my courage to go into the pub, knowing that I will be a curiosity. Not many thirteen year old girls are seen in pubs, particularly at this late hour. And of course it is illegal to buy alcohol under the age of eighteen. As I walk inside, there is a lot of noise and chatter and I recognise the faces of many of the locals, all male. The room goes very quiet as I go up to the bar and ask for a bottle of gin, and I become aware that some of the regulars are talking about me in low tones. I hear my mother's name mentioned. I suspect they are mocking her. We live in one of the big houses in a small village and everyone knows who I am. When Ben, the publican, hands me the bottle wrapped in a paper bag, I try to say as quietly as possible, in a matter-of-fact tone: "Please could you put it on the slate." The room is silent as the men wait to see what will happen next. A sign above the bar reads: 'A refusal often offends, so please don't ask for credit'. Ben hesitates for a split second, then he looks at me, irritation softened with pity, and with a tiny smile he nods his head. I can still remember the delicious taste of the bar of chocolate on the way home, my mission accomplished, and singing a song I had learnt at school as I walked up the hill, clutching the bottle of gin:

"Soft the moon o'er field and wood, steals by brook and tree, soothes my brow and calms my blood, sets my spirit free."'

Five decades later, as I set about writing this chapter, I heard the song, a Schubert lieder, on the radio. It's called *To the moon*.

My mother's alcoholism made her inaccessible for me. I got to know the pattern intimately: one double gin, she would mellow as her anxiety reduced and she might show me a little kindness; a second gin, apathy descended on her, she lost interest in everyone and everything, and after the third, hostility, bitterness, you knew to keep out of her way. This was her pattern, twice a day, every day, for probably fifteen years. At the time I didn't realise she was an alcoholic. I felt many things towards her as a result of her addiction, mainly anger and contempt but also pity. The way her mood changed with each drink was beautifully illustrated for us on the German drink coasters we used each day at mealtimes, I now realise, but at the time I was oblivious of the fact. There were six coasters, depicting a man going through the stages of inebriation: Morose, Verbose, Jocose, Bellicose, Lacrimose and Comatose. Sometimes, my mother bypassed Verbose and Jocose. Throughout all those years, I remember thinking of a bottle of gin as my enemy. It was like another person in our relationship, her companion, keeping my mother at a distance.

Rehab? Not for me!

In her forties my mother went into a rehabilitation unit in a public hospital in London to be dried out. For her courage and humility in attempting to free herself of alcohol addiction, I still feel great admiration. That she didn't succeed in staying away from alcohol when she came home is understandable. Her life was empty, her marriage over, her children had all moved away and she had nothing with which to replace alcohol. In spite of an excellent brain, she couldn't hold down a fulfilling job. She needed to be able to drink at lunchtime. Besides, she told me she thought all non-drinkers were boring. What hope did she have?

The last time I saw her before she died, she was in hospital. She wasn't drinking any longer because she was too ill. If only *this* woman could have been my mother growing up. I could relate to her easily. During that visit, when we talked honestly with one another possibly for the first time, she told me of a memory from her youth: She came home late one evening to find her mother, who never accepted a drink in public, staggering in the living room. My mother, incredulous, asked: 'Mummy, are you drunk?' whereupon her father shouted at her to go to her room.

On the last day of my visit, before returning to Australia from England, I was worried as to how I could say goodbye to her for what was obviously going to be the last time. How does one say a final goodbye to a parent? A nurse I had got to know well during my time at the hospital told me it was important to say goodbye and not to avoid it because I would regret it later. She was right. I decided to take some of my mother's favourite things in to the hospital — hand cream and expensive soap and a framed photo of her children and grandchildren — plus a bottle of French champagne in celebration of the time we had spent together, assuming that we could share half a glass when my brother came to collect me to take me to the airport. My mother's eyes lit up when she saw the champagne, and she insisted I open it straight away. By the time my brother arrived, the bottle was almost empty and my mother and I were in a relaxed and happy state, our last goodbye made so much easier by the champagne. It was the one time in my life I thanked God for alcohol!

In my late twenties I began to drink heavily, but the memory of the damage it had done to my mother's health and to her relationships with everyone in her life, particularly her children, was enough to frighten me. Recovering from an operation in hospital in my early thirties, I had time to contemplate my life. I was divorced, drinking too much alcohol, smoking too many cigarettes and my health was beginning to suffer. I could see clearly that this was my mother's path. I knew I had to find another for myself. I am now one of the fortunate few who can enjoy a glass or two of alcohol and not look for more.

Drinking alcohol in moderation is such an enjoyable and acceptable way of socialising with others. It is only when it begins to destroy a person's health, functioning at work, family life and relationships that it becomes a problem. Not surprisingly many of my clients have abused alcohol and/or drugs at certain times. It is hard to avoid if your friends are heavy users and nearly all social gatherings involve alcohol and drugs. Drinkers want you to drink along with them.

At times I am surprised at what intelligent, outwardly successful clients tell me about their escapades with alcohol and drugs at parties and raves. Sometimes, just hearing themselves telling me is enough to make them aware of what they are doing to themselves. A close friend of one of my clients fell down the stairs, drunk, at a nightclub. She spent several weeks in intensive care. It was a powerful warning to her friends and colleagues.

I have worked with many people who have an addiction — alcohol, drugs, gambling, sex or shopping. One client confessed to owning 300 pairs of shoes. Acknowledging an addiction is a very big step. Addicts are often in denial. They are able to convince themselves that no one knows of their problem, that family and friends are unaware of their secret habit. My mother's decision to go into rehabilitation resulted from her overhearing some friends discussing her drinking when she was out of the room. She was shocked as she was convinced that no one realised, that we older children might have had a suspicion but that everyone else was fooled. The truth, I discovered later in life, was that most people we knew were aware my mother had a drinking problem.

A number of my clients grew up with alcoholic fathers and sometimes mothers. Others lived with parents who used drugs regularly and not surprisingly many follow in their parents' footsteps. You have in front of you the example of what to do when life gets too hard and if you behave like a parent, you feel closer to them.

Research suggests that many people have a genetic predisposition to alcohol addiction. When I was a student Ray Hawkes introduced me to the idea that clients engage in addictive behaviour as a matter of choice and that the addictive behaviour is directed towards the achievement of some end (Hawkes, 1998). In a recent interview Gene Heyman put the same point of view, arguing that 'addiction is not a disease. It has the highest remission rates of any psychiatric disorder and it is the disorder that is most susceptible to the factors that influence our decisions' (Sheean, 2011). In contrast, the National Institute on Drug Abuse states on its website that drug abuse and addiction is 'a chronic relapsing brain disease expressed in the form of compulsive behaviours'.

In my work what I usually see most clearly is what lies underneath the need to drink heavily and/or use drugs, and why each individual opts for a particular addiction. I find that as clients address those painful events in their lives they often lose the compulsion for their addiction. The need just disappears. Over the years I have learnt how important it is to allow the client to decide when the time is right for them to address their addiction and to change, however tempting it might be for me to try and speed up the process.

Giving up smoking

I started smoking cigarettes when I was fifteen. After her first drink of the day, feeling a little relaxed, my mother would look to me for company, welcoming an ally in her vices. She would offer me a cigarette, a glass of wine. When I arrived at the hospital to say goodbye to my mother for the last time, I was in my thirties and still a smoker. On leaving the hospital, a few hours later, I had lost all desire to smoke. Had I smoked for twenty years to feel closer to my mother? Had I freed myself by telling her honestly how miserable I felt in my teenage years? I only know that I never wanted a cigarette from the moment I walked out of the hospital.

Both my parents smoked heavily. (You only have to watch old movie classics to be reminded that it was considered sophisticated at that time. Everyone smoked). As mentioned earlier, my parents were very different people and the way they gave up cigarettes illustrates this clearly. My father suffered a heart attack in his forties and gave up smoking instantly. My mother also suffered a heart attack in her forties but continued to smoke. She tried, unsuccessfully, to give up periodically. I recall a fake plastic cigarette she would suck on from time to time, but it would irritate her so much she would replace it with the real thing. At one stage she tried hypnotherapy and would travel to London by bus once a week to 'see my quack.' The hypnotherapist had given her a large photograph of himself to take home. In the photo, his eyes were protruding, I remember. She was told to gaze into his eyes before beginning her 'therapy', which involved listening to a gramophone record of the therapist urging her to: 'relax, relax, you are drifting off ...' I remember seeing her lying on her bed one day, listening to the record dutifully but smoking a cigarette as she did so. Eventually she stopped going to see the hypnotherapist. She told me he had asked her not to come any more as he was worried he might take up smoking. I think she was disappointed; it was probably the only therapy she ever experienced. One of the last letters I received from her announced: 'The big C has got me — I knew it would'. Her diagnosis, throat cancer, came at the age of 64.

Whatever form an addiction takes, the underlying need is usually the same: to boost self-confidence in a social setting, to feel a sense of belonging and/or to numb the emotional pain of earlier, often unacknowledged, experiences. The disowned parts of us are often hidden in the addiction.

It is tragic to observe clients trapped in an addiction and crippled with guilt, lashing themselves because the worse they feel, the more they need to escape into whatever it is that dulls the pain. What many don't know is that alcohol is a depressant. When the effects wear off, depression can set in and the only solution seems to be more alcohol (the famous 'hair of the dog'). Several young women I have worked with found themselves in risky situations as a result of getting drunk when out with friends. One woke up in the apartment of a man she couldn't remember meeting, another found herself stranded in the early hours of the morning, having lost her wallet and car keys and a third woke up in hospital, with no memory of how she came to be there. A young man came to a few counselling sessions to address his alcohol problem when his partner ended the relationship, but he repeatedly cancelled appointments. I assume he was not ready to address his drinking problem. At times clients will have great difficulty freeing themselves from an addiction because their partner wants to continue and the relationship works best when both people are involved in the addiction.

Relapse — 'will I / won't I?'

It is common for people to relapse, even when committed to freeing themselves of the addiction. I worked with a man for some time who was addicted to heroin for a number of years. For several months, he succeeded in abandoning heroin but then found he was thinking about using heroin again. I had spoken to him previously about taking time to consider his actions, if he were tempted. What would be the gain for him? And the loss? An opportunity presented itself when his wife was away on business. He contacted his dealer, bought the heroin, prepared 'the gear'. Then he contemplated what he planned to do. For half an hour he sat and looked at the drugs, the needle. Then he reached his decision and threw it all in the bin. He was proud of his will power that day and didn't touch heroin again.

When I reflect on the clients who have left counselling before being able to bring about the change they were hoping for, the majority are those with an alcohol or drug addiction. It requires enormous dedication to free oneself.

Why is change so hard?

One of the difficulties faced by people who are trying to change their life is the notion that they have to 'give up' the addictive behaviour, whatever form it takes. If a client's life is painful and bleak, giving up the one thing that eases pain means he is placed under extreme pressure. Where an individual is able to replace the addiction with something positive, whether it be an activity, a good relationship, a new interest or merely a commitment to a healthy lifestyle, he will stand a far better chance of freeing himself from the addiction. Sometimes it is also a matter of timing. What is acceptable, normal even, in one's teens and early twenties is inappropriate once an individual decides to settle down and have children. A client, about to turn thirty told me: 'I don't even like myself when I'm drunk any more. I can't listen to myself or learn anything about life when I drink too much. I'm sick of living like this.'

Case study — remorse, the morning after

Annie (whose father abused her sister — see Chapter 2) began drinking in her teens:

'I was brought up in a small country town and alcohol was a big problem. Boredom and alcohol just seemed to go hand and hand. From the age of sixteen I would go out drinking, having a 'big night' with my friends. In saying that, I was enjoying myself. It wasn't until later on in my life that I realised the drinking wasn't doing me any favours. I would drink far too much and end up saying things to friends and to people I didn't know, things I didn't even mean. I would wake up the following day and often I couldn't remember what I had said or done. Then I would have to apologise. The day after one of these nights was always very, very bad. It wasn't often that I would upset my friends, but it did happen occasionally, and that would upset me terribly. I would beat myself up for ages. If I were dating a guy, I would become paranoid that he was doing something wrong when in fact he wasn't. For many years alcohol ruined my relationships.

'I remember going through a stage where I would become emotional, when I was drinking, about what Dad had done to Rhiannon. I hated having to tell a guy I was dating that my father abused my sister.

'Nowadays, when I have a massive night out, I wake up next morning and I try to go over the night with a fine tooth comb to ensure I haven't upset anyone. I feel I have grown up in the past year as a result of addressing my drinking in counselling sessions. I definitely drink much less than I used to. For me, having a few drinks with friends is like a release after a week of work. I can't wait for the weekend to come around, so that I can catch up with friends, particularly as I live on my own. But I know I am lucky to have very supportive friends who look out for me when we are out.'

A rare badge of honour

A client with his own successful business admitted to spending more than $60,000 a year on cocaine. It was clear in counselling sessions that he felt ambivalent about abandoning his drug use. While he felt uncomfortable at the way his work, health and relationships were governed by his addiction, he believed that he was far more creative when using cocaine and couldn't imagine a life that did not include drugs. When I asked him to tell me what he thought he might be like, if he didn't use drugs, he replied: 'I'd be normal, average, boring, invisible.' He added that it was a 'badge of honour' that he could consume vast quantities of alcohol and drugs and still be highly successful in his work. Not surprisingly, he didn't continue in counselling. Clearly, at that stage of his life, he was not ready to choose a different lifestyle. He was already in his forties.

Case study: a lesson from a client

One of my first clients was a heroin user who had come to see me with his wife for marriage counselling. At the time Jerry was also seeing a drug counsellor, a fact which I found reassuring since I didn't think I knew enough about heroin addiction. A few months later, Jerry told me that he wasn't seeing the drug counsellor any longer. Alarmed, I asked why. He replied: 'Because the drug counsellor always focussed on heroin and every time I left after my appointment, I would catch the train to Footscray and score.

'You don't ask me about heroin. When I am here I talk about other aspects of my life, the things that went wrong for me when I was growing up and why I feel I need heroin.'

Jerry's parents had divorced when he was eighteen and were then forced to sell the house he had grown up in. He was devastated at the loss of his home and family. Jerry felt that both his parents forgot about him: 'I was like a souvenir from their marriage, something you put in a drawer and forget about.'

Two years after his parents separated, Jerry attempted suicide. In hospital, when his parents came to see him, he wondered: 'Did I have to go to these lengths just to get them both here?'

I have always felt grateful to Jerry for teaching me a sound lesson when I first started as a counsellor. He confirmed for me that, as with any presenting issue, the focus in counselling is about what hasn't worked for a client in terms of their relationships and sense of self. By the time he finished counselling Jerry was no longer using heroin. I sincerely hope that is still the case.

Case study: Nicola and her 'bitch friend'

It was the start of her second counselling session. Nicola looked anxious, uncomfortable, and close to tears. She said that the first counselling session had been extremely positive and was exactly what she needed. She was, however, afraid that I would be shocked when I heard what she had to tell me: that she had been an alcoholic for many years. I replied that I considered myself to be fairly unshockable, particularly where alcohol was concerned, because both my parents were alcoholics and I had been fortunate to have escaped. Nicola was clearly surprised and relieved at my reply.

There is much debate about counsellors' self-disclosure and many believe that the client should know nothing, or at most very little, about their counsellor. I find it difficult to maintain that role when I feel that disclosing something about myself will benefit my client. Nicola fully expected this would be her last session because she felt ashamed of her addiction. Once she knew that I was familiar with her problem, that alcohol had defined my childhood, we were able to work together.

Nicola felt very sad when she started in counselling: 'I

was living very internally at that time, an incredibly insular life. I was so miserable that I didn't feel comfortable unless I was under the influence of something or other, and then a few hours later I would feel desperately guilty and desperately unhappy. I was living a roller-coaster life.'

Nicola had hoped that when she had a child, things would be different and her life would fall into place, but she found it was too hard to avoid alcohol. She was consumed with guilt and felt she needed to keep away from her one year old son when she was drinking. Nicola was in a good relationship and when she began counselling it was for her child's sake that she wanted to change. Later, Nicola would begin to feel she deserved to enjoy life for herself as well as for her family.

When Nicola was young, the family lived in Melbourne. On a whim her father decided to move to New South Wales when Nicola was twelve, to pursue his passion for water sports. Nicola was at an impressionable age and the change of schools was difficult. She felt that she didn't fit in at her new school and found it hard to make friends, always feeling like an outsider. Nicola's mother was desperately unhappy as a result of the move. She had started drinking alcohol prior to the family moving and this escalated following the move to New South Wales.

Nicola was the youngest of four children, two boys and two girls. She still recalls a day when she was around 22: 'I was shocked to find a change of name certificate under the paper lining of the wardrobe in my childhood bedroom. I showed Mum and she told me reluctantly that she had been married before and that my eldest brother and sister were children from her previous marriage. Mum and Dad had decided to keep it from us so that we wouldn't feel any different from one another. Dad would be father to all four of us. The two older ones were told just before we moved to New South Wales. Mum and Dad decided not to tell my brother and me, one reason being that they didn't think I would cope, that it would cause problems for me and in turn for the others.

The four children were treated differently by their father (biological father of Nicola and her brother Anthony). Anthony and his father were inseparable when he was growing up and it was obvious to everyone that he was his father's favourite. Nicola commented that while there were large photos of her father and brother all over the house, the only photograph of her was the ultrasound of her son, in her uterus, on the fridge. As a small child, Nicola idolised her brother and father and was desperate to be included in the things they did together, but even though she became a tomboy, she was excluded and felt it deeply.

When Nicola was 8 she saw her mother take a bottle of vermouth out of the cupboard (strangely the cupboard in which she had found the change of name certificate) and drink from the bottle. It was late at night and Nicola's mother thought she was asleep. Her mother attempted to conceal her drinking, but Nicola's father became aware of it. He would involve the children in his criticism of his wife's drinking and encourage them to take his side against her. He would embarrass his wife in front of the children, and told Nicola, when she was fifteen, that it was her job to count the bottles every day and check up on her mother. At the time it felt to Nicola that she had been given an important job to do.

On one occasion he involved Nicola in confronting his wife, accusing her of being an alcoholic and threatening to leave her and take the children. Her mother, terrified that he would carry out his threat, gave up drinking. Nicola, just fifteen at the time, stepped into her mother's shoes and started drinking in earnest. By the age of sixteen she was drinking heavily and had continued to do so for twenty years. She also used marijuana when it was available.

When I explored what purpose alcohol served for Nicola at this time, she replied: 'It numbs me, so that everything doesn't hurt so much or panic me so much.' We looked at what lay underneath, what feelings were buried which Nicola needed to numb. I asked her how she would describe her addiction. What part did it play in her life? She replied: 'I would describe it as my "bitch friend".'

Nicola was fortunate in being close to her mother who was immensely supportive and she began the hard work needed to understand her complex relationship with her father. He was a strong, self-disciplined man, enthusiastic about life and his family. He was also opinionated and judgemental and capable of hurting Nicola by his tactless comments and personal attacks. When she was growing up he would say to Nicola that she was just like him. In her early teens she tried hard to be 'a little Dad'. Underneath the tough exterior, Nicola's father was a wounded man. His mother died when he was only seven. His father remarried quite quickly, but his new wife would not accept Nicola's father, who was sent to live with his grandfather.

Drinking alcohol brought Nicola closer to her mother, 'a little Mum' instead of 'a little Dad'. She felt enormous admiration for her mother who had had a difficult life. Her first marriage had been to a man who abused drugs and alcohol, father to the two older children.

Nicola was in a vulnerable and weakened state when she came to counselling, suffering from anxiety and panic attacks. She was critical of herself as a result of her addiction. But she was also blessed with a strong will. She set about freeing herself from alcohol and marijuana. The desire to be a good mother was a strong incentive.

The main focus for Nicola in counselling was to separate from being a child to her parents, whereby she was aiming to model herself on either her father or her mother. She began to appreciate her personal strengths and to value herself.

When I contacted Nicola some five years after counselling to discuss her story, I was quite prepared to hear that she was drinking alcohol or using marijuana, as it is common for people to relapse. It was heartening to hear that she had recently given birth to her second child and was no longer drinking or using marijuana. Three months earlier she had also given up smoking cigarettes. A trifecta! She described herself as one of my major success stories, adding: 'I do feel it is something pretty major that I have achieved.' She brought some photographs of her children with her and told me: 'They are my world. They are my life. They are my reason for changing!'

Nicola also told me that her marriage is stronger than ever and throughout all the years her husband has been 'a wonderful partner, friend and support to me and my family.'

Case study: food as protection and comfort

Lily initially came to see me with her ex-partner, many years ago. She was eighteen at the time, and he nearly twice her age. While they grew as individuals, the relationship didn't last. Following the break-up, Lily came to counselling sessions intermittently. When one reads her story, it isn't hard to understand why she would be reluctant to address the pain of her early life. As mentioned earlier, for the purpose of this book, I invited ex-clients to contribute their story, in their own words. What transpired, as a result of writing her story, was that Lily was able to face the trauma of her early years, to find the will to commit to counselling and address the hurt of her childhood. If it weren't for this book, Lily might never have done so. Hers is possibly one of the saddest stories I have heard. I was not aware of the extent of her suffering, when I first knew her. It seems that Lily's only companion along the way was food.

In Lily's words: 'The first time I was criticised about my weight was when I was around seven years old, by my great aunt. "Geez Lily, you're getting chubby," was what she said. I remember feeling hurt and my face flushed with embarrassment.

'Every now and then I was called 'fatty' by my brother and sister, and by my peers in primary school. Looking back, I suppose I believed what they said and I started filling myself with food. The sad thing is, when I see photos of myself around that time, I was a completely normal young girl — not fat, not skinny, just normal. Writing this sentence has brought tears to my eyes, all these years later.

'Growing up, I was heavily beaten by my mother. My parents had a terrible relationship and I suppose my mother took it out on us children. I remember some nights being woken up by her throwing our toys around because we hadn't cleaned up properly or for some other trivial reason. At these times she was like an angry beast. I was always scared of my mother and tried to be the mediator in the family, keeping things happy so no one would be upset. I didn't allow myself to acknowledge just how upset I was. As the oldest in the family, I felt responsible for my younger brother and sister.

'I don't remember Dad being there much when I was

growing up, but I do remember feeling safe whenever he came home because Mum was a little more controlled when he was around. Mum never had any motivation to do anything. She would sleep all day and stay up all night.'

For Lily and her siblings, life became even more painful as her mother's mental state deteriorated. Much of Lily's early life is a blur. I would imagine she doesn't want to remember those times too clearly. At one stage, when Lily was about ten, her mother left all three children with their father and grandparents and went to America. She stayed away for six months. During this time her father formed another relationship and moved out. It was the end of family life, as the children knew it.

'When she came back from America, she was very different. She didn't seem to take anything too seriously and she had started smoking marijuana. I first knew about it when I found a bong in her cupboard and confronted her. I didn't know exactly what it was, but I knew it was bad.

'Not long after this, we moved out with my grandparents into a small two-bedroom unit and it was then that Mum went off the rails. She was out partying until all hours and was heavily involved in drugs. We had many arguments when she was 'coming down'. She would say terrible things to me and blame me for things I had no idea about and didn't even understand.

'One Sunday, when I was about twelve years old, my grandparents told me that Mum was in trouble and they had organised a friend of theirs who drove a taxi to take me to Sydney (from Canberra) to collect her. I couldn't understand what was going on and I remember feeling very scared. My grandparents handed over $500 cash and put me in the car. We set off, me and a man I didn't know. When we finally managed to find Mum in Sydney, she was in a paranoid state and was insistent that people were following her, trying to kill her.

'Later that year, Mum was admitted to a psychiatric ward on an involuntary order by the police. My grandparents rushed to take us to see her. Only one person was allowed in to see her at a time, so I went in alone. Thinking of this memory scares me to the core. I remember looking at her thinking she was possessed by the devil. Her eyes were red with dark bags under them, her skin deathly pale. At first she accused me of having set her up so as to have her confined in a psychiatric ward. When I calmed her, she told me what I had to do and who to contact to get her out. It was the most terrifying experience. From what I can remember, she was there for several more days.

'Throughout all these years, I kept eating. I always had a sweet tooth. Maybe that was to compensate for the bitterness of my life. From the age of ten onwards, I was often sick. I can see now I was like a hypochondriac, constantly willing myself to be sick so as to get my Dad's attention. Most of my teen years were filled with thoughts of suicide, but I never felt I could go through with it because I cared too much for my family and didn't want to hurt them.

'It was at this time in my life that my relationship with my father was at its worst. All I wanted was his love and affection. I became ill with glandular fever and was bedridden for four weeks. One night my glands were so swollen that I was having difficulty breathing. Mum called Dad to take me to hospital, but he didn't come. An ambulance came instead.'

For the next few years, life with Lily's mother became even more chaotic. The family moved numerous times, sometimes staying in motels and boarding houses. Lily missed more than two years of schooling. The authorities seemed not to notice. Finally they settled in a house in Queensland and Lily was enrolled in year 11. She loved the routine and stability of school. Her mother, however, was unable to free herself of her drug addiction and lived a disordered life, the children coping as best they could. Lily's relationship with her mother became increasingly conflicted and they fought on a daily basis. No one was caring for Lily, apart from her elderly grandparents, and she still felt responsible for the entire family.

When Lily was nineteen, she awoke from a bad dream, feeling something was wrong inside her head: 'I decided to see a doctor and get a CT scan. I was told that they had found a small tumour in the third ventricle in my brain. It was called a colloid cyst and is very rare. Not much is known about them. It was benign but could cause sudden death from blocking the spinal fluid to my brain.

'I was eventually put onto one of Australia's top neurosurgeons, a pioneer in non-invasive surgery, one of the world's leading specialists in tumours in children. I spent a year on the waiting list, which was a really difficult time. I felt very frightened.

'At some point that year, I contacted my father to let him know about the tumour. His wife managed to convince him that I was making it up to get money out of him. I can't begin to explain how crushing it was that my own father let me down at a time like that. One day I showed him my CT and MRI scans to prove that I was telling the truth. He asked me: "How do I know that's actually a tumour?"

'I was eventually called to Sydney for surgery and it was a very tense period.

'Deep down in my heart, I feel there was a part of me that wanted to die. Selfishly, it was more to hurt my father in the hope that he would realise how he had hurt me. But everything went well and three days later I was released from hospital.

'By the time I was twenty and in a relationship, I was huge. I knew I had only myself to blame, but I couldn't stop eating. I suppose I didn't care really. I was ashamed of who I was, ashamed of my past. I just hated myself. I felt that everything in my life had been hard.

'It took me a long while to find the strength to face the pain and fear of my early years through counselling and to understand my relationship with food. In some ways, eating was my only comfort growing up.'

What I have included is only a part of Lily's story. Through having counselling, Lily learnt to value and care for herself. It is to her credit that she has managed to avoid drugs and alcohol for many years. She is learning to care for her body and she is now a normal weight. She has also preserved her personality, in spite of the terror and pain of her childhood. Currently Lily is spending six months in Europe. She feels happy for the first time in her memory.

Case study: the anonymity of a gambler

When we first met, Shirley had lost her direction in life and was filled with despair. She was isolating herself from family and friends. (Shirley's dreams were explored in Chapter 6.)

If families have a motto for the way life should be lived, Shirley's family's would be 'Just get on with it'. Getting on with anything became a challenge. Getting through each day was a hard task. Sensitive and emotional from her earliest years, Shirley felt bruised by some of the family, in particular her mother, who judged her for her failings and appeared incapable of understanding her. In her mid thirties when she came to see me, she was at a low point in her life.

Shirley described her family as 'a typical 1950s family with large chunks missing, in particular love and emotion.' At home everyone had their roles. The children knew what was required of them in terms of behaviour, 'and you were yelled at or hit if you didn't do what was expected of you.'

Shirley was an intelligent, well-educated young woman with strong ideals and a kind and warm nature. For a number of years in Australia she had been working in the finance industry and was realising that, while she was good at her job, it didn't offer her the sense of fulfilment she wanted from a career.

After moving to East Timor, enjoying her freedom and fulfilled as a teacher of the native children, she was feeling happier than she had in a long time, free to be herself, to be accepted and valued for who she was without judgement and to be away for a period of time from the normal stresses of work, family and peers. But tragically Shirley was raped by a man she knew, a man she believed she could trust. As someone who prided herself on being a good judge of character, she was devastated by the betrayal. She thought he was someone she could rely on. Following the rape she lost her trust in everyone, including herself: 'He took everything from me. I'd always trusted people, had faith that people did the right thing. I thought I could read people. I tried to stop him. He stripped away a part of me. He struck at the heart of who I am as a person ... or who I was.' The rape destroyed her happiness and her enjoyment of life.

Soon afterwards, Shirley married an Indonesian, someone she knew as a good friend. She was aware, deep down, that her hasty decision to marry was a reaction to being raped. She wanted to feel secure and cared for. Not surprisingly the marriage was problematic, largely due to language and cultural differences. After eighteen months, even though they remained close friends, Shirley returned to Australia alone.

Shirley had always assumed she would marry and have a family. Of the three siblings, she was the one expected to settle down early in life. Part of her sadness stemmed from the fact that marriage and children now seemed a remote possibility.

Within a couple of years, feeling lonely and unable to heal her wounds, Shirley began to gamble. As she allowed herself to sink further into the darkness of her addiction, she became her own harshest critic and attacked herself mercilessly for gambling and for not getting on with her life.

In our sessions I asked Shirley why she had chosen gambling and whether there was any gain for her in her addiction. She told me that she could enjoy a feeling of companionship and connection with other gamblers without having to socialise or account for herself. There was certainly no risk of her being judged by her gambling companions. We discussed the possibility that her addiction also served to keep her isolated. Was this in part a choice for her at the time? Was gambling also a means of distracting herself from the rawness of her life?

Shirley felt that she had repeated the sense of being trapped which she experienced in her childhood as a result of her mother's judgement: 'I feel lost, struggling for a sense of who I am, where I am going, what I can offer … a sense of urgency … time is running out.'

As she struggled to find the way forward and to discover a way of valuing herself, support came suddenly and unexpectedly, from the dream world. A few months after beginning counselling, Shirley had a number of vivid dreams about three sea creatures. Her soul animals, a turtle, an albatross and a seal became Shirley's 'guardians and protectors' and helped her to find her way out of the darkness. Shirley's dreams are addressed in detail in Chapter 6: *Trust your dreams.*

She began to feel happier, to enjoy pottering at home and in her garden, to smile and laugh again. She told me one day that she was tired of gambling and didn't want to be a gambler any longer. I asked Shirley if she had experienced any positive role models in her life. It brought to mind her grandfather, who had died when she was very young. Shirley described him as 'solitary, independent, someone who did his own thing, and he was always laughing.' She remembered with sadness the day of her grandfather's funeral. She was not allowed into the church, because she was upset and crying. She was made to remain outside. Shirley recalled staying with her grandfather on the farm as a small child, being up early in the mornings on her own with him, 'whooping around and laughing.'

Shirley was surprised at how potent the sense of her grandfather was and how reclaiming the memory of her time with him strengthened her. She was able to reconnect with a happier Shirley, because her grandfather had loved and accepted her for who she was. The knowledge that he saw her, that he felt no judgement towards her, was significant. Following this discovery, Shirley visited her grandfather's grave in the country. Years later, he was still a source of strength and love.

To be appreciated by someone, to know we are acceptable and lovable just as we are, offers us the opportunity to value our true self.

When I contacted Shirley several years after counselling, I was pleased to hear that she was close to completing a teaching qualification. Her guardians and protectors were still important in her life. After we made contact she began writing poetry, with her soul animals as inspiration.

The clients discussed in this chapter were able to commit to the counselling process. Over time they succeeded in improving their self-esteem and also clarifying positive, healthier goals for themselves. They were then able to exercise a degree of choice and to opt for a way of life in which their addictive behaviour no longer had a place.

Chapter 9

Join the living and let your dead go

My grief lies all within,
And these external manners of laments
Are merely shadows to the unseen grief
That swells with silence in the tortured soul.
—Shakespeare *(Richard II)*

Death is part of being human, a part of living. We are all going to die. In view of this fact, it seems extraordinary that as a society we are so reluctant to speak about death and dying.

When someone dies, family and friends rally, send flowers, letters and cards, leading up to the time of burial or cremation, and perhaps for a couple of weeks afterwards. Then everything goes quiet. The bereaved are left alone and expected to 'get over it' fairly quickly and move on with life. It is common to hear someone say of a friend who has lost someone close to them: "She's being really strong. She's coping well". It's what we want to hear. If someone we know isn't coping, what can we do?

Previous chapters discussed the emotional difficulties that children may suffer as a result of parents' inability to meet their need for love and attention. The focus is different in this chapter because death is often a traumatic and sudden event. The impact of the death may be profound for each family member and for the family as a whole, but each person may respond differently to the trauma.

In relation to my clients, it is generally the death of a parent, a sibling or grandparent that causes greatest emotional disturbance. The men and women who come to see me, however, are often unaware that it is, in fact, the death of a significant person in their life — maybe years earlier — that is causing them to feel distressed. Often other triggers, such as relationship difficulties, anxiety or depressive feelings, persuade an individual to seek counselling.

This chapter explores the impact of a particular death on a number of my clients, beginning with the death of a parent. It also looks at the way a number of men and women were traumatised when they were young, by the death of a sibling or grandparent. Some were young children when the death occurred, while others were adolescents. The deaths were all unexpected and came as a huge shock.

A number of factors determine how severe the impact of the trauma is likely to be on a child, including the child's age at the time of the death, the child's position in the family but most significantly, the way the death is handled by the surviving parent and family members.

The stages of grief

In 1969, Kübler-Ross challenged society's prevailing attitude towards death and bereavement (i.e. don't talk about it, sweep it under the carpet). In the forty years that have elapsed since Kübler-Ross's book, considerable progress has been made in hospitals and hospices but it would appear that little has changed in the public arena. Where death is concerned, denial and suppression are still the norm. Most people still cannot talk about death, or the possibility of someone's death, with any degree of ease.

Kübler Ross's grief model addressed five stages of grief (denial, anger, bargaining, depression, acceptance). She added that these stages do not necessarily follow in the same order and not everyone experiences all stages but she maintained that everyone will experience at least two. Since Kübler-Ross's work, others have added to the literature, and increased our understanding. Stages may overlap and, for example, a person may exhibit anger while still in the denial stage.

Denial — 'This cannot be happening to me'

Many years ago, a young woman had been seeing me for a few months to address a number of difficulties, particularly her distress that she was still single and often experienced problems in her relationships with men. She phoned me one evening, extremely upset. That afternoon, without warning, her mother had died, sitting in a chair in front of the television. Her daughter found her some hours later. She saw me for her normal counselling session two days later.

This was my first experience of working with someone in a state of shock and denial following a significant death. (My client would probably not, under normal circumstances, have been seeing a counsellor within two days of her mother's death). The extent of her denial was such that she behaved, for several weeks, as though nothing significant had happened. She told me later it was as though her mother had gone on a holiday. She and her mother had had a very close relationship and she was still living at home. Her mother appeared to be in excellent health so her death came as a great shock.

Later, my client's feelings of anger were extreme; she was angry with everyone in her life, including me. The fact that all the people around her went on with life as before, busying themselves as though oblivious of her suffering, angered her most of all. While still angry, she terminated her therapy. In a phone conversation, she told me she had consulted a psychiatrist, who had prescribed antidepressant medication.

Denial — 'It was fine after Mum died'

A man who saw me with his partner to address relationship difficulties, did his best to convince me that his mother's death, when he was nine, had had minimal impact: 'It was fine, because after Mum died, my dad met my stepmother and she was great.'

Many sessions later, when I felt he was strong enough, I encouraged him to tell me about that time once again. I learnt that it was in fact two years after his mother's death that his father and stepmother met. In the interim his father sought solace in alcohol, returning home regularly from the pub late at night, often drunk. My client and his brother were on their own in the house every evening, lonely and afraid. He was just nine years old and his brother fourteen. Twenty years passed before the brothers revealed to one another how desperately alone and frightened they felt following their mother's death.

Deep mourning — stuck in a painful place

Many clients I have worked with were reluctant to confront the feelings they had buried as a result of a parent's death. It is common for those who lose a parent when they are young to suffer extreme anxiety, often described by clients as a hollow feeling in their chest. Following the death of a parent, a child inevitably looks to the other parent for reassurance. Several clients described the way their surviving parent succumbed to alcohol or drugs to deal with grief and as a result was incapable of parenting their children. A number of men and women I have worked with, whose mother or father died when they were teenagers, were offered no help at all. Family and friends avoided speaking of their parent in front of them.

There is a wealth of information available nowadays for people dealing with grief and loss, starting with the Internet. The Australian Centre for Grief and Bereavement lists on its website a wide variety of resources, including many good books available for helping children. In my experience, those who lose a parent when they are young are unwilling to seek advice or help for themselves, because they are frightened of taking the lid off their feelings. They are also afraid of what they might discover. Time and again my clients tell me they have avoided *even thinking* about their deceased parent, sometimes for decades. This is not documented as a known stage or phase in the literature, and yet in my experience it is a common reaction.

Case study: A father's death, the loss of a whole family

Steve came into counselling to address relationship difficulties. At the time he was in his late twenties and was in a relationship with a woman in her early forties. His partner was keen to have a baby but Steve knew he was not ready to be a father.

As I asked about his family, Steve started to tell me about his father's death and to cry uncontrollably. His father had died in an accident when Steve was fourteen. Steve was shocked at his own response. It was the first time he had talked to anyone about his father and allowed himself to contact his feelings. He had come to see me to discuss concern over his relationship — he hadn't expected to be speaking about his father's death in our first session.

When his father died, Steve's mother fell apart. The family doctor referred her to a psychiatrist who prescribed heavy medication, which she had continued to take from that time. Steve's father had been central to the whole family, loved and respected in the farming community where they lived, someone to whom others turned in times of crisis. Following his death, Steve's mother was clearly incapable of adjusting to life without her husband or caring for her children.

In the fifteen years that had elapsed, no one in Steve's family, or the extended family, had talked about his father because no one could handle the pain and sadness. The children took their cue from their mother who was reluctant to allow others to see her distress and therefore unable to speak about her husband.

Steve recalled that day, fifteen years earlier: 'We came home from my under 14 football match and we were making pizza for tea. Dad was still working. Suddenly our neighbour John was at our back door. He looked very worried and said he had to talk to Mum. He took her for a walk up through our backyard. The next thing I knew, his son James, a great kid who was just five at the time, came running into the house and blurted out: "Your dad's dead. He just died. My dad tried to wake him up, but he couldn't … he's dead."

'My father died in a freak accident on the farm. Our family is Catholic. The priest came to our house and said we should pray. He then said it was terrible what had happened, but it was all right because Dad was in a better place. I was stunned. My dad was gone. How could that be all right for anyone — for my family, for me, for our friends? It didn't make sense.'

In order to enable him to access the feelings he had buried, I encouraged Steve to write a letter to his father. He went home after the first counselling session and wrote a seven-page letter to his father that turned into an extended letter to his mother and siblings, the brothers and sister who were also locked in grief, unable to talk about their father. His two brothers had turned to alcohol following the tragedy. Steve's family had been devastated by his father's death and his mother's collapse. He was shocked and surprised at the feelings locked inside him. Writing the letter gave him a great sense of relief.

Steve realised in his first counselling session that it was time to address the trauma of his father's death in order to take up his life once again. He was able to appreciate why he was in a relationship with a woman who was much older. His partner was able to replace the love and security he had received from his father. Steve decided to end their relationship.

Steve was also concerned at how competitive he had

become. He was driving himself to a point of exhaustion in his work and exercising compulsively, believing he needed to be strong, physically and mentally. He put himself under great pressure playing competitive football even though he often dreaded having to play. It was not hard to understand why he was placing such demands on himself. In a counselling session, Steve told me that nothing he did was ever good enough, but he didn't understand why he was so hard on himself. When I asked if it were possible he was still looking for his father's approval, wanting to hear his father say to him: "Steve, you're doing well," he started to cry. It was the start of significant change. Steve abandoned being so tough on himself.

It was clear that Steve was suffering in part because he no longer had the support of a strong male role model, at a crucial stage of development. Steve's father was seen as a man of strength in the community. If he could just die in an accident in this way, (when a rock flew up and hit his head when he was driving his tractor) what did it mean for a young boy?

Steve's first task was to come to terms with the loss of his male role model, a *good* father, who would always be absent from his life. He had filled the void by focussing on masculine aspects of his personality. At times overwhelmed by his suffering, he would display his anger and aggression, deliberately hurting other players on the football field. He exercised fanatically. Following his father's death, his mother was no longer able to nurture the family or care for herself adequately. In effect, Steve lost his mother as well. No one was there to look after him and he had no idea how to nurture himself. Steve's older brothers were lost to him too, as they had turned to alcohol. It was the end of family life as Steve had known it.

Steve felt unfulfilled in his career of personal trainer

and made the decision to re train as a secondary school teacher. This career move could be seen as Steve beginning to explore the more nurturing aspects of his personality. His first year was extremely confronting. He wanted to appear in charge, to assume an air of authority with his students, but he told me that inside he still felt like a fourteen year old boy, 'no older than my year 9 students.' He was uncomfortable in his dealings with students, particularly the year 9 girls, whom he saw for half an hour (as their home room teacher) before school each morning.

Our counselling sessions became a blend of therapy and teaching supervision. Over time Steve was able to acknowledge that in part he had stopped maturing at fourteen and had joined his father in the grave. It was time to climb out. I encouraged him to be more honest with his students and to relate to them, to let them see the real Steve, someone with genuine feelings, rather than the tough disciplinarian he was trying hard to be. Steve was aware that his expectation of his students' achievements was quite unrealistic. He asked me: 'What should I say to them?'

I told him it was something he would have to decide, but perhaps he could tell them something honest about himself.

In our next session Steve told me that he walked into the classroom the morning after our discussion, and said to his students: 'I've decided to tell you something about my life. When I was your age, and in year 9, my father died in a freak accident on our farm ...'

Steve was surprised to discover that being a teacher became 'a piece of cake' overnight.

Aged thirty, still an adolescent

Edward came to see me initially with his girlfriend to address relationship difficulties. It was clear both he and his partner needed to face their own complex emotional problems and I was not surprised when they told me they were separating a few weeks later. Edward came to a number of sessions, on his own, after the separation.

Like Steve, Edward's father died in an accident when he was fourteen (in Edward's case a car accident). He was nearly thirty when he came to see me. He had spoken to no one about his father's death in the sixteen years that had elapsed. Edward recognised very quickly how he was stuck in adolescence. He was feeling lost, and he had no idea of the direction he wanted to take, in terms of career, relationship or home. He had returned to live with his mother.

Edward was ready to address the feelings he had buried as a result of his father's death. What came to light was that his earlier reluctance stemmed from the fact that some of those feelings were negative. His father hadn't always supported him as a young boy or helped him to feel confident as he matured. Edward felt his father saw him as a "wimp", who preferred reading books and playing computer games to riding a motor bike or playing football, which his father obviously saw as "manly pursuits".

After delaying for several months, Edward wrote a letter to his father:

> I've been asked to write you a letter. I can't tell you just how long I've put off writing. It's a letter that's been 16 odd years in the making — 16 years of the same day recurring. I'm writing this letter as a man of 32 who still feels like a 14 year old boy. I'm writing out of pure necessity. I can assure you I've procrastinated, distracted

myself and delayed the inevitable in every possible way, fearing this moment for a very long time.

Edward was surprised at what transpired as a result of writing the letter: 'Quite a few truths came to light. It was as though a curtain was pulled back and I could see the real issues that were affecting me. It wasn't my father's death. What shocked me most was the realisation that things were the same before Dad died'.

Freeing himself of the guilt for feeling angry towards his father at times led to rapid change. Edward knew he had to take responsibility for himself. From the age of fourteen he had always had a girlfriend to depend on. When his current relationship ended, he understood he needed to become independent, to stand on his own two feet and take charge of his life.

It is both rewarding and exciting to see clients take the step forward in life that is vital for personal growth. When they reach that point, they are able to see clearly that they need to begin the process of change. It can come as a shock to see that the reason they are stuck may be in part because they are choosing to be, in order to avoid facing difficult feelings.

Fear — 'What if I lose all connection to my father?'

An emotion that many clients have experienced following a significant death is fear. If my client hasn't addressed the loss of a parent, it often means that the surviving parent and extended family have also avoided doing so. There is a wall of silence and life just continues on as though nothing important has taken place. If the death is not spoken of, it is very difficult for a child (even a grown-up one) to initiate a discussion which he is afraid could have disastrous consequences, for other family members but also for himself. Fear prevents him from taking the lid off his feelings — fear of the unknown, fear of falling apart, fear of upsetting others and fear of losing the thread of connection he still feels with the parent who died.

Jemma, (Chapter 3), had avoided facing her father's death for many years because she was afraid she would lose all connection to him, that in saying goodbye he would simply disappear from her memory. Once she was ready to let him go, Jemma felt calmer and more accepting of his death: 'Although it was very hard to face the death of my father, I'm grateful that I have done so. You were right in that I now have him back but in a peaceful sense. I realised this on the anniversary of his death. It was the first time that I have been able to cry for him in sixteen years and it felt really good.'

Drowning in grief

Sometimes clients come to see me struggling to deal with grief, particularly when dealing with more than one death. Louisa was one of these people:

'My father and a close friend of mine died within a short space of time. I expected to feel better after a few months but instead I felt worse as time passed. My grief had the effect of disconnecting me from the world. I felt removed from everyone and everything. I felt I was going through the motions — work, food, sleep — everything felt strange. I sought counselling because it seemed that grief was taking me over. At times I had a physical pain in my chest and felt heavy and slow. For me the grief I felt for my father tied into other areas of grief in my life. I felt I was drowning in a sea of grief, as though grief at my father's death held hands with other grief — a long chain of grief.

'I don't think I necessarily believe in the five stages of grief, but I do think I got stuck in depression. It felt like I was lost in sadness and that death was deep in my bones. It was the opposite of life.

'I came to understand that I had to let myself feel sad. To not be afraid of what I was feeling and just accept that it was how I was feeling. To be *in* my feeling.

'Counselling helped enormously, for many reasons. It gave me a place to check into. During the week I would just try to stay with my feelings, knowing that I would be seeing my counsellor before long. Then the sessions gave me a space in which to try to put into words what I was feeling and to be reassured that I wasn't going crazy.

'My counsellor was able to join together other events in my life where I felt grief. Just knowing that my appointment was coming up, that it was my time, that I knew I could say virtually anything, no matter how strange — all this was a tremendous help.

'There were other things that helped too. Writing helped a lot. And nature — walking by the sea, feeling the wind. And little things that friends did that showed me they cared. That helped a lot too'.

The death of a child

The death of a child is obviously a far greater tragedy than that of an elderly person who has had 'a good innings'. It is not uncommon for a marriage to break up following a child's death. This is particularly the case where there is guilt or blame. Parents may grieve in different ways and as a result may not be able to help one another. Where one parent may need to talk about the child who has died, for the other, speaking about the tragedy might be impossible. Unable to handle their own and one another's grief, parents are sometimes oblivious of what the surviving children are experiencing.

When a child dies, the effect on the siblings as well as the parents is profound. It generally means that a child will occupy a different position in the family. A middle child becomes the eldest or the youngest, and there may be a big gap between surviving children. Sometimes an only child remains.

A *fear of angels*

Max's sister died when he was five and she was three. No one talked to him about what had happened to her at the time. He buried the experience because his parents didn't talk to him about her death. It was a very long time before his little sister's death became a conscious memory: 'It upsets me that I can't remember anything about her. When she died my mother told me the angels had taken her. She said she heard the angels' wings. My sister's name was never mentioned again in our family. She was my only sibling at the time and suddenly I was an only child.

'My feelings were not considered by my parents when she died. In a counselling session, more than forty years later, I became overcome by feelings of loss and sadness at her death. I had no idea those feelings were buried inside me. I felt terrible because I couldn't recall her face. I now know that my sister's death had a profound effect on my ability to form close relationships. In those years there was no thought of counselling, particularly for children.'

Not surprisingly, from that moment, Max was highly suspicious of angels.

Case study: 'It should have been me that died'

Katie came to counselling in her late twenties, twenty years after the death of her sister. Katie was seven and her younger brother Carl five when their eleven year old sister Lina died.

Katie had grown up feeling uncomfortable as the middle child, largely because her big sister seemed perfect in every way. She was intelligent, pretty and popular. Carl, the youngest and the only boy, also had a special place in the family. Katie felt like the black sheep, in the middle. In spite of this, Katie felt they were a close family before her sister's death: 'Mum and Dad did everything for the family. I remember the day Lina died as though it happened yesterday. The previous day she went riding and fell off her horse, and I can still remember what I was wearing that day. I should have gone riding with her, but I was eating chicken wings and I wanted to go on eating, so I didn't go. She came home, and she seemed fine. She lay down on the couch and went to sleep. That was a special treat because in our family you had to sleep in your bed.

'Next morning, I remember we all woke at the same time and went into the lounge room, but Lina wouldn't wake up. I remember my brother screaming at my father to get the belt, to belt her so she would wake up. And I remember I didn't say a word for ages. Then I remember being put into our bedrooms because the coroner or someone was coming to take her. It was horrible as we had no idea what was going on, no one talked to us, or explained what was happening. We just got put in our rooms with lots of lollies. They were meant to make us feel better. We were taken to a friend's house and left in a room with more lollies.

'I don't think I saw my mother for about two months after that. She just didn't get out of bed and we were passed around from one relative to another. My parents had no idea how to cope.

'Before the funeral we went to see Lina in the coffin. I remember going in and seeing my sister lying there and my mother wanted me to kiss her. Instinctively I believed I shouldn't, but my mother insisted. I didn't want to kiss her because that wasn't my sister, but my mother made me kiss the corpse and I don't think I've ever forgiven her for that. I've had a problem pleasing my mother since that day.

'The family dynamic changed enormously after Lina died and I know I have forgotten large chunks of my life. I felt I should have been the one to die, not Lina, because I never believed that I would be anything in life or that I would do anything worthwhile. Lina, on the other hand, was perfect.

'Years later I found a note I had written to my parents: "Dear Mum and Dad. It should have been me that died, not Lina. It was my fault".

'Mum was always inviting people to the house when we were teenagers and they often stayed with us, as though we were all one big happy family. I suspect she couldn't bear us to be alone, just the four of us. I had a friend from high school who left home and my mother took her in. One night Mum got drunk and she started calling my friend Lina.'

Katie had to work at restoring her relationship with her father, which changed radically when Lina died: 'When I was little I was 'Daddy's girl'. After Lina died something happened to him. I don't know why but through my teens I didn't even want to get close. I don't know if it was because I felt he wasn't there after she died. What I understand now is that he had to go to work and provide for the family. I feel most sorry for my father because he had no time to grieve. My mum stayed in bed, we got pushed around to friends and relatives with lollies, but he had to go back to work.'

Lina's death was a life-changing tragedy for her little sister. Katie was aware that her sister's death had altered the way she was with everyone in her life and later affected her relationship with boyfriends. She lived with the expectation that all relationships would inevitably end.

When I asked Katie what her relationship with Lina was like, she replied that it was, 'Little sister looking up to the big sister.' She remembered an episode when she was having her photo taken and wouldn't smile, and then Lina came and sat next to her and she started smiling. She also said that Lina 'used to put me to sleep every night.' I said it sounded as though Lina really loved her little sister. Katie had never considered that before, and felt comforted by the thought.

Katie recalled her great-grandmother's funeral: 'That was the first funeral Mum allowed us to go to, and I just sat there and cried and cried. I wasn't crying for my grand-mother, I was crying for Lina.'

I encouraged Katie to remember her relationship with her sister rather than attempt to push all thoughts of her out of her mind. She spent some time looking at photo-graphs of the two of them as children, reading old cards and letters and a diary she had written during her child-hood years. Listening to music, one song in particular, helped her to remember life before her sister died.

On the anniversary of Lina's death, Katie went to a

beach and released balloons on which she had written all the things she wished she could say to her, and the feelings she needed to let go of. It was the first time she had celebrated her sister's life and acknowledged the anniversary of her death in a positive way.

'For twenty-five years all we ever did was go the cemetery, take flowers, sit down and miss her.'

I contacted Katie three years after her time in counselling. She was aware that she had changed a great deal. She was no longer controlled by grief and she felt that she was able to pursue the things she wanted to do with her life. A significant part of that change was that Katie no longer felt like 'the wallflower surrounded by two big, big flowers.' She no longer felt defined by the death of her big sister.

A mother's death, a helpless father

I have worked with several clients whose mother died when they were very young. Generally a mother is at the centre of the family, the main caregiver, the one who is there before and after school, who cooks meals, runs the household and provides most of the nurturing. As discussed earlier, young people often find it easier to talk to their mother about emotional issues because their father is reluctant to do so.

For some clients, overwhelmed with grief when they come to counselling, their mother's death is the one issue we cannot address in the early stages because it is simply too painful and too frightening. Once I feel the client is able to trust me we can begin the work of looking at the loss of her mother. Until that time we walk around the trauma as though approaching a wound from many different sides, waiting until the client is ready and closely observing any dreams that may act as a guide. Clients are often not prepared to write a letter to their mother to say goodbye, because they are not ready to make the death a reality.

It is common for a man to re-partner fairly quickly in order to provide the children with a mother figure (and himself with a partner). In some cases the introduction of a woman into their lives is the last thing a child wants because it can feel as though they have been abandoned again by a parent. If a mother dies, the father may be at a loss as to how to handle the role of sole parent, particularly if he has not been involved in the running of the family. A client told me that she got her period a month after her mother died. Her father, thrown into a panic, rang the family doctor (a man) for advice. It didn't occur to him to speak to a female relative or friend. She still recalls her distress. All she wanted was her mother to be there for her: 'The next embarrassing experience was telling Dad I needed a bra. I put it off for months and months. He said he would drive me to the shop and wait outside. When we got to the shop, Dad reluctantly agreed to come in with me but stood awkwardly inside the door, embarrassed to be surrounded by female underwear.'

Shock, denial, sadness — a grandfather's death

In my years as a counsellor I have seen how vital grandparents are in providing stability and love to their grandchildren. Sometimes a grandparent is the one who is able to offer unconditional love to a child and to make the child feel they are acceptable and lovable, however difficult their behaviour. Several of my clients said they were called 'over-sensitive' and 'drama queen' by their parents, who obviously had difficulty handling them. Nothing the child did, however, appeared to upset or anger a particular grandparent.

Rosie came to see me, concerned over relationship difficulties. She discovered in her first session that what lay behind her tears was grief at her grandfather's death when she was a teenager. It came as a surprise. She went home and wrote him a letter the same evening. She felt quite changed as a result:

Dear Grandpa,

When you died I was only sixteen years old. Oh my God, it was the biggest shock of my life. It still feels like yesterday that I lost my grandpa and you meant the world to me. Even though some of the family thought I was a little loud and a drama queen at times, you were always there to take care of me, calm me down, call me your princess and say to me "My Rosie." Growing up there were so many little things like playing cards, family gatherings and Sunday lunches, when I always sat next to you at the head of the table. All that is what gave me my character and the personality I have today.

At your funeral it felt like someone had stolen my heart. They had taken my arms so I couldn't reach out to you and my legs so I couldn't walk to you. I felt helpless, a feeling that over time didn't go away; it just got easier. When you died the family fell apart — no more poker, no more morning coffee and biscuits, no more Sunday lunches and no more you. Dad has never been the same. He keeps a little to himself now. Grandpa, when you passed away, did part of me do the same? All I know is that I didn't have my grandpa long enough — my graduation, my first car accident, going to Italy and seeing where you were from and staying with your family. Everyone loves you, but now the family seems empty without you.

I always felt a big connection to you and I still feel you speaking in my heart when I need you there. I feel I am so much like you — culture, attitude, sense of humour and sometimes laziness!

If you were here I would be asking you for some guidance and advice and asking you why was it you always won at poker? And asking how you did those magic tricks. You made me believe that I too can do magic and I know now that you meant I could be anything I want to be.

You are my angel. I am blessed to be your granddaughter.

Rosie.

Rosie had come to counselling concerned over relationship issues. As a result of facing her feelings about her grandfather she could understand much more about her choice of partners. She was surprised at the feelings that had been controlling her since her grandfather's death.

Perhaps it is difficult for families to recognise the impact on a child of a grandparent's death. Other family members may be prepared because of the age or ill health of the grandparent. Death might even be seen as a relief. For the child, however, a grandparent often occupies a vital role and for most it will be their first experience of death. It can come as a great shock if no one has alerted them to the possibility of their grandparent dying. Parents sometimes are caught up in all the practical matters that need to be taken care of and may not consider the child's loss.

Shock, guilt, anger — May's pop

May's grandfather died on her sixth birthday. It was an overwhelming shock. There were a number of similarities in her reaction to his death and Rosie's when her grandfather died, but there were significant differences too. The day her grandfather died was the first time May had seen her mother upset and this also came as a shock.

It is the morning of May's sixth birthday. She is the first out of bed and hurries to her parents' room, filled with excitement at the thought of her presents and a birthday party later in the day. She hears unfamiliar sounds coming from the bedroom and as she reaches the door she sees her mother, in tears, being comforted by her father. Shocked, she goes into the kitchen and hides under the table, feeling guilty and afraid. She stays under the table for most of the day, refusing to come out. It must be her fault, because she has been bad. It is the first time she has seen her mother cry.

No one talked to May about her grandfather's death. He was the person she loved most in the world; she knew that he adored her and she was his favourite grandchild. At mealtimes she liked to sit on Pop's lap, leaning back on his big tummy. She knew she could trust him implicitly. How could he die, and on her birthday?

Later in our sessions May contacted the anger she also felt that day (but needed to suppress) because her sixth birthday was totally spoiled. A sixth birthday is a very important day. May was no longer the focus of attention the day her grandfather died.

In counselling sessions, it was some time before May's grandfather's death surfaced as one of the major traumas of her life. May was too distressed, for a long time, to talk about his death. The shock, the confusion of feelings, fear, guilt and suppressed anger made it almost impossible for her to comprehend. From that day, she was unable to trust anyone completely.

A year or two after she had been in counselling, May's dog died. She suffered enormous sadness, and it helped her to access some of the unresolved grief over her grandfather's death because with her dog she had also experienced a deep bond. What she also experienced was profound guilt, which lasted a long time 'How can I go out and have fun, when my dog is dead?'

The loss of man's (or woman's) best friend

Many clients have worked with me to address the grief and loss they experienced when a pet died. Pets are often one of the family. As one client told me: 'Much better than family'.

Jemma (Chapter 3) contacted me to tell me her beloved dog Beau had died from poisoning when a neighbour put down bait to kill a fox. She was traumatised by his death, because he was her only companion in her toughest, most depressed years:

'There were some days, I felt I couldn't drag myself out of bed, but I did because of Beau. He gave me a purpose, a reason to get up. When I was at my lowest, Beau knew it. He would climb onto my chest and put his head on my neck. He would sigh heavily as if to say 'I know how you feel'. He saved my life during my loneliest times.

'I realise I had never loved as purely as I loved this fluffy, tail wagging dog. I will forever be in his debt for giving me the gift of love, something I had not experienced previously in my life. He was without doubt the most special animal I have ever known.'

A taboo topic: a parent's suicide

It is with some reluctance that I am writing about parental suicide. As with sexual abuse in the second chapter, it is rarely addressed. When my husband read this section, he advised me to make it 'more lively, a bit less depressing'. It's not easy to put a cheerful spin on the topic of traumatic death and especially suicide. But however depressing, this chapter needs to be written because it is a tragic reality of life — some parents (and others) do commit suicide.

The Australian Bureau of Statistics reported in 2006 that suicide remains a major external cause of death, accounting for more deaths in Australia than transport accidents. I know that many clients, men particularly, often contemplate the possibility of committing suicide. One man referred to it as 'the permanent solution'.

I would like to think my writing about suicide might help even a few people who read this book and encourage them to seek counselling if they need to. What I know is that the clients who addressed buried feelings about a parent's suicide in our sessions were helped considerably by the process. In time they were able to speak of the death without feeling as upset. More importantly, they were able to see how the relationship with that person had helped to shape them and had enriched their life.

As death is rarely spoken of in our society, children who have experienced the suicide of a parent feel they have to remain silent for fear of revealing a shameful truth. As one client told me at her first session: 'It's taboo to talk about dead people, much less suicide. So how could I possibly tell anyone my father killed himself?'

Without some form of help it is a nearly impossible task for a young person to address the hurt and shame of a mother or father's suicide. Where the surviving parent is able to deal with their own grief and also help their children, the trauma is considerably less. The men and women I have worked with in counselling spoke to no one of their feelings, until deciding they had to get help. A client told me she had a 'fantasy mother' in her mind. When asked about her mother by people she met in her daily life, she would speak of the imaginary person. Revealing that her mother committed suicide was something she could not contemplate. Even thinking about the circumstances of her mother's death was too overwhelming.

Melissa, (see Chapter 3), told me she wanted to address her mother's death, thirteen years earlier, but was too scared. Her mother had suffered from a mental illness and had taken her own life: 'Something might happen to me ... I might fall apart ... I might find out things I don't want to know ...'

No one, including her father, ever talked to her about her mother's death or the fact that she took her own life.

'I was too afraid to ask, so I drew my own conclusions. It was horrible. I was so frightened. I made myself not feel. I became desensitised.'

Melissa told me of a night when she was just eight or nine years old. Her bedroom was next door to her parents and she remembered being woken in the night, coming out of her room and seeing her mother being taken out of the house on a stretcher. She heard her father say they were going to pump her mother's stomach. She was left in the dark. No one told her what was happening and she was left wondering: 'What can I do? Why is this happening? Who can I turn to? Who will help me?'

A client who came to see me ten years after her mother committed suicide told me when she started counselling that she felt sad approximately seventy per cent of the time, and then added: 'I just want to feel sad.' She told me that her sadness allowed her to feel close to her mother. Several months later she told me she felt sad approximately fifty percent of the time. It was getting easier for her. Until persuaded by her older sister to seek counselling, she felt totally stuck in her life: 'I didn't know how to grow up without a mother.'

Avoidance — a father's suicide

Ted, who separated from his partner after their first counselling session, (Chapter 5), saw me for individual counselling in the weeks that followed. His father had committed suicide when Ted was twenty. He told me that his version of events, for anyone who asked, was that his father died in a car accident.

'I don't think I ever dealt with my father's death. I was very upset when he died, but I didn't let myself think about him. All those feelings, his memory, everything, I just swept it under the carpet and never looked at it. I didn't want to feel sad, so I would lie about his death. A lot of people think he died in a motor accident. His own son feels ashamed, the son he would have done anything for. I've totally shunned his memory. I can't remember the date he died. I can't even remember his birthday. In no way at all do I celebrate his life. I never think of the things he did with me, how he took me hiking, fly fishing, birdwatching, playing in the snow, all the things kids love doing. I just focussed on the negatives of his life and determined never to make his mistakes — get divorced, let my wife down or allow myself to get sick. The truth is I am similar in character and how I go about dealing with life. My marriage has ended and for several years I've relied too heavily on alcohol. Now I know I want to turn things around and learn how to live a positive life.'

It is hard for a child to admit to feelings of anger when a parent commits suicide. If they are unable to do so, the feelings remain and prevent the child (however adult) from healing and feeling positive.

From time to time, a mother has come to see me, concerned for a child (generally a son), terrified that he is a suicide risk as he is using drugs. What I suggest is that she tell her son how devastated she would be if he were to kill himself. Sometimes people who attempt suicide fool themselves into believing no one would miss them, and that some people would even be better off. No parent is better off, if a child commits suicide.

The death of a partner

People mourn in different ways and in their own time. Some have a very practical 'no-fuss' attitude to death, even the prospect of their own. Not everyone reacts in this way.

Clients often say to me: 'It's been six months/a year, I should be over it by now!' I tell them they don't need to 'get over it', but the pain will lessen with time as they adjust to the loss and find a different way of living which does not include the person who died.

For some, a significant death can be followed by a period of turmoil and chaotic emotion. A client described her reaction to her husband's death over the following months: 'One day I'm absolutely fine and feel happy to be alive, but the very next day I can be overwhelmed with feelings of sadness and loss and I don't even want to leave the house.'

This is a very normal reaction to the death of someone close. Emotions can fluctuate for no apparent reason.

In her book *Grief and Dreams* (see Chapter 6), Mary Symes described her personal journey through grief and her difficulty in handling her pain, in part because she couldn't get the help she needed from those around her: 'I am sad that in our society, where we tend to see ourselves as well-adjusted, rounded people, coping with the complexities of life, that so few among us are prepared or able to talk about the one thing we all have in common which is death. I feel sad because this inability, this resistance, this fear made my grieving so much harder to bear.' (Symes, 1987).

Mary was conscious that others felt uncomfortable about her situation and desperately wanted her to do something so they would feel better about her: 'Poor Mary. Why doesn't she go back to work? What does she do all day? No wonder she's getting depressed. Why doesn't she go out and find a man?'

Mary's husband was lost at sea. There was no 'ending' or 'resolution' for her. As mentioned previously, it was only through the exploration of her dreams that she was able to heal from her loss. Mary believed she was changed, utterly, as a result of her trauma: 'My old self would not recognise the person I am today'.

Grief and mourning is encouraged in some cultures. Family and friends come together over an extended period of time, joining in ceremonies and rituals as a way of dealing with shared grief. This gives the extended family the opportunity to come to terms with their feelings about the death. Many who have lost a partner, parent or child are in a state of shock until well after the funeral. There are many practicalities to be seen to immediately after a death. Grieving is put on hold for a time. Anyone who has lost someone close to them knows that it can take a long time to mourn. It is not as though we ever forget those who really matter to us.

A therapist's experience of death

When I began as a counsellor, significant deaths in the lives of my clients, particularly the death of a parent, would affect me greatly. There were times I had to hide the fact that I felt tearful. This was particularly the case when the client was concealing their suffering, to the point of denial at times. Throughout my teenage years I struggled in my relationship with both my parents, but at least they were there to engage with and knowing them gave me a basis for understanding myself.

An uncle who was very important in my early life, and at times an ally against my parents, died when I had settled in Australia. He was a fighter pilot in the war and contracted polio when he was only twenty-one, so he spent two years in an iron lung in a hospital in India. I later understood that his death, at fifty-four, was not so surprising, but it came as an enormous blow to me. I felt that I needed him to be a part of my life, even though I saw him rarely as I was living in Australia. My brother told me of his death in a letter which arrived ten days later. You didn't phone, at that time, to announce a death. (Nowadays you might find out in a text message or on Facebook.) I was told that my aunt had asked for no flowers or letters, so I didn't write. I know now I would have been helped had I done so.

For a long time I felt there was a wound inside me. It was ten years or more before I came to the understanding that what my uncle gave me would always be there, that the loving relationship he offered me played a big role in making me who I am.

I remember when I was in my teens and feeling self-conscious about being taller and more developed physically than my friends, my uncle assured me that at thirty I would be happy with how I looked. When I left for Australia, at the age of twenty-two, he wrote a poem for me. Re-reading it I can see he knew me better than I knew myself.

Looking back, I suspect that it was my uncle's death that was still affecting me, when clients spoke about a parent's death, because he was able to parent me in a more trustworthy manner than either my mother or father. In a letter that my aunt wrote me, a year after his death, she described how the family was (or wasn't) coping: 'We are all, in a sense, in a state of shock — we find it difficult to concentrate on one thing for very long — and the pattern of our lives has been completely altered. No longer do we watch for hidden obstacles to a wheelchair or crutches, no longer do we have a resident male — a husband and father. There is a terrible sense of loss. And yet we go about our daily business and we hear people say: "Aren't they taking it well?" and "Aren't they good?" And we don't feel good at all. We feel very brittle.'

In 2005, while I was writing this book, I visited a cousin in Scotland I hadn't seen since we were about ten years old. When he was sixteen tragedy struck his family. Both his mother and father died within a few months of one another. I remember my father in tears (one of just two occasions I saw him cry) when he heard about his sister's death. What I find hard to accept now is that we lost touch with my cousins following their parents' death. How can it be that my parents didn't keep in contact, or make sure we did? We lived at opposite ends of the UK, it is true, but I find it shocking and very sad.

When my father was in his seventies he renewed contact with my cousins and encouraged us to do the same (by then we were all middle-aged and living in different parts of the globe). It was in fact wonderful to spend time with my cousin, in spite of our advanced age. We both remember the holiday we spent together as children.

The majority of the clients I have discussed in this chapter came to counselling presenting with a wide range of concerns, often linked to anxiety or depression. They were mostly unaware that it was disowned feelings over the death of someone close to them that was still affecting them, years later. Through finding the strength to contact buried feelings, they were able to address their grief. Healing could begin.

As a society, we need to be able to face death and accept that it is a part of life. We need to talk about it, to show our feelings and to help those around us to do the same.

Afterword

*We shall not cease from exploration, and the end of all
our exploring will be to arrive where we started and
know the place for the first time.*
—TS Eliot (*Four Quartets*)

I find it hard to believe that it has taken me
nearly six years to write this book. During those years, I often invited ex-clients
who had spent a considerable time working with me in
counselling, to write of their experience. I generally did
so when at least a year or two had passed since their final
counselling session. I was curious to know how ex-clients
were doing in their lives; this is not something you normally hear about, as a therapist. I was also interested to
know *how* they believed change had occurred as a result
of their hard work.

When I was close to finishing the book, I sent the clients' stories to them, expecting some to be happy to have
their journey in counselling included, others to tell me
they would prefer not to be involved. These last pages
emerged as a result of the clients' reactions to their stories,
sometimes very many years after finishing in counselling.

Their responses amazed me. All but one person wanted
to be a part of the book, and to have their story told. But
many also wanted to add to their story, and to tell me
what they could now appreciate — that they had changed
dramatically as a result of the work they did in counselling.

The word 'surreal' kept coming up in their replies. Was that really me? Was I really so lost? So sad? So anxious? While they could acknowledge that the words were theirs, the events and stories were true, they no longer felt they were the same person. They had matured, grown and changed and now understood themselves in an entirely new way. 'I feel like a different person' was a comment I heard frequently.

I expected that many clients, men and women, would want me to remove some of the more personal details, particularly criticism of parents. I would not have been surprised, or disappointed. It was up to them; the stories, the parents, families and partners are theirs. But only two people asked that I take out a few comments about their respective mothers.

There were some surprising responses. Reuban told me that he had forwarded his story to his parents, who contacted him immediately, concerned about him and determined to see that his brother gets the help he still needs. Rosie emailed her story to her mother. The following day there was a ring at her front door. Her mother was standing on the doorstep and when Rosie opened the door, her mother hugged her.

There were others too. Priscilla was surprised to learn I was worried she might have been too challenging for me, in my early days as a counsellor. Barry told me that he felt my care, encouragement and humour all over again when he read his story. Jemma was happy to see her words and mine, blending, in the telling of her story. Shirley wrote that she was quite fearful before reading hers, but afterwards felt a great sense of achievement. By far the most common response, on reading their stories, was the awareness that they had achieved a great deal as a result of all their hard work. As Patrick wrote: 'I am absolutely blown away. Looking back on my time in counselling in that way, I can see just how far I have come. Others have seen it in me too. Thank you'.

Tanya wrote a long reply, detailing the significant discoveries she had made about herself and her time in counselling. She ended with: '… a part of me feels honoured that you included me in your book … I feel wanted and important and I know this is because I never felt wanted or important during my childhood and teenage years, as a result of the way I was treated'.

I was struck, when reading the clients' stories, how often their involvement in weekend groups, or the monthly group that followed, seemed to feature as a vehicle of change. While I have been aware of the power of group therapy for a long while, it was surprising to hear how often clients attributed real change to their involvement in a group experience. One of these, Annabel, wrote of being stuck, for a very long time, in spite of doing everything to bring about the change she wanted: 'I didn't understand why I couldn't shift. What was in it for me, to remain stuck, unseen and unloved. I knew it felt safe and comfortable. It was what I had known all my life, but I wanted to change. At a group meeting, over a year of searching later, I shifted. They were the first people I had shared my life with honestly. That night, despite my resistance, they not only saw me but they let me know that I had been seen and that they wanted to see me, not for any other reason other than to know me. I sat with that feeling. I felt *seen* in my bones, and it felt good. It finally dawned on me that that's what I had to do — *be seen*. It was *my* responsibility and it required action and effort'.

The book, it seems, has a life of its own. If it weren't for writing this book, I wouldn't know how my clients had fared since their days in counselling. These men and women were all able to work with me in counselling and to change their lives. It is important to say, however, that I was not able to succeed as a therapist with everyone who came through my door. It is crucial that people seeking counselling find the person who is right for them. I was not always that person.

For those who commit to the process of exploring their inner world, I believe it is a life-long journey and one that certainly continues long after the last counselling session.

I should like to end with a tribute to my own parents, whom I have written about in the pages of this book, sometimes in an uncomplimentary manner. Like most parents, they did their best with what they knew. They both acted out of their own pain as a result of their earlier experience. My mother died in 1982 and my father in 1993, and I forgave them a very long time ago. When I became a counsellor, my brother told me I was making my childhood pay for me, and in a way it is true. I don't believe you can be an effective therapist unless you have experienced suffering at some stage in life and done the work to heal yourself.

There was, in fact, much to admire about my parents. In my early years I felt loved by both of them. I still remember watching them dancing together at a New Year's Eve party at our house, when I was a child. They were a striking couple and looked very much in love. Life changed for all of us when addiction took over and their marriage fell apart.

One of the most important things they gave me, I can see now, was an appreciation of the arts through their love of books and writing, music and theatre. My life has been the richer for it.

Bibliography

Biddulph, S. (1994). *Manhood.* Sydney: Finch Publishing.

Biddulph, S. (1998). *The Secret of Happy Children.* Sydney and London: Bay Books.

Biringen, Z. (1988). *Raising a Secure Child.* New York: The Berkley Publishing Group.

Estes, C. (1992). *Women Who Run with the Wolves*. Sydney: Random House Australia.

Gottman, J. (1997) *Raising an Emotionally Intelligent Child.* New York: Simon & Schuster.

Grant, I. (1999). *Fathers Who Dare Win*. Auckland: Pa's Publishing.

Greenberg, M. (2003) *Mastering Emotional Skills.* In D. Goleman (Ed.), Destructive Emotions. London: Bantam Books.

Hawkes, R. (1998). *Counselling a Couple with a Gambling Problem*. A.N.Z.J. Fam Ther., 19, 195-200.

Kübler-Ross, E. (1969). *On Death and Dying.* New York: McMillan.

Miller, A. (2007). *Free from Lies*. New York: W.W. Norton & Co.

Miller, A. (2006). *We can identify the causes of our suffering*. From http://www.alice-miller.com/articles

National Institute of Drug Abuse. (2011). From www.nida.nih.gov/pubs/teaching/Teaching6/Teaching.html

O'Connor, P. (1993). *The Inner Man*. Sydney: Pan Macmillan.

Potter-Efron, R.P. & E.P. (1989). *Letting Go of Shame*: Hazelden.

Satir, V. (2008). *In Her Own Words*. Phoenix: Zeig, Tucker & Theisen.

Siegel. J. (2000). *What Children Learn from their Parents' Marriage*. New York: Harper Collins Publishers.

Sheean, L (2011). *Addiction: A disorder of choice. An interview with Gene Heyman*. Psychotherapy in Australia, 17.

Symes, M. (1987). *Grief and Dreams*. North Balwyn: Rene Gordon.

email: amandastuart@bigpond.com
web: www.amandastuart.com.au